Texas A&M University Press
publishing since 1974

OUTLAW COUNTRY REPORTER

WITTLIFF COLLECTIONS MUSIC SERIES

The Wittliff Collections

Hector Saldaña, General Editor

SAM KINDRICK

OUTLAW COUNTRY REPORTER

MISFITS, MADAMS, AND HANGIN' WITH WILLIE

Texas A&M University Press
College Station

First edition

♾ This paper meets the requirements of ANSI/NISO Z39.48-1992
(Permanence of Paper).Binding materials have been chosen for durability.

Library of Congress Cataloging-in-Publication Data

Names: Kindrick, Sam, 1934– author. | Saldaña, Hector, writer of foreword.
   | Wittliff Collections (Albert B. Alkek Library)
Title: Outlaw country reporter : misfits, madams, and hangin' with Willie /
   Sam Kindrick.
Other titles: Wittliff Collections music series.
Description: First edition. | College Station : Texas A&M University Press,
   [2024] | Series: Wittliff Collections music series | Includes index.
Identifiers: LCCN 2023052504 | ISBN 9781648432040 (cloth) | ISBN
   9781648432057 (ebook)
Subjects: LCSH: Kindrick, Sam, 1934– | Nelson, Willie, 1933– | Music
   journalists—United States—Biography. | Alternative country
   music—Texas—History and criticism. | Country musicians—Texas. |
   LCGFT: Autobiographies.
Classification: LCC ML423.K57 A3 2024 | DDC 070.4/4978092
   [B]—dc23/eng/20231201
LC record available at https://lccn.loc.gov/2023052504

*Unless otherwise indicated, all photographs are from the Sam Kindrick Papers,
located in the Wittliff Collections, Texas Music Collection.*

This book is dedicated to my Aunt **Rayola Chenault Proffer** and **Chester (Red) Smith**, two powerful people who taught me things I needed to know while growing up fatherless in the Hill Country of Texas. Rayola was the greatest horsewoman many ever knew, and Red Smith was the alpha and the omega when it came to breaking broncs and training saddle horses. My father, Grady Kindrick, died before I was a year old, and I grew up on a learning curve heavily influenced by Red and Aunt Ray, who was my mother's baby sister.

In later years, Aunt Ray was the family historian. But as a young woman, she could fearlessly ride a horse as well as anyone. She was like an older sister to me.

Red was my father's friend, and he worked tirelessly alongside my cowboy-lease-rancher maternal grandfather, Clarence Chenault. Red remained close to my mother's family until his death. He taught me to shoot a rifle. He taught me how to gut a deer. He taught me not to lie, cheat, or steal. And he taught me how to stand up to the school bully. He was the personification of tough. I loved Red Smith. Without Aunt Ray, this work would be sadly lacking. Rayola supplied me with all of the family history before her death on April 6, 2021, in an Aurora, Missouri, hospital. My love for Rayola grew exponentially as she tirelessly supplied me with family facts. She was ninety-three.

I can recall her tenderly caring for my little dog Tippy after a fatal rattlesnake bite, and I can still see her spurring her big brown gelding through cedar brakes where the devil wouldn't go.

I regret that Aunt Ray didn't live to see this book in print. But it really doesn't matter. She's out there in the good place with Red, where both of them see and know everything worth knowing.

Red Smith, my surrogate father and the toughest cowboy who ever lived.

When I was jailed and facing prison, son Grady attempted to raise bail money.
He was my visitor at the Bexar County Jail. He never gave up on me.

Contents

Sam Kindrick drunk on a mechanical bull was an impromptu stock show feature. Photographer unknown.

Series Editor's Foreword

Clarence Samuel Kindrick is an offbeat Texas original. He has been his entire life. For a good part of his nearly ninety years on this earth in these South Texas parts, he's been a legend—whether as a brash newspaperman, an outlaw country music insider and publisher, FM radio renegade, menudo cookoff founder, or patron saint to misfits, madams, and a madman or two. Rogues, losers, and dreamers were all welcome. He was outlaw, gonzo, and iconic long before those terms became clichés. He earned every heap of praise and every curse word hurled his way in the Alamo City.

Of course, no one ever called him Clarence. That was his maternal grandfather's name. And only his mother and closest relatives called him Sammy. Sam Kindrick was the name. He was the man who agitated editors and publishers, who befriended gangsters, professional wrestlers, politicos, barmaids, musicians, bikers, drug dealers, booze hounds, speed freaks, fortune tellers, and the vampires of the night. The vices that came with the territory nearly killed him.

He chronicled in real time the rise of outlaw country music and Americana music in Texas. His aim wasn't to define it. He was not a music critic. He left those arguments to others who called it redneck rock, progressive country, and cosmic cowboy music. Sam was there to give it oxygen. But he brought game.

As a kid, he watched Hank Williams perform at Cherry Springs Dance Hall, albeit through a window. At Sul Ross State College in West Texas, he plunked along to the radio on a Gibson electric guitar. That's where he met Elvis Presley in February 1955. It was in the days when the future "King of Rock and Roll" and guitarist Scotty Moore and bassist Bill Black still shared driving chores and posted their own flyers in places like Alpine. By the 1970s, Sam Kindrick simply swaggered into the underbelly of the outlaw country beast. He understood it.

He had transformed himself from the hundred-dollar-a-week bow-tie-wearing newspaper reporter and then alcoholic polyester-suit newsroom veteran to a gruff-talking, turquoise-bejeweled cowboy god on the burgeoning Texas music scene. Cranked and ornery.

He was born again in a way that made his Baptist mother shudder. His gonzo writing and tirades could peel paint. The precursor had been his 1973 book, *The Best of Sam Kindrick: The Secret Life and Hard Times of a Cedar Chopper*. Now, he was all in. Untethered.

His silver-and-turquoise belt buckle, complete with a real bear claw among its stones, was a gift from a murderous gangster. With a black cowboy hat and unruly beard and long hair, he announced himself like a bad man out of *Hang 'Em High*.

His calling card was bolstered by friendships with the likes of legendary musicians Johnny Bush, Augie Meyers, and Willie Nelson. While he was simpatico with Nelson, his reporter's antennae picked up on an aura of mystery and aloofness fostered by the ambitious pigtailed singer-songwriter. "It's important to study what he never says," Kindrick observed in a haze of cocaine, angel dust, alcohol, and marijuana smoke. He could've been a permanent fixture on Willie's bus in those early days. But Sam Kindrick didn't see himself as a hanger-on or groupie. The truth was he wasn't ready to get straight. There were many more boozy, clenched-jaw twists, and drug busts to go in the story of the outlaw journalist.

Music fans and historians will get plenty of the good, the bad, and the very ugly in this book. But don't call it a confession. It's simply the same way Sam Kindrick has been telling his stories for decades in newspaper columns and in his own *Action Magazine*.

As a longtime musician, music journalist, and now curator who oversees his archives, I can attest that some of the source material for this book is shocking, brutal, outrageous, crude, and downright weird. He had friends on the right—and wrong—side of history. His journalism reflected the xenophobia, racism, prejudice, stereotypes, bigotry, gallows humor, delusions, and deep flaws of the era and within himself.

But Sam was always honest, insanely humorous, stylized, self-deprecating, and an accurate barometer of the times and its characters. He told it like it was. He had a moral code. He didn't pretend to control what came out of the mouths of his subjects—or his own. I've witnessed his cautionary redemption tale.

My favorite part of his story is when he was a boy with a dog raised by a single mother in Junction, Texas. This is what truly shaped the man behind the manual Royal typewriter. He adored his tough little Terrier mix named Tippy. The dog was a beloved part of the country family. Tippy loved to ride on the front fender of his grandmother's old car when she went shopping for groceries. I would loved to have seen that dusty road scene.

His aunt Rayola, a horsewoman as tough as any cowboy, often gave Tippy a ride on her horse Brown Jug. He sat behind her in the saddle. The dog had been a gift from the family doctor. Sammy raised it from a puppy, and they played along the banks of the South Llano River. They fished together, Sam in cutoff jeans, barefoot, and wearing a floppy straw hat. Tippy was a spotted, colored blur of light sniffing out squirrels and raccoons. Rattlesnakes, too, led to eventual tragedy. A lifetime later, a different dog—Petey the Wonder Dog—a bundle of "twisted steel and panther piss" would grace Sam's stories.

In the late 1930s and early 1940s, the rambunctious child was mischievous and a handful for his young mother, a deeply religious, highly educated schoolteacher, and, later, award-winning poet. The roots of Sammy's tenacious writing skills can be traced directly to her. Bernice was the family historian and his best friend.

She indulged him with his pet beaver, who chewed the leg off a dining room chair, and Samson the pet donkey and Possie the possum. Sam collected the wild animals. He was a friend to the high-spirited horses with names like Pinto, Leather Britches, and Redbird. That fascination was reprised decades later in one of his "Offbeat" newspaper columns about pet piranhas and tall tales of thousand-pound mutts.

His father died at age thirty-two when Sam was only nine months old. It's believed he died of a ruptured appendix. Grady Kindrick was a mystery, an untouchable presence for the imaginative boy who grew up in the small stucco house that Grady had built. There's a photo of the young family posed in front of it. The baby is on his mother's lap, and his father looks like a character out of *O Brother, Where Art Thou?*

Grady's passing was, Sam's mother would write, "the death of happiness." According to the undated tribute typewritten by his pious mother, Grady softly sang religious songs in his final moments in his hospital bed, succumbing as he sang, "Going to shout all over God's heaven."

It was an impossible standard. Sam often wondered what other attributes he might have inherited from his father. A childhood story of how his father had once cut down a mighty pecan tree after a flood in a show of defiance could be connected to his own explosive temper. His father was an excellent golfer and wagered on games. Sam heard his uncle's stories of how his father loved to hit into sand traps just to blast out of the sand. Sam longed for any information, any connection. He still has a couple of his father's hickory-shaft golf clubs. He reveals that it's a mixture of sorrow and curiosity whenever he holds his father's clubs.

Maybe it's because it's as close as he could ever get to holding Grady's hand. A family ranch hand, a hard-drinking horseman named Red Smith who slept in his spurs and had a face as rutted as the canyons of the Big Bend, was Sam's father figure. When young Sammy was bullied in school, Red advised him to find a strong cedar stick and hit the culprit "upside his head." He also taught the boy to shoot pool and make cowboy coffee over a fire in an open pan.

His mother held on to ghosts, too. Among her possessions at the end of her life was the pocket-sized *Red Letter New Testament* inscribed in Grady's beautiful handwriting: "I love you, Bernice."

She rarely revealed herself, even in her poetry. Usually, they were testaments to religious faith, work, nature, and the "tears of the years." Writing lifted her soul. A peek inside was another thing. The closest time, perhaps, was an untitled poem with the working title "Portrait Unveiled." A stanza offered this glimpse: "But she is truly hostage here, within her own confines, and viewed as odd occasionally, devoted to her lines."

And she was in pain, too. Did little Sammy truly understand? A tortured poem titled "A Psalm on the Death of a Young Father of an Infant Son" is a window into her sorrow. Little Sammy would surely find solace in such lines as "Lord, he was overjoyed to have a son and was eagerly planning life with him." But her sorrow verged on desperate: "Lord, you are so rich up there, couldn't Heaven have waited and let the daddy have his chance to love and guide, know his child?" It's not clear Sam ever saw these words.

In a poem called "Mother and Young Son," she recounts how "lacking a father's presence was a true problem." There is an occasion where she recounts catching her two-year-old child with a stick and asking him what he was going to do with it: "I'm going to whack Munny."

When he was three, she placed the Easter baskets in the tree branches because the rain had left the ground too wet. Her son tearfully came to the realization this was not the work of the Easter Bunny and threw a tantrum. "Now, you told me a story," he said to his mom. "This is not Easter. No rabbit can climb a tree."

Bernice taught him to swim at Flat Rock Crossing on the South Llano River. She was a natural athlete who had played basketball as a girl. Sammy later lettered in football, basketball, and track.

I first met Sam Kindrick in early 1976. I was onstage at the old Warehouse Club with my power pop band, the Krayolas. It was a hideaway near the airport where the owner liked to flash his pistol when he paid you. I should say, I didn't meet him so much as I saw Sam. You couldn't miss him. I was a teenager, and we were intimidated, if undaunted. Look who just walked in.

Action Magazine was new on the streets, and we had read the stories and seen the pictures. The dude looked tough and talked tougher. He was a badass. He sat near the back, I recalled. Then, I heard that drawl I've come to know so well. "Play 'Johnny B. Goode,'" he yelled out.

We were as green as they came, a Chicano boy band, really. We all looked at each other. We didn't know the most basic of rock songs. The closest thing we knew was the Beatles' version of Chuck Berry's "Roll Over Beethoven." We played it at a breakneck roar. He didn't boo. I still remember he gave us encouraging applause and may have even snapped some pictures of us. He always had his camera with him.

My real first connection to Sam, however, was through his son, Grady, the oldest of his three children. And it had come years earlier. We were the same age and went to the same junior high and high school. I didn't know him that well. But we were friendly. We had a class or two together. He was thin as a rock star and had really long hair. In the early 1970s, he wore faded jeans with color patches on them, the kinds favored by hippies. I was impressed that he had the courage of such self-expression. I was on the football team with a buzz cut and liked David Bowie's glam rock music but didn't dare say it. He was quiet and sensitive, but there was a rebellious air to him, too. I was vaguely aware that his father was a newspaper columnist and later the wild, rebellious publisher of *Action Magazine*. Over the decades, Sam and I would become friends. He was a mentor and a terrific source when I became a professional journalist.

When Grady died by suicide in 1993, I began to see Sam in a different light. I was a father by then. I was saddened by the news and imagined the depth of pain that he was feeling. I could relate. A few years earlier, my mom's sister, my aunt Sara, was murdered in Laredo. She was thirty-nine and the mother of three. I understood Sam's horror. This was deep and wasn't going away. Fifty-seven years earlier, Bernice had lost her Grady; now, Sam had lost his second one.

All these years later, nearly a half century, my affection and respect for Sam are the same as any loving son would have for their own father. I'm very proud of Sam for writing this book and for entrusting the Wittliff Collections at Texas State University in San Marcos to preserve his archives, which includes personal papers, his newspaper columns dating to the 1960s, more than four decades of *Action Magazine*, and more than forty-two hundred photographs. His mother's poetry is also preserved at the Wittliff. Both Sam and his mother were students here, so it's doubly sweet.

This memoir is only the beginning of the conversation with future historians interested in researching the origins of outlaw country and Americana music in Texas, the characters inside and on the periphery of that scene, and the cavalcade of misfits, rock 'n' rollers, barflies, rogues, and jesters that intersected with Sam's world—the way they really were. Sam's "Offbeat" columns in the *San Antonio Express-News*, hundreds of them, are a colorful treasure trove.

And at its core, this book is the voice of a man who is now on his way to thirty-five years of sobriety and one who has love in his life with his wife, Sharon. He is a survivor of many traumas, but one is central. Sam is a man haunted and inspired by the Grady he never knew and the one he didn't know long enough. Both died too young. Their memories live here.

—*Hector Saldaña*
General Editor

OUTLAW COUNTRY REPORTER

THE DEVIL IN JACKSON

This is about Willie Nelson, *Texas Girl Magazine*, and my face-to-face meeting with the Devil in Jackson, Michigan. I felt obliged to include it in this book.

I took my two sons, Grady and Steven, to Willie Nelson's first July 4 picnic in Dripping Springs, Texas. That was in 1973. I was present during planning stages for the epic cow pasture blowout, so I had knowledge in advance of the surprise rock superstar who was to appear.

The scheduled lineup included Willie, Waylon Jennings, Tom T. Hall, Kris Kristofferson, Loretta Lynn, Tex Ritter, Rita Coolidge, Charlie Rich, and Hank Snow. Nobody in the country would have suspected that Nelson would have Leon Russell as a surprise guest on that first July 4 picnic. I knew that Nelson and Russell had been friends for years, and I knew in advance that Willie was planning to spring rock star Leon on the country music crowd at Dripping Springs.

In 1973, Leon Russell was a rock-and-roll god, a much bigger draw than Nelson at the time, and my sixteen-year-old son Grady's absolute musical higher power. Grady played nothing but Russell on his record player, and his room in our San Antonio home was a Leon Russell shrine, with Russell photographs and posters on all four walls and even the ceiling.

I could hear Nelson's distinct voice as we crawled out of the truck. He was sitting on a log near one of the campfires, and the man sitting across from him had his back to us. Willie was playing his battered Martin guitar Trigger. The two of them were singing the old Willie tune "Family Bible." When I spotted the cascade of waist-length golden-blond hair, I knew instantly who was singing with Nelson. Leon Russell had arrived. Good spirits were in the atmosphere on that warm July night. We could all feel it.

When they finished the song, I distinctly remember leading Grady up to the campfire. Steven had wandered away. I knew Leon from a previous meeting, but Grady had never before laid eyes on his rock idol from Oklahoma. Nelson seemed to grasp the moment. When I introduced my son, Willie shook Grady's hand and then turned toward Russell. "I want you to meet my friend Leon Russell," Willie told my kid. Then to Leon, he said, "This is Sam's son Grady."

Leon promptly reached out and grabbed Grady's hand. "Mighty pleased to meet you, Grady," Russell said in his inimitable Oklahoma drawl. "I hope you enjoy the music and have a good time tomorrow."

I don't recall Grady's mumbled response to his idol. I will never forget the look of incomprehensible shock and joy on my kid's face. His speech was frozen. He looked at me and smiled for a split second. He knew his old man had pulled off this impossible scenario for him. Leon Russell sensed it too, something spiritual and really special. I have no words to explain the love I felt at that moment for my son. And for the long-haired Oklahoma rock star who reached out to my kid. I became a Leon Russell fan for life.

That first Willie concert was the beginning of an era, the birth of redneck rock, a cultural awakening that was felt all over the South and beyond. The hippies and the rednecks would lay down their arms and light up the joints of peace. I looked out over that great roiling sea of youthful humanity on the morning of July 4, 1973, and what did I see? I saw a cloud of marijuana smoke. I saw a huge sign that read "E Pluribus Willie," and I saw more naked titties than one could imagine existing in one Texas cow pasture at one time. Another significant chapter in my life was beginning to unfurl. That next chapter would prove to be rowdy and exciting, very dangerous, exhilarating at times, heartbreaking, educational, and scary as hell.

That first Willie July 4 concert drew a crowd estimated at forty thousand. I had my boys at the first four—Dripping Springs, College Station, Liberty Hill, and Gonzales. The crowds swelled exponentially. The Gonza-

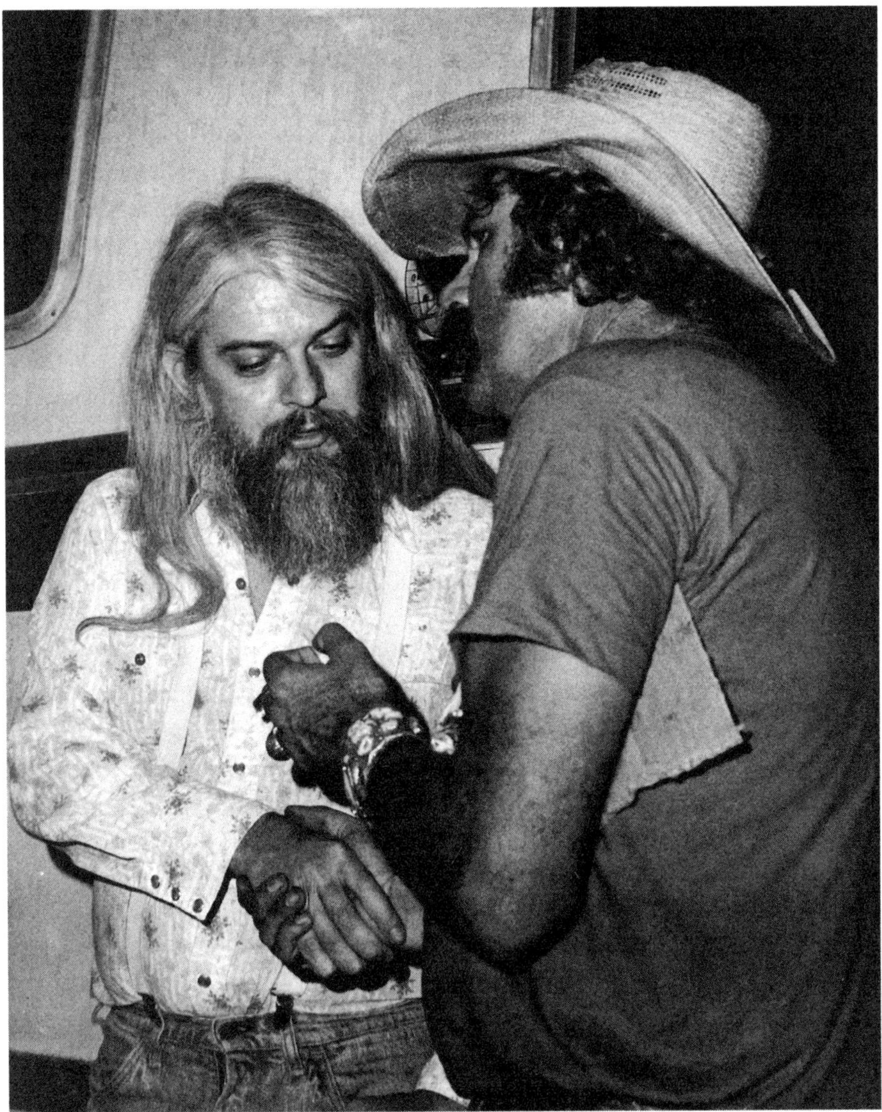

Leon Russell (*left*) and Sam. At the early Willie Nelson picnics they came to see Leon.

les turnout was estimated at eighty thousand, and I lost count as Nelson moved the show to other states before returning to the Austin area.

I met Willie's two older daughters, Lana and Susie, at Dripping Springs when they were teenagers. His son Billy I met later. These kids were all by Nelson's first wife, Martha, a lady I never met. The only Nelson wife I was to know was Connie, the blond beauty and mother of two of Willie's girls and who remains my friend today.

There was driving rain at the Gonzales picnic, and it was here that I met David Allan Coe, self-described "Mysterious Rhinestone Cowboy and Death Row Killer." I was intrigued by the big tattooed entertainer, and we were to become friends as we remain today. David Allan Coe is one of the most talented people I have ever known. David Allan and I exchanged books—*The Best of Sam Kindrick* for Coe's *Ex-Convict*. The Coe book features a young Coe mug shot from an Ohio State penitentiary and detailed survival instructions for anyone preparing to enter a penitentiary. It tells you when to talk, when not to talk, and how to survive with the worst of the worst.

"The key to prison survival," Coe told me, "is learning how to mind your business." The Bandidos Motorcycle Club outlaws were starting to hang around Coe shows at that time, and the one on Coe's tour bus when I climbed on that day in Gonzales was a surly San Antonio biker called Dead Weight. I had never been a Dead Weight fan, and he wasn't crazy about me either. Someone had shot him in the belly, and surgery had left him barely holding his guts in place on that muggy day in Gonzales. He smelled about as bad as he looked, and the two of us were exchanging minor unpleasantries when Coe pitched me a glass container of cocaine in a sack that also held a mirror and a soda straw.

"I'm going to change for the show," Coe said as he headed for the bus sleeping quarters. "I hope you boys can cool it. Dead Weight is so fucked up with bullet holes he can barely walk."

Dead Weight saw Coe hand me the bag. He was duly impressed. "You and David Allan must be really tight," the biker said. "I can hardly believe he would turn his back on you with you holding his personal stash." After that, Dead Weight and I were civil to each other. Coe and I, if anyone is interested, gave up drugs years ago. That is why we are both still alive.

In those early years after Executive Editor Charles O. (Charlie) Kilpatrick fired me from the *San Antonio Express-News*, and while I was still holding my air job at KEXL FM, I hatched the crazy idea of starting my own improbable publication, a small tabloid that I would name *Action Magazine*. I wanted to focus on the Texas outlaw music explosion out of Austin, from Austin's Soap Creek Saloon to the Armadillo World Headquarters where

Willie Nelson was sharing the stage with everyone from Kinky Friedman and the Texas Jew Boys to Commander Cody and the Lost Planet Airmen. Yet I didn't want to be limited to only music. I wanted my publication to cover the action, whether it be talented musicians or colorful preachers like the "Chaplain of Bourbon Street" Bob Harrington, bare-knuckle street fighters like Bobby (Kid Death) Thomas, or shotgun-packing pimps and infamous killers like Arthur Harry (Bunny) Eckert. *Action Magazine* ran no record reviews. I never wasted my time in the pretentious business of passing judgment on someone's music. I wrote more about the musician than the music. I wanted an honest balls-to-the-wall publication that would kiss no corporate asses or take any prisoners. And that's exactly what I told Lone Star Brewing Company president Harry Jersig when I made my pitch for a back-cover advertiser. I noticed a thin smile on Jersig's lips while I was talking.

I didn't have a dime to my name, and Jersig knew it when I outlined what I had in mind. He was already in tune with Willie Nelson's growing impact on the burgeoning Texas music scene. I knew that Jersig had little use for the *Express-News*, and I knew that his music advertising promotions man Jerry Retzloff liked me. Retzloff was also connecting with an exciting new breed of new age musicians like Jerry Jeff Walker, Marcia Ball, Ray Benson, Janis Joplin, Asleep at the Wheel, Willis Allen Ramsey, Rusty Wier, Ray Wylie Hubbard, and B. W. Stevenson.

"I will write about these people and more," I told Harry Jersig. "I want to sell you the back cover of what is now a nonexistent magazine." Jersig wrote me a check for a thousand dollars on the spot, and the rest is history. That first little twelve-page issue of *Action Magazine* was printed on March 25, 1975. It featured Willie Nelson on the front cover and Lone Star Beer on the back cover. And Lone Star was to stick with me for years to come. Talk about pathetic defiance. I actually pitched a bundle of fifty copies of that first issue through the front lobby door of the eight-story *Express-News* building on Avenue E. I think I also yelled "Fuck you, Charlie" at the top of my lungs.

I felt like Daniel standing naked in front of the lion's den and shooting the finger with both hands. I know I was as crazed and out of control as a Hunter S. Thompson dope dream. Earlier I had been offered a job with the *Houston Post*. No, by God, I would take no newspaper job in Houston. I would stay in San Antonio and haunt Charlie Kilpatrick until the day one of us died. He died June 27, 2013. And Daniel finally relaxed the double "birds."

Charlie's daughter Kye is a classy lady who was nice to me one time. In the recovery program that eventually saved my life, I learned that resentments are my number-one offender. I have still got my share of resentments, but I finally let Charlie go before that resentment killed me, and I wish his daughter and the Kilpatrick family nothing but the best.

When I told Willie Nelson of my plans for *Action Magazine*, he encouraged me. "Give the musicians who have never been written about a shot," he said. "There are some good ones out there who have never had any recognition in print. Give them all some ink when you can."

Those early issues featured only one colored ink, red on the magazine logo. The four-color process necessary for full color required publishing film separations that were more than I could afford in those early years. "Print them all in black and white," Willie said. "The black-and-white papers will appeal to the poor people."

The first run of eight thousand copies of the *Action Magazine* tabloid was printed on a web press at San Antonio Press, which was then located on Fredericksburg Road and owned by the Medellin family. Jose Medellin headed the business with assistance from his two younger brothers, Luis and Raul.

Most web presses around Texas in those days required service by technicians in Chicago and on the East Coast, but not San Antonio Press. Joe Medellin worked on his own equipment, and I can recall him in those early years, crawling wrench in hand from under one of the big iron monsters. I can remember Joe smeared with printers' ink from head to foot. He even had it in his eyebrows. He had it in his blood as well. I know the excitement. The big newspaper web presses used today rumble and roar like a freight train. When they hit full speed and printing velocity, literally shaking the building, I never fail to feel a goosebump playing along my spine.

Action Magazine would never have been if not for Jose Medellin. Joe has a heart and a soul and I will love him forever. He carried me with no charge for printing over a few tight spot early months and the better part of one year, and I know he never did get paid in full for all he did. In later years, Joe's brother Luis became the company head. He, too, was kind to *Action Magazine*. Other printers made lower bids for my business

Redneck Rock Hits San Antonio

Let this column be an introduction to our first issue of "The Action."

In this publication, you'll find exactly what our name implies--ACTION!

You can't keep a squirrel on the ground in timber country, and this staff doesn't like flat land.

If you don't know me, you're lucky. If you do know me, I'll sympathize with you. But I won't apologize for being born, nor will I apologize for what we intend to be San Antonio's number-one entertainment vehicle.

Sprawling San Antonio has been starved for a genuine entertainment publication. Here it is. "The Action" is designed for one purpose. To entertain.

WE INTEND TO keep the juices flowing. This publication is not written for any clique. It's published for all of the folks who love to boogie.

"The Action" will cover the nightclub circuit. It will also offer some meaty, gutsy reading material, complete with top-quality photographic art.

But we'll do more than sandwich a bunch of stiff-necked cocktail talk around our advertisements. It ain't the meat, it's the motion, brothers and sisters, and I'll bite off both thumbs in front of the Alamo before I'll allow this vehicle to bore anyone.

If it's a big, fancy cocktail party, we might be there. If it's an arm wrestling contest between Circus Face Flannigan and Jo Jo the Dog-Faced Boy, I'll guarantee you we'll be there.

FROM MY GOOD friend Willie Nelson to the kid with holes in his tennis shoes and a rented flat-top guitar, "The Action" staff will listen. And we'll report.

We will cover the clubs, we will cover the music scene of San Antonio and surrounding areas, we will cover anything that involves fun, frolic and folks--restaurants, concerts, armadillo races, or goat ropings.

San Antonio is filled with fine musicians who have never been given a fair shake. That's what we're here for. I've got a reputation for all sorts of things. Some bad. I've been commode-hugging, knee-walking drunk, and so hungover some mornings I couldn't make a fist until noon. But I've never been accused of failing to tell it like it is.

That's exactly what this column and "The Action" will do.

My title is editor and co-publisher. But I've always adhered to the adage that titles are no better than the man behind them. And most titles won't buy you a short beer at Mom's Baitstand.

GRANTED, THIS ISSUE of "The Action" is not too large. It's up to you, the reader, to help us expand and grow. This publication belongs to you.

I've been around pompous, hypocritical, rednecked typewriter jockeys most of my life. The majority of them are like guitar pickers with a tin ear for music. They've got a tin ear for living, breathing, human folks. And we feel that we can swallow a bottle of ink and sweat out a better story than the majority of them can write. Because "The Action" is where it's all at--with you the people.

We want this publication to be light and breezy, flip and factual, stern in some ways, and maybe a bit sophisticated in a raw-boned, countryfied sort of way.

"The Action" looks down on no man. If we offend you, it's purely intentional. If we entertain you, that's intentional, too. But if we toss a bundle of floss and gloss and glitter at you, sans rare meat and zingy copy, then it's time for us to go out and play in the expressway.

I'LL PROMISE YOU that "The Action" staff will never be caught crawling around on an expressway.

Willie Nelson sums up my sentiments well when he sings that walking is better than running away, and crawling ain't no good at all.

"The Action" won't crawl. We might walk. But we'll genuflect before no tin god. And most of the time, we'll be blowing out our tennis shoes in an effort to bring you the finest in down-to-earth literary entertainment.

This column will be dedicated to that end. And so will this entire publication.

We want to be proud of this publication. And we can't be proud of it unless you are proud of it. And you can't be proud of it unless you are part of it.

"The Action" wants to blow and go like a big wheel in a South Texas cotton field. And we want you wheeling right along with us.

It's like Peter Cedar Stacker said: This magazine will make haunted houses uglier, and ugly girls prettier.

We want you to appreciate things you've never even thought about.

Sometimes, we'll be as pretty as hoar frost glistening on a cow chip in the moonlight. Or as pretty as a speckled pup sitting under a red wagon.

And sometimes we'll come on like a burst of dirty thunder. Action is the game. And "The Action" is our name.

A new brand of music has wafted upon the San Antonio scene like a gentle spring breeze.

It can't be labeled and hung on a musical peg--nor can the untidy fellows who pick and sing it.

Author Jan Reid tried to explain this musical phenomena in his book, "The Improbable Rise of Redneck Rock."

Yet this music and its creators and disciples just don't fit into a mold.

They have one common characteristic': In some aspects, they're all rebels. Nice rebels. Friendly cats in cowboy hats, willing to share their last swallow of beer with a "cross-country" brother.

Call it what you like -- redneck rock, progressive country, or just plain, down-home, foot-stomping music.

It's here in San Antonio. And it's going to bust the musical seams of this city before men like Willie Nelson, Rusty Wier, Steve Fromholz, Augie Meyer, and an army of others are through.

Some refuse to accept this new style of music for what it is--a loosely-knit combination of country, rock, jazz, blues and cedar stump story-telling.

But Willie Nelson, the king of it all, sums up the feelings of his bearded, unshorn legions well when he grins through his red whiskers and says: "I don't put music in

Continued Pg. 3

WILLIE NELSON
. . . The Cross-Country King

THE ACTION NEWS WILL BE DISTRIBUTED AT OVER 500 RESTAURANTS, HOTELS, MOTELS, LOUNGES, NITE CLUBS AND LIQUOR STORES THROUGHOUT SAN ANTONIO.

IF YOU DID NOT GET YOUR COPIES OF "THE ACTION NEWS" OR YOU HAVE RUN OUT, PLEASE CALL 494-7475. AND WE WELCOME NEWS TIPS AND STORY CONTRIBUTIONS.

Action Magazine first issue, March 1975. I staked my territory with Willie Nelson on the cover and popularized terms like "redneck rock," "progressive," and "cross-country." Printer Joe Medellin carried us for months when I couldn't pay him.

over the years, but I remained with the Medellins until they sold San Antonio Press.

With help from my son Grady, I delivered those first free-distribution magazines to nightclubs, restaurants, ice houses, and other people spots. Grady never finished high school, insisting on working for me and passing his General Educational Development (GED) test in the meanwhile. We were not well received by all. Cappy Lawton ordered Grady out of one of his restaurants when the boy tried to deliver the magazines, and I took rejections involving my son personally. I recall refusing later to do radio commercials for the Lawton eateries when I was on the air at KEXL.

I will never forget the response I got from musicians who were to grace the pages of my little rag over the next forty-four years. I became very close friends with Johnny Bush and Augie Meyers. They remained close through the years. Others I formed friendships with include Gary Stewart, Doug Sahm, Darrell McCall, David Allan Coe, and many hundreds more. I feel like I helped raise Dub Robinson, Randy Toman, and Robert (Cotton) Payne of the old Drug Store Cowboys group. We shared an office at one point. And I was there when Claude Morgan formed his Buckboard Boogie Boys group with fiddler Ron Knuth, drummer Larry Robison, and bassist Larry Patton. These three had been part of Hank Williams Jr.'s band, all finding themselves out of work when Williams was seriously injured in a Montana hunting accident.

I met and interviewed the legendary Ernest Tubb at the Kicker Palace in Poteet. In discussing various country musicians during the course of the interview, the Texas troubadour had little good to say about David Allan Coe, who had mimicked Tubb in a song Coe called "If That Ain't Country."

"I think he's a disgrace to country music," Tubb said of Coe. "He can sing a little, but all that long hair and tattoos and cheap-looking Indian jewelry has no place." Then Ernest Tubb stared straight into my eyes and I will never forget his words: "And you could do with a haircut yourself, son." The old Nashville troubadour was nowhere ready for the evolving era of progressive country music, or redneck rock as some were calling it.

During the mid-1970s and 1980s, I had frequent interaction with Willie Nelson and that unlikely gaggle of followers and hangers-on who were to establish themselves as the Willie Nelson Family. Willie paid some of them; some he just fed. Others just followed along. But a T-shirt emblazoned with the Willie Nelson Family stamp would gain you access to the hallowed halls of a Nelson tour bus, various backstage sanctuaries, and hotel suites where marijuana smoke hung like a Gulf Coast cloud bank.

When Willie moved into his Pedernales Country Club holdings near Austin and purchased a pool hall on South Lamar he called Willie's Pool Hall, we had a new center for the universe. This was in the 1970s when South Austin was the place, Willie's was booming, and Manny Gammage was attracting national attention with his Texas Hatters on South Lamar. Willie Nelson, David Allan Coe, Rusty Wier, and other figures of prominence were wear-ing the handblocked Manny Gammage hats with the distinctive curled brim. I always wanted one but could never find the bucks when I was in Austin.

Willie and his sister Bobbie Nelson were both raised by their grandparents in Abbott, Texas. Willie's mom left shortly after he was born. His father, Ira, was an automobile mechanic who came back into Willie's life to help out around the Austin pool hall. I did an early *Action Magazine* article on Pop Nelson. Everyone called him Pop. Willie's stepmother was known as Mom Nelson.

Willie called me when the story on his father was printed. He never mentioned anything about the father waiting until his son was established as a music star before coming back into Willie's life. "I want to thank you for writing about my dad," Willie said. "It means a lot to me."

Asked once about Willie's long-haired outlaw look, the father said, "With the money he is making today, I think it would be fine if he grew his hair down to his shoe tops."

To know Willie, to know the real Willie Nelson, I think it is important to study what he never says. His lyrics have established him as a world-class poet with the guts and gall and compassion and love to show most of his soul to the world. He raises millions for farmers. He rescues and shelters old and abandoned horses. His respect and genuine love for fellow musicians is a given. His insight is stunning. But an aura of mystery has always been part of Willie's psyche. I think it must have something to do with humility. He doesn't talk much about death.

I was especially fond of Paul English, the Nelson drummer who dressed in black, often with a satanic cape and cowboy boots with silver, pointed toe guards. Paul was a former Fort Worth pimp and gangster who talked nasally through a nose that had been broken more than once. A fierce and dangerous body guard who would have defended Willie with his life, Paul English was inspiration for the Willie Nelson song "Me and Paul."

We were at John T. Floore Country Store in Helotes when Willie sang this one before a live audience for the first time. It details his trials and tribulations on the road with his former gangster drummer, with one verse encapsulating it all. I had already heard the story. There had been a bomb threat at the airport in Milwaukee, Wisconsin, and Paul's sinister appearance had resulted in the entire band being temporarily detained. "I wrote a song about Paul," Willie told me that evening at Floore's. The verse about the airport incident goes like this:

> At the airport in Milwaukee
> They refused to let us board the plane at all
> They said we looked suspicious
> But I think they want to pick on me and Paul

I wrote a cover story for *Action Magazine* on Paul English. The cover photograph was of Paul in his black attire and holding a stuffed devil in his lap. "Willie saved my life," English told me. "I was living on borrowed time in Fort Worth. There had already been two contracts on me. I was a shuffle drummer and Willie took me in. We have been brothers since that day. I would lay down my life for him."

I went on the Willie Nelson tour of state and county fairs in the early 1980s, starting in Mississippi and ending somewhere around the Great Lakes. Willie flew me back and forth from various tour engagements to San Antonio so that I could work on *Action Magazine*. Poodie Locke was the stage manager back then, while David Anderson was the road manager on that tour. I was in for an education that was to include the most harrowing drug scare of my life.

Nelson was getting hot during those days. His *Redheaded Stranger* album was on its way to turning platinum, and strange pale-skinned Northerners in states like Illinois, Michigan, and Wisconsin were out on summer afternoons in straw cowboy hats and Willie Nelson T-shirts.

I don't know how it is today, but Chicago was an exciting otherworldly metropolis with an Al Capone aura that made me feel like I needed a tommy gun for safety. I recall we were milling around in an outdoor city park shortly before Willie's show on Navy Pier. Uniformed Chicago cops were standing hock to hip with husky dudes in black T-shirts who were snorting rock cocaine off knife blades in plain view. Nobody was attempting to hide anything from anybody. They were spooning the dope out of plastic bags with little thought to hundred-dollar cocaine rocks that fell and bounced unnoticed on the ground.

They were freely sharing the coke with any of us who were interested. Cops were interspersed among the official-looking cats in the black shirts. It was obvious that they were Willie fans and eager to make the Texas visitors feel at home. Jane Byrne was mayor of Chicago at that time, and one of the cops had a message for me.

"Hey," he said in that strange Chicago accent. "I hear you are a writer in Texas. You ought to write something about this fucking bitch mayor we got up here name of Jane Byrne. This fucking bitch wants to take our guns away when we are off-duty. Hey, this is fucking Chicago, man. A Chicago cop without a firearm is dead meat. You really should write something about this dirty fucking bitch."

The Navy Pier chicken-wire phenomenon is mentioned elsewhere in this book—women crawling like monkeys up a chicken-wire shield in front of the Nelson stage on Navy Pier. But I was soon to learn that the Willie appeal ran far deeper than a surface of starstruck women. Songwriters the country over were taking notice. The Nelson lyrics were galvanizing the same types of songsmiths and storytellers who once sat at the feet of Hank Williams. I was soon to see it firsthand.

As the tour moved through one Wisconsin city, the bus air conditioner went on the blink. Those were the days when a tour bus had windows that opened manually. The road crew had the bus windows open when I saw something sail through. Then I saw another object sail into the bus. I heard clicking and clinking sounds, like hail or sleet was hitting the bus. Objects were hitting and bouncing. Then something landed in my lap. What the hell? It was a cassette tape in a plastic container.

Willie's stage manager Poodie Locke explained. "These are cassette tapes of original songs. Those are songwriters out there trying to get their original songs into the bus in the hope that Willie might hear one and want to record it. It happens a lot. Sometimes they try to throw the tapes on stage during a performance."

I asked Locke if Nelson ever listened to one of the songs. Did he ever record one? "It ain't done that way," Locke said.

This was around the time that Nelson decided to quit doing hard drugs and stick with marijuana. He demanded the same of his musicians and road crew. He was more than adamant, posting signs on the tour buses that read "IF YOU'RE WIRED YOU'RE FIRED."

Some members of the Willie Nelson Family dutifully stopped the dope. Others hid the cocaine, pills, and methamphetamine from Willie. I was snorting both coke and meth at the time, and I refrained from commenting when Willie suggested that it might be better if I followed suit. "I talked it over with the boys," Willie said. "They have agreed to pull up."

Such was the tour bus climate that summer when we pulled into Jackson, Michigan. Willie was scheduled for two performances at the Jackson County Fair, one in early afternoon and the other a night show. The afternoon show was well under way, and some of us were still on the bus, smoking weed and just kicking back. Poodie Locke was still on the bus, as was Don Bowman, a country comedian who was opening for Willie, and roadie Billy Cooper, a longtime friend of mine.

The only other person on the bus that afternoon was a woman who, we later learned, owned a massage parlor in Jackson. She was a big woman with curly red hair and wearing a lot of costume jewelry. She had no official authorization for being backstage and on the tour bus, but there she was. And such is a common occurrence amid the hustle and bustle of setting up and tearing down for a road show. Someone just winds up backstage and nobody really knows how the person got there.

The big redhead was laughing and joking like she belonged, and I gave little thought when she produced a little silver pipe and passed it to Don Bowman. Like the rest of us, Bowman assumed the pipe contained marijuana as he took a hit and passed it on to Cooper. I had barely inhaled one lung full of smoke when I knew something was direly wrong. I was starting to rise up toward the roof of the bus when I saw Billy Cooper's anguished face. His eyes were as big as banjos. I looked down at Bowman and saw that he was rigid as a fireplace poker, grinning like a vapid Mardi Gras mask with drool dripping out of his mouth.

"It's the pipe," Billy Cooper cried. "The pipe, the fuckin' pipe."

Poodie Locke was a big guy in cowboy boots. He didn't smoke the little silver pipe, sensing instantly what was happening. As my body rose up through the roof of the bus, I remember Poodie grabbing the female massage parlor owner by her tangle of red curls and dragging her off the

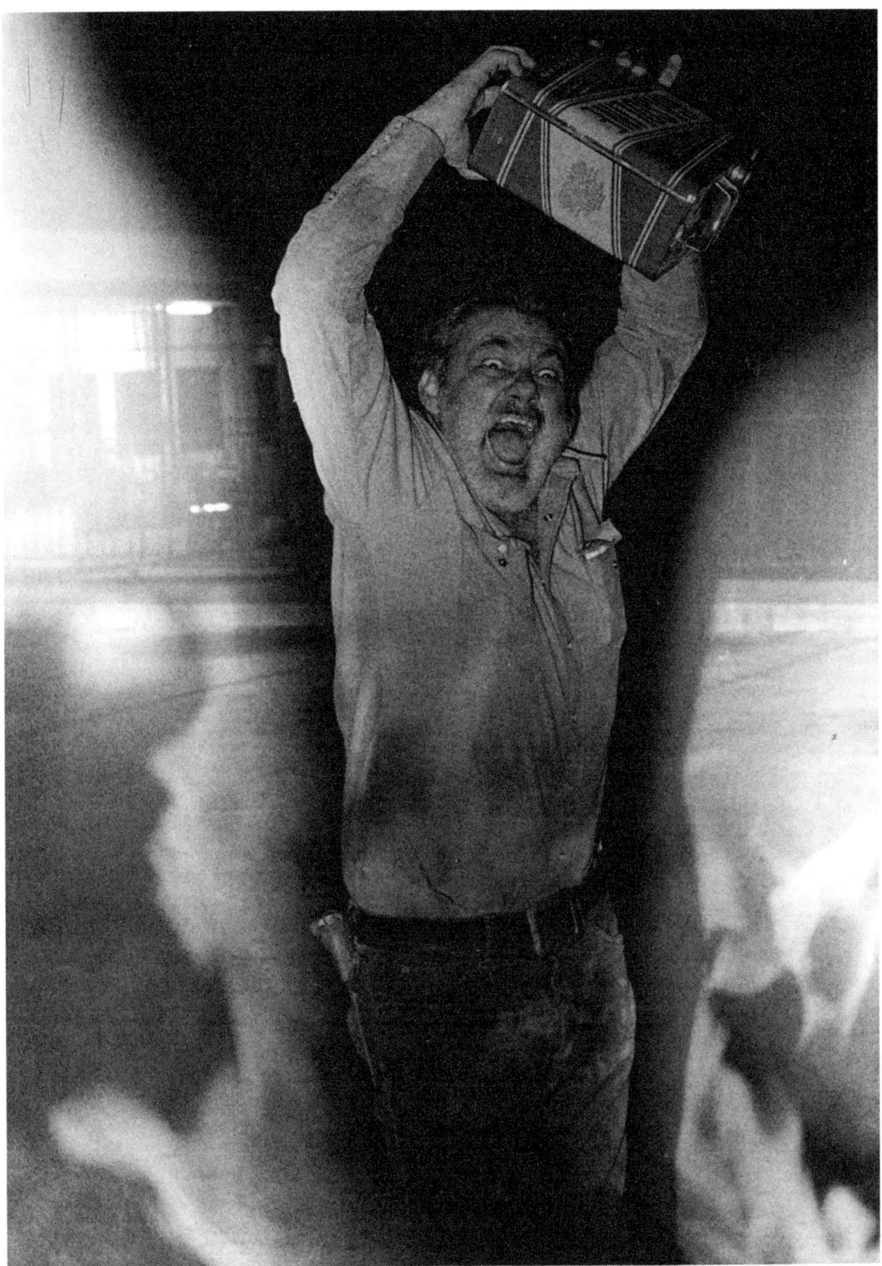

Sam on fire. For the magazine, as an inside joke, I recreated a dangerous incident that had occurred under the influence. I'd set myself on fire: "I was fucked up, man."

bus and across the gravel parking lot. I remember the woman howling at Locke. "Those guys knew what they were smoking." Willie might have been a recipient of the evil pipe and Locke knew it. Poodie was still dragging her by the hair as I floated on up out of the bus for at least a mile where I was to meet the Devil.

The Devil and I were high up above the county fair and the stage where Willie was playing. I never saw anything or anybody as horribly scary looking as this sonofabitch. He had long sideburns, pimples on his face with purple pus running out of them, and long rotten fangs that made him look like a walrus with cavities wearing a straw cowboy hat. And I will swear to this day that the Devil had a hand-tooled leather hatband that read "E Pluribus Willie."

Suddenly, and without warning, the Devil was gone and I was back on the tour bus, shaking like a dog passing razor blades and clinging to Cooper and Bowman like they were my mothers. We were all scared shitless, and it seemed only reasonable that we lock the bus doors. The terrifying thing about being this scared is that you don't know what you are scared of. Fear becomes terror.

Don Bowman had some measure of wits intact when he suggested we eat something. "We get something to eat and we might come down off this shit," he said. Cooper agreed. I looked out the bus window and could see lighted carnival rides down a small hill. I didn't see the Devil anywhere, but I knew he was out there somewhere. I was still terrified, but I volunteered to go for hot dogs.

With Bowman and Cooper locked in the bus behind me, I ran down the hill and found a hot dog stand. With a dozen hot dogs in a sack, I ran back to the bus like the hounds of hell were barking down my shirt collar. We gobbled down those hot dogs like contestants in a hot dog–eating contest. We were still scared out of our skins when Nelson and the band returned to the bus. The band members were pounding on the side of the bus and yelling like hell when one of us finally unlocked the door.

I don't recall what he said, but Willie wasn't happy about being locked out of his own bus. We never learned exactly what was in the little pipe, but most of us figured it was a pure form of angel dust, the street name for phencyclidine (PCP). I later looked it up. It is known for producing severe hallucinations, and one semiofficial source designates it as "the scariest motherfucking drug on the planet."

Sam with Willie Nelson. I was one of the first to hear the early mixes of
***Redheaded Stranger*. I loved it but didn't think it would sell. On the surface,**
Willie acted like he didn't give a rat shit about anything.

I have never fully accepted the possibility that the Jackson Devil was a hallucination. I looked into his yellow eyes and smelled his fetid breath. I saw his hatband, and I could read every word on it. Cooper, Bowman, and I suffered pounding headaches for two weeks after the Jackson show.

This was the last Nelson road tour for me. My next close contact with Willie came in December 1979, when I did a cover story on Nelson for *Texas Girl Magazine*. To read the article, search online for "Willie Nelson Interview; Texas Girl."

The article is a general feature on Willie, combined with the new magazine's statewide search for the most beautiful woman in Texas. With headquarters in Houston, the slick new enamel-cover magazine had everything necessary for success but enough seed money to get it over the initial hump.

Printer friend Joe Cardenas was an early consultant with the Houston publisher of *Texas Girl*, as was ace photographer Bill Spence, the man behind the camera for our big *Texas Girl* photo shoot, which was to include the final candidates for the search for a Texas beauty queen. It all took place at Willie's country club. Western artist Clinton Baermann was present, and he appeared in photographs with me, Cardenas, and numerous scantily clad beauty candidates who frolicked around that afternoon on the Pedernales Country Club hill. A few of them were stark naked, and photographer Spence didn't miss a one.

The magazine was billed as the Texas answer to *Playboy*, which it hardly was. While *Action Magazine* lasted forty-four years on inexpensive Canadian newsprint paper, beautiful full-enamel color *Texas Girl Magazine* went belly-up after two more issues. I don't think a Texas beauty queen was ever named. Willie said, "Too damn bad. It was one hell of an idea."

2

GROWING UP ON THE LLANO

I never knew for sure what first inspired me to write. Looking back now, I know that a major influence was Fred Gipson, the Mason County writer who penned books such as *Hound Dog Man* and the nationally acclaimed best seller *Old Yeller*, which became a major motion picture. I grew up on neighboring ranchland in Kimble County. *Hound Dog Man* was the first book I ever checked out of the Junction school library. It was classified as a children's book.

J. D. Salinger also caught my eye when I was still a kid. I read Catcher in the Rye three times. Salinger was an early-day outlaw, as was Scantlin, the rapscallion hero of Gipson's first book.

I will always count San Antonio Evening News front-page columnist Paul Thompson as a significant influence. He was a word mechanic with few peers, a literary hatchet man with a fascinating command of the written word. Paul Thompson became a mentor of sorts. I was intrigued by his ability to kill, gill, and gut political panjandrums with his writing while skating successfully along the fine line of libel. Paul Thompson probably wielded more political power than any other single individual on the San Antonio scene. He epitomized the term "Poison Pen." He was damn sure the most feared writer in this part of Texas.

And I read gonzo journalist Hunter S. Thompson (no relation) with the weird feeling that I might have known him in an earlier life. I had to read Hunter Thompson. Perhaps because his weird behavior and scattershot writing style offered proof that you don't have to be sane in order to make it. Whatever make it is. I never was sure about this. Hunter S. killed himself at the very end of his zany career.

As mentioned earlier, when I was a kid growing up in Junction, Texas, and surrounding Kimble County ranchland, my first interest in any kind of literature was focused on writer Fred Gipson. Gipson's interests centered on dogs and kids. He wrote several books, gaining national acclaim with the touching dog yarn *Old Yeller*. I was always taken with Fred Gipson's knack for describing our part of Texas—there is nothing prettier than hoar frost sparkling on a cow chip in the moonlight. But it was Gipson's earlier novel that caught my fancy and fired my imagination, a story of a boy and the lovable but fiddle-footed rake the boy idolized.

The title of the book is *Hound Dog Man*. The setting is Mason County in West-Central Texas. The main actor is a raccoon hunter who never managed to completely grow up. Blackie Scantling is his name. He was never referred to as a raccoon hunter. He was a coon hunter, the greatest in the world, and his coonhounds were called Rock and Drum. People from that neck of the woods still refer to raccoons as coons. I do so myself.

Hound Dog Man is told from the perspective of twelve-year-old Cotton Kinney, a country boy who yearned for a dog of his own. After dropping by the Kinney home for a visit, Blackie Scantling was to captivate young Cotton with antics and trail hound stories alike. The two even went on a magical adventure that saw the hound dog man get down on all fours and back down a bewildered bull. And as was his custom, author Gipson eventually returned the boy to reality and his responsible, hardworking father and the qualities that such men instill in their sons. There was always a moral to a Fred Gipson story.

I had two Treeing Walker Coonhounds while growing up in Kimble County, of which Junction is the county seat. And wouldn't you know I called my dogs Rock and Ruby. I also had a tough little terrier mix I called Tippy.

My childhood hero, William Chester (Red) Smith, however, was no coon hunter, although his lifestyle was as free spirited as was the fictitious Blackie Scantling's. Red was the toughest cowboy in the world and the greatest horse trainer who ever lived. Of Red Smith, I once wrote: He was a hell-raising whiskey-drinking cowboy with no teeth and a face like a rock slide. Red Smith was my Blackie Scantling.

My father, Grady Exa Kindrick, died before I was three months old. I never got to know him. He died on an operating table in San Antonio's old

**Sam with father, Grady, and mother, Bernice, in front of the
Junction house that Grady single-handedly built. This photo was
taken about two weeks before Grady's death when I was about
nine months old.**

Nix Hospital after being rushed by car from Junction, more than a hundred miles distant. The year was 1934. My mother, Bernice, always told us
that Grady died of locked bowels. His younger brother, my uncle Bennett
Kindrick, told his son, my cousin Roy Kindrick, that my father's death
could probably be attributed to a ruptured appendix accompanied by pneu-
monia.

My mother was a beautiful, brilliant schoolteacher and published poet who retired with a master's degree after teaching in Comstock, Comfort, Junction, and the Fort Sam Houston Independent School District in San Antonio. She taught me in fifth grade. It was my hardest school year, as my mother wanted no hint of favoritism. Her last job was at Cole Middle School at Fort Sam Houston.

When I was in school in Junction, she married an Edwards County ranchman by the name of Temple Deats. This marriage was abusive and was annulled by a county judge. She later married Horton Howard, a retired chief in the US Navy and a really good guy who treated me with kindness. They stayed together until Howard's death.

When Bernice was eighteen months old, she was voted the prettiest baby in Junction. My aunt Mary Helen (Polly) Majirus, one of my mother's younger sisters, remembered a picture of the event, my mom crying and holding a little silver cup she was awarded. Always active in church and civic organizations, she published two books of poetry after retiring from school teaching for forty-five years. She was a member of the National League of American Pen Women and the Stella Woodall Poetry Society International, among many other organizations.

I know she was brilliant, and at some level I believe she loved the little boy Sammy she raised, but we were never what one might call close, as Sammy grew up to become Sam the daily newspaper columnist and later the publisher of *Action Magazine*. My mother's taciturn disapproval was always there. She never mentioned anything I wrote, and the words *Action Magazine* never escaped her lips. Alcohol consumption was anathema to her. The first issue of *Action Magazine* in 1975 had a back cover advertising Lone Star Beer. I'm sure my mother never looked at another issue. And I had my part. My own drinking problem and the drug arrests that followed did nothing for the relationship with my rigidly religious mother.

But there was another side to my mother. After I was divorced from my first wife, Vicky, and before I was to marry my forever wife, Sharon, my mother washed every stitch of clothing I owned, and she lovingly hand-mended my shirts, pants, and even the bed sheets I took her to be washed. She always loved little Sammy, and the love for that little boy endured until her death.

Mom the teacher and poet. She was a good writer. She taught me how to survive, sticking with it. But she hated *Action Magazine*. She wouldn't have anything to do with it. She was an old-school Baptist, and we had a Lone Star Beer ad on the back cover of the magazine.

I can also recall those times so long ago when I really wanted a father. One instance has been lodged in my memory like a river bottom rock. I must have been in grade school. Red Smith was working with my cowboy grandfather. A larger and older bully was tormenting me when school turned out for the day. My mother being a teacher in the Junction school may have exacerbated my situation. The bully, Bob Wallace, was shoving me down, then daring me to get up and fight him. I guess I was ashamed to alert my grandfather, but I finally told Red what was going on.

He told me what to do. "You get you a strong cedar stick. Then you go upside his head the next time he messes with you."

"Upside his head?" I remember asking.

I never forgot Red's reply: "Upside his head means you knock hell out of him anywhere you can hit him. And you stay with it. If you don't do this, it will only get worse for you. This kid pushing you around ain't got good sense. Sometimes people like this need to have sense knocked into their heads."

I was prepared to take Red's advice, but when I showed up outside school with the cedar stick, my adversary backed off. There was fear-fueled fury in my eyes, and I was probably foaming at the mouth like a rabid fox as well. It was enough to stop the bully. He reported me to the school principal for threatening him with a club. But he never again tried to shove me around.

For as long as I can remember, Red Smith was intertwined with both sides of my family. He was a close friend of my father, and he worked for years alongside my cowboy maternal grandfather, Clarence Frank Chenault, a lease rancher who survived for years in the rugged Central Texas cedar brakes after a mortgage foreclosure cost him his own ranch on Kimble County's Cedar Creek, just a few miles south of the town of Junction. He bought the ranch from his grandmother, Susan Abigail Wood Harmon Kelly. He later lost the ranch in the mortgage foreclosure, due to heavy rains that kept him from reaching the bank in time to make his mortgage payment. Ironically, it was Weaver Baker, law partner of my grandfather's friend Coke Stevenson, who signed the foreclosure. I don't believe my grandfather held a resentment. He told me once that it was "just business" and that Baker was only doing his job.

People who loved and admired my grandpa affectionately referred to him late in his life as "Old Shinny." Although he was nearly stone deaf, Clarence Chenault was not mute. Shinny could cuss like a China marine on a blue streak. He lost almost all of his hearing as a young man. He always blamed his hearing loss on an old Model-T Ford freight-hauling truck that he drove with no muffler. Our family always maintained that my grandfather was said to be a distant cousin of General Claire Chenault, commander of the famed Flying Tigers of World War II.

I loved my grandfather Chenault. He could read my lips fairly well, but his hearing impairment probably kept us from being any closer than we became. He taught me to boil cowboy coffee in an open pan; he taught me to shoot pool in the Junction Pool Hall. But it was Red Smith who taught me to shoot a rifle and gut a deer, and it was Red who got drunk with me repeatedly in later years when I was a reporter with the *San Antonio Express-News*.

My grandfather was poor for most of his life. All but dirt poor. Lease ranchers in the Texas Hill Country were akin to the poor sharecroppers of the South. They worked hard just to stay on the land and provide for their families.

During the late 1940s and early 1950s, the hated screwworm was threatening to obliterate the livestock industry in many parts of Texas. The screwworm hatched and thrived on living animal flesh, eating away until the animal was dead or too far gone to survive. This was before experiments at Texas A&M University produced a sterile screwworm fly that, in effect, sterilized other flies, eventually bringing the hated scourge to an end in Texas. This happened in about 1957 in Kimble County, about four years after I graduated from high school.

I have vivid recollection of livestock crawling with screwworms. I once saw a doe deer with worms working in her face. She was stumbling blindly until Red Smith ended her suffering with a single shot from a .30-.30 Winchester rifle. The doe had wandered into the long-since-abandoned Evergreen School House on the South Llano River, one of numerous elementary schools in Kimble County before students were bused into town for the advanced grades and high school. Members of my family had attended the Evergreen School.

The powerful stench of Smear 62, the foul black goop that was the only answer at that time for screwworms attached to living livestock, will remain in my nostrils until I die. My family experienced the worst of the screwworm epidemic in Kimble County when my grandfather Chenault was lease ranching on one of the Coke Stevenson ranches on the North Llano River.

I was just a boy in those days, but they had me out doctoring the worm-infected sheep, goats, and even cattle. My aunt Rayola Chenault, my mother's baby sister, was a cowgirl who rode like a man with my grandfather Chenault and Red Smith, both driving and carrying infected livestock from the ranch pastures to a fenced area near the ranch house that was called a "worm trap." We doctored the wormies in the trap area daily, turning them back into the open pastures only after they healed, making room for new wormies in a never-ending battle with the screw-worm fly. Any small wound, even a tiny scratch, would invite the hated flies and the "blow," eggs that would quickly hatch into flesh-eating larvae.

I can remember Red, Aunt Ray, and my grandpa carrying new wormies across the pommels of their saddles to the ever-populated worm trap. And there was a constant influx of babies—lambs and goats that were orphaned by the flesh-eating worms. My grandmother called them "sanchos," and to this day I don't know where she found the word. The sanchos were fed daily with diluted cow's milk in Coke bottles equipped with rubber nipples my grandmother fashioned from discarded car inner tubes.

My mother's side of our family was headed by my cowboy grandfather Clarence. He graduated from Peacock Military Academy in San Antonio, and when a young man, he and Texas governor-to-be Coke Stevenson hauled freight by mule and horse team between Junction and Brady, the nearest railhead to our part of the state. They also hauled goods in and out of Menard, another railhead, often camping together on the trail. The two of them were lifelong friends. And through the years as I grew up around my grandpa Chenault and Red Smith, much of that time was spent on ranchland that my grandfather leased from Coke Stevenson.

Both sides of my family, the Kindricks and the Chenaults, were inexorably enmeshed with the Stevenson attorney brothers, Coke and Bascomb. When Coke was elected governor of Texas (serving from 1941 until 1947), my Chenault grandparents were living and working on Stevenson property my grandfather leased from his longtime friend. Bascomb Stevenson continued on with the law firm when he became engaged to my father's oldest sister, Kimble County beauty Anga Lillian Kindrick.

I was always told that Bascomb was a heavy drinker and probably an alcoholic. He and my aunt Lillian had announced their plans to marry when Lillian died in a one-car rollover near Junction. Bascomb had been at the wheel and was unhurt in the wreck that killed my beautiful aunt. Everyone said Bascomb was probably drunk. My father's brother Bennett Kindrick said Bascomb killed his sister. He swore on Lillian's grave that, from that day forward, he would never drink a drop of alcohol. And he was true to his vow. He stayed sober until his death at age ninety-eight.

Coke Stevenson organized the First National Bank in Junction. He served as a county attorney, county judge, and state representative before he was elected lieutenant governor and then governor. The only political race he ever lost was the one that made headlines all over the nation, his fall by eighty-seven votes to Lyndon Johnson in the infamous "Box 13" race for the US Senate. Everyone in Junction always said that Lyndon Johnson stole the election from Coke Stevenson by virtue of the dubious Box 13 in Jim Wells County, which was delivered by vote broker George Parr. Names for some of those who allegedly voted in Box 13 had been copied from tombstones.

My grandmother Chenault, Lula Burt Hodges Chenault, had the nicknames "Oudie," "Toodle," and "Evie," but we all called her "Mama." My aunt Rayola, her youngest, said Mama used the name Lula the most. Her death was a tragedy that my old cowboy grandpa never got over. I was in junior high school when my mother pulled me out of class. I will never forget that awful morning. My grandmother Chenault had been killed by a train. The circumstances were devastating.

My grandfather's last attempt at lease ranching was on Kendall County property located a few miles out of Boerne on the Sisterdale Road. The owner, who lived in San Antonio, hired my grandparents to act as caretakers on the ranch. My grandparents lived on that ranch for about a year before they made the decision to move into a Junction house my mother had found for them. They were leaving the Boerne ranch when a freight train hit their 1938 four-door Plymouth sedan on the northern outskirts of Boerne, killing Mama Chenault and seriously injuring our Papa. The circumstances, later recounted by my heartbroken grandfather, were hard for any of us to take. All but impossible for our Papa. He finally recovered from his physical injuries, but his tormented mind never healed.

The car had stalled on the railroad track. Mama was desperately trying to get my hearing-impaired grandfather out of the vehicle with her while there was still time. The train engineer was blowing the whistle full blast. Clarence couldn't hear it. Lula was desperately trying to push Clarence out of the car. She would not leave him. He couldn't understand her frantic words. She loved him. We all knew it. She stayed with him in the cab of that old car until her death.

My aunt Rayola Chenault Proffer was my greatest helper in piecing together much of my family history. Aunt Ray died at ninety-three on

Above, **Sammy Kindrick, Cub Scout. On my scouting experience, I may have learned to start a fire. But that was it.**

Left, **Sammy with clarinet. That was something my mother wanted me to do. In college, I bought a mahogany-colored Gibson Les Paul and taught myself to play "Orange Blossom Special."**

April 6, 2021, near her home in Aurora, Missouri, while we were still texting back and forth. She told me the following: "Papa never talked to me about what all happened—at a later time, the only thing he ever told me was that Mama was tugging on his shirt sleeve with tears in her eyes and was pointing to the train. I still do not know if they were thrown out of the car or not. Someone told me that right after it all happened and this person got there, they saw Papa and Mama on the ground with Papa holding her head. Mama was taken to the mortuary in Boerne, and an ambulance took Papa to a Fredericksburg hospital. To this day I do not know if Papa had any serious injuries or not. I don't think he had anything broken. And I don't know how long he was in the hospital. This all happened close to noon on a Wednesday, May 12, 1948. The funeral for Mama was at 4:00 p.m. Friday, May 14.

Aunt Ray said a coroner who investigated my grandmother's death said she may have died of a heart attack when the train hit. There was little blood, he said. "This would have been a blessing if it were true," Ray said, going on to note that she saw traces of awful bruising on Mama's face as she lay in her casket. "The undertaker had tried to cover it up, but we could see the damage."

I was just a youngster at the time, but my grandmother's violent death and my old cowboy grandfather's anguished grief gave me an early look at what true love really looks like. Old Shinny Chenault was done cowboying after my grandmother's death. My mother had another room built for him on our little white stucco house in Junction. He spent most of his time shooting pool in the Junction pool hall. I never heard my grandfather say much of anything about the horror on a Boerne railroad track.

But I heard enough to know. My room was next to the add-on room that was Papa's until his death a number of years later. I heard. Late at night. Every night. Not loud. The soft sobbing of an old cowboy mourning a lost love, the only love he had ever known, the mother of his seven children, and the one he might have saved if not for the damnable hearing loss that denied a train whistle. The whistle tried its mechanical best to warn them, but the human frailty was the rapacious creditor, not to be denied. She would not leave him. She never did. And he never stopped loving her.

Aunt Ray sent me a copy of the letter of condolences former governor Coke Stevenson sent his longtime friend after my grandmother's death. The letterhead proclaimed: "Stevenson Ranch. Cattle, sheep, goats. Junction, Texas." It read:

Dear Clarence:

I have wanted to come and see you and try to express my friendship for you in your time of tragedy and loneliness. You know, of course, of my friendship, and have known of it for many years. There isn't much that a friend can say in a time like yours except to let you know that you are remembered often and in the spirit of a fellow man who would be helpful if he could.

The temptation is strong, Clarence, to men in your situation, to give up and let go. But don't do it. All of us have a purpose to serve in this world, and while you and I can never understand why we have been called upon to suffer tragedy in our lives, yet there must be some reason for it and it is our duty to accept it and make the best use of our situations for our families, our friends, and our communities. We can still do some good in the world. It may not be much but every little bit makes life worth living for someone. I am satisfied that you feel a great deal like I do and that you have the determination to carry on. I hope so.

   With kindest regards, I am sincerely your friend.
   [The letter was signed:] *Coke R. Stevenson*

My mother was the oldest of the Chenault children. After her there were, in order, Nunelee Harman, John Blake, James Allen (Jimmy), Mary Helen (Polly), Joyce, and my aunt Rayola. Jimmy was the child prodigy who applied for college entrance and passed with flying colors when he was in his third year of high school. He then joined the army with parental consent when he was seventeen, only to die in a Denver hospital of tuberculosis. My mother traveled to Denver to be with him during his final days. His entire army career was spent in Denver's Fitzsimmons General Hospital.

My father's side of the family was always more of a mystery to me than my mom's side, largely because my father; my maternal grandfather, Samuel Bennett Kindrick; and my aunt Anga Lillian Kindrick all died before I got to know any of them.

I was born November 10, 1934, and named Clarence Samuel Kindrick after my grandfathers. My birth took place in the old Nix Hospital in San Antonio, the same hospital where my father died.

My paternal grandmother was Iva Lou Miller Kindrick, known to her grandchildren as "Nanny." She lived in the family home in Junction until her death when I was still an adolescent. My paternal grandfather was a postmaster in Junction and also at the Telegraph Post Office and Store on the South Llano River, but he died before I was born. My father's brothers were Ur Dee (Turk), the oldest in the family and a Junction postmaster himself, and Miller Bennett, the youngest. My aunt Lillian was second of the Kindrick kids, and my father was number three. Of all the Kindricks I was closest to my uncle Ben and his two sons, Freddy and Roy. Fred passed of natural causes, and my cousin Roy Kindrick, an oral surgeon, was retired from his surgery practice in Denton at this writing.

Sam's baby picture at the Junction home.

Bennett Kindrick was hired as business manager of the Gatesville State School for Boys by Robert Winship, who was superintendent of the state reformatory at that time. Winship had been a Kimble County rancher, teacher, and Boy Scout leader. The Kindrick and Winship families had been close for some time. I always figured that Coke Stevenson may have played a role in Uncle Ben's hiring for the state job.

My uncle Ben started as business manager but worked himself up from the state school business office to be named superintendent. A humanitarian who loved the boys under his supervision, he did away with such harsh punishment practices as the dreaded "busting block," a greasy, filth-encrusted mattress where boys were stripped of their pants, laid face-down, and whipped with a thick razor strop until their buttocks were striped with blood and torn flesh.

These facilities have been converted into a state women's prison, but I can recall our summer visits to my uncle Ben and aunt Eleanor when my cousins Fred and Roy were romping and playing baseball with the reform school inmates. Bennett Kindrick was slight of build, but he had an amazing way of handling even the roughest of the inmates, some of them eighteen or nineteen and built like adults. They respected him, and many of them loved him. He even adopted and helped educate a few of them. Uncle Ben always said that most of the reformatory inmates were not bad boys, just neglected boys who needed a loving home.

When I was a baby, my grandfather S. B. Kindrick owned and operated the Kimble County Telegraph Store and Post Office on the pristine headwaters of the South Llano River. Telegraph consists of a store and ranchland and was once a US Post Office. Residents of Kimble County refer to it as Telegraph, Texas, now a ghost town. My grandfather was the postmaster and grocer-owner of the general store, which sat on ranchland that bordered the Coke Stevenson Ranch, which bordered both sides of the river. During the1927 F5 tornado, which destroyed the little neighboring town of Rocksprings in Edwards County, my grandfather Kindrick was said to have given away groceries and drinks to the tornado victims.

The store and beautiful riverfront ranchland, known as the Telegraph Ranch, were passed from my grandfather to my father, who kept the property until his death. During that time, my father allowed my maternal grandparents to live in quarters attached to the store, and for a time my grandfather Chenault was the Telegraph postmaster. "I feel sure," said Rayola, "that Grady and Bernice allowed Papa and Mama to live rent free in the Telegraph store quarters as long as they wanted."

My Chenault grandparents moved frequently, barely managing to keep the wolf from the door. From the Cedar Creek Ranch, they moved to Hays County and then back to Telegraph and Coke Stevenson property on the South Llano River. From there they moved to ranchland on the North Llano owned by Stevenson, and they stayed there until Coke sold that ranch to J. M. Livingston. I think they then moved back to Stevenson property on the South Llano before they moved to Kendall County ranch property near Boerne.

After my father's death, my mother sold Telegraph Ranch and Store to Ernest Boyette, an Austin lobbyist. Ernest's younger brother Pat was a TV weather pioneer in San Antonio. I think he was on Channel 5. When Bernice sold Telegraph, she was frightened and grief-stricken, a young schoolteacher with an infant son and no comprehension of ranch real estate value. She let Telegraph go for a pittance, and she grieved over the loss for the rest of her life.

The ranch, store, and riverfront property would have been mine had my mother held on to property, which is worth multiple millions today. I never faulted her. At the mere mention of Telegraph, tears would spring into her eyes, and my heart would mourn with her. I was spiritually connected to that piece of heaven on earth, and my soul roams those riverbanks to this day. I fished there, I hunted coons and ringtail cats there, and I swam in the prettiest and cleanest waters on earth. So who, I have often wondered, really owns Telegraph? It couldn't matter who holds a paper deed. Who really owns Telegraph? Ask the Dalai Lama and he might tell you: Sam Kindrick.

The South Llano and the North Llano Rivers of Kimble County merge just below Junction, hence the name of what I believe to be the prettiest little town in Texas. After confluence of the north and south streams, what we always called the Main Llano, it meanders on through Mason County to join the Colorado River near the town of Llano.

The South Llano, where I spent most of my boyhood, is the gem of spring-fed Texas rivers, and the great flood of 1935 was the water event most discussed throughout my early years. I was a year old when the flood hit. My mother told me she stood on the front steps of the First Baptist Church to watch both rivers raging on either side of the town. And sixteen miles up toward the headwaters of the South Llano, my father's Telegraph Ranch and Store weathered the storm, but not before a beautiful riverfront pecan orchard was leveled by the mighty rush of water, leaving one gigantic and majestic pecan still standing.

Red Smith was staying with my family at that time. He recalled my father's reaction. "Grady had a double-bit cedar axe in his hand," Red told me. "He told me to grab an axe and help him. Grady said, 'I can't bear to look at that one tree. Let's take it down and start all over again.' So that's what we did." Red Smith and my father worked the better part of a day in waist-deep river-bottom mud before that last pecan sentry was to fall.

I think I know now where my once-explosive temper and defiant attitude might have come from. Grady was a Christian Church man who might have let his self-will run riot on occasion. God took almost all of

Grady Kindrick. My father was an idealized and mysterious presence in my life. He was successful, beloved, and great at golf, too. I don't remember my father. I always wondered what he would have taught me, how it could have been.

his beautiful pecan orchard, so he and Red finished the job. Was this tree cutting an act of defiance? Anger? Grief? I always wondered if Grady felt remorse over destruction of that tree.

Everyone I have ever talked with who knew my father would attest to his sharp business acumen. "He could fix a broken-down bicycle and sell it for three times what he paid for it," my uncle Ben told me. "There is no way of knowing how far in the business world Grady might have gone had he lived. He was the master of the deal."

By the time he reached the age of thirty, he owned two large produce trucks, a grocery store, the Telegraph Ranch and Post Office, and our white stucco Junction home, which he built himself. Oliver Lynn Verlin was the rock mason who built our fireplace. My mother was a devout Christian and member of the Junction First Baptist Church. She and others said my father was a staunch church member who also sang in the choir with a strong tenor voice.

I never knew for sure if my father was a gambler, but many of the old-timers who knew him said he was known to wager at golf, the sport he loved and reportedly excelled at. While Grady's truck was being loaded with produce and other goods in preparation for his return to Junction and other towns along the way, he often frequented the Brackenridge Park Golf Course where he was a known winner. An old-timer in the produce business by the name of Guggenheim, who I think had a company in Boerne, recalled my father's skill with the golf clubs.

I don't recall Guggenheim's given name, but I recall his words when defining my father's prowess with the golf sticks: "Grady could hit out of a sand trap like few others. Sometimes he deliberately hit his ball into a trap. When he blasted out of the sand, his ball would almost always land near the hole. His opponents called it luck. But it was not luck. Your father could hit out of sand like the pros. I watched him win this way time and time again."

When I was young, I had my father's full set of golf clubs, all with hickory shafts. I lost many of them through the years, and the only two I have left are a driving iron and a 1920s-era niblick, which is shaped much like the modern day 8 or 9 iron. While talking with friend and fellow writer and musician Hector Saldaña about writing a possible autobiography, I mused: "Hell, Hec, what to write and how to start?"

Hector came right back. "Hold those old golf clubs of your dad's and write what comes into your head."

I did it. I held the clubs and closed my eyes. Stories and events from my past began to form. But the two most notable sensations were sorrow and curiosity. I felt an almost palpable sorrow that I never got to know my father and a profound and almost overwhelming sense of curiosity about what might have been. I have always wondered what Grady Kindrick might have taught me had he lived into old age.

The Chenault family horses and my cowgirl aunt Rayola's keen observations and heartfelt remembrances speak volumes about who we are. She was ninety-two at this writing. The horse members of our family included

Pinto, Brown Jug, Leather Britches, Dunny, Redbird, and Buckskin. Pinto was my grandfather's pride and joy, a high-strung paint cow pony that had been broken to the saddle by Red Smith. The first time Aunt Ray laid eyes on the two-year-old paint colt, Red had Pinto jump the hood of a car parked in front of the Telegraph Store. That did it for Papa. He bought Pinto on the spot.

Only Aunt Ray could give firsthand and beautifully descriptive information on the Chenault family horses and the hard times my grandparents survived. The Great Depression of the 1930s was ending, but it was still tough for hard-scrabble lease rancher Clarence Chenault and his brood as the World War II years materialized. Of my grandfather's favorite horse, Aunt Rayola said:

> Pinto was a paint or pinto horse. His coat was white and spotted with bay mane and tail. Red Smith broke Pinto. Red was working for Debs Boone at the time, and he rode Pinto to Telegraph one day [from the Boone ranch]. Pinto was just two years old then. That is the earliest age for a horse to be broken. There was a convertible parked across the road from the store. Red was so proud of the way Pinto handled. He showed off a little by having Pinto jump the hood of the convertible. Shortly after that Papa bought Pinto [from Debs Boone].
>
> Pinto was the most high-spirited of all our horses. Not temperamental, just hyper. His energy was limitless. When you were riding him, if you didn't pay attention, he would throw his head back and hit you right between the eyes. Any morning that Papa saddled Pinto, they seemed to go through the same routine. Papa would start to put his foot in the stirrup, and Pinto would know exactly when to sidestep. So they would literally go around and around, Pinto making noises by blowing through his nose while Papa's leggings were flying. Pinto would get his bits jerked and a few whacks from Papa's old floppy hat across his withers and a whole bunch of "dad blame its," as "dad blame it" was Papa's favorite cuss word, with the threat of "I'll wrop my rope across your withers." Papa always pronounced wrap with an "o" as in "hop." With all of this out of the way, Papa would mount up and off they would go, Pinto stepping lively and both of them sniffing the wind.

Our Papa Chenault could never afford ranch help. Red Smith worked with him for enough money to get drunk on the weekends. Mama did all of Red's laundry and kept him supplied with the buttermilk he loved. Aunt Rayola worked stock with my grandfather from the time she was big enough to mount a horse.

"Papa always tried to run a thousand head of sheep and a thousand head of goats," Rayola said. "When it was time for the roundup, Mama would have breakfast made and get us up at four." Rayola said it took them almost a week to complete the roundup. They pulled out before daylight in the mornings, Ray on the big brown saddle horse she called Brown Jug, and Papa on Pinto.

Aunt Rayola hoarded her most treasured memories like some women stockpile diamonds. "Papa would never let us kids race the horses," she said. "But sometimes as we started out early in the morning, Papa would pull his hat low over his forehead and say to me, 'I don't believe old Crow Bait (my horse Jug) can beat Pinto.' Then he dug in the spurs and the race was on, me on Jug and him on Pinto, neck and neck and full speed for about a quarter of a mile. Then it was down to business for the rest of the day."

She said Pinto was nosy and always wanted attention. "When we lived on the North Llano, there was no fence around the house. Pinto would come up to the screen door in front of the house, snort a little, and twiddle the door with his upper lip. One day we gave him a slice of light bread, or 'wasp nest' as Papa called any bread that was not homemade. Pinto caught on quickly how to get his treat. Pinto had a bad habit of biting or kicking the other horses. He didn't do it to us, just the horses. We had to watch him when they were all fed. He would gobble up his oats and grain and then run the other horses away from their feed boxes."

After a long day's ride, Rayola said, from five in the morning until nine at night, Pinto would still be going strong. "After the other horses were all turned out in the horse pasture for the night—when they should have been grazing or resting—you could hear Pinto at any hour running the other horses. From the sounds they were all making, you knew he was biting and kicking. The next morning he would be full of vinegar and ready to ride. I'm sure if we had inspected the other horses, they would have had bloodshot eyes. Papa tried hobbling Pinto at night, but hobbles would never hold him. I suspect he chewed them loose. Papa next tried a big chain about six-foot long with a heavy leather strap on one end, which was buckled to a foreleg. Pinto mastered that. At night you could hear him sling that chain with a certain rhythm—clank of chain, then hooves, as he ran the other horses. I suppose Papa gave up after that."

Rayola could still produce the wonderful little memories that might have slipped through the cracks for less attentive people. "We were out in the pasture . . . stopped for a shady rest, the horses hot and sweaty. They liked their heads rubbed where the bridle fit. Pinto would go up to Papa's back, rub his head up and down really hard. Almost push him over. Then he did it. Papa was on hands and knees, drinking from a spring. Pinto ducked his head, shoving Papa's backside until he went headfirst into the creek."

When Papa left Boerne and after my grandmother's death, he knew he had to find Pinto a proper home. He found it on the Coke Stevenson ranch. Coke took Pinto in, and my grandfather's great paint cow pony and longtime friend was allowed to live out his remaining days on the Stevenson ranch near Telegraph where he started it all by jumping over a car hood.

Rayola's horse was Brown Jug, a powerfully built animal we all called Jug. Rayola told me:

> He was part Morgan. Had a dark reddish-brown coat with black mane and tail. Before Papa bought him, he was used in rodeos as a roping horse. During that time he got his foot caught in a fence, leaving a bad cut on his foot and leg. The wound didn't leave him a cripple, but he could no longer be used in rodeos.
>
> Jug stood out from the other animals—always with a look of elegance. Neck had a graceful arch. Pretty rounded forehead and ears always pointed alertly forward. He was larger than most saddle horses but was sure-footed and could stop, start, and turn just as quickly as any quarter horse. He had a gait that made riding him as comfortable as sitting in a rocking chair. He was usually good-natured and gentle, but you couldn't always count on it. He wasn't too good to bite you, and of all the horses we had, you couldn't trust him not to kick if you walked behind him. Especially when he was eating. He got me only once, leaving a horseshoe print on my backside, which I wore for a while. I had fed the other horses

and was walking behind Jug, still carrying the feed bucket, when
he got me. Jug kicked me and the bucket into an agarita bush.

Rayola recalled Jug using the old breath-holding trick that many horses have known to pull when the saddle girth is being cinched up. "Only Jug probably did it a lot more than most horses," Ray said. "He would puff up like a blowfish when I was cinching the girth, then let his breath out when we were on our way. Of course, the girth cinch would be so loose the saddle would almost fall off. It made me so mad I felt like murdering Jug. But he loved me, and contrary as he could get, I loved him."

Red Smith was my grandfather's most loyal stock wrangler, but a drifter by the name of Doc Curtis was there for some of the roundups. And Rayola recalls that Doc was helping them round up sheep when Jug threw her for the first and last time. "We were rounding up the sheep and it was hot. That was when we lived in the rock house on the Stevenson Ranch. We had stopped to rest and loosened the saddle girths on the horses. When it was time to go, I tightened the saddle girth and Jug nipped me. This was one of his contrary days. I suppose horses have days they don't feel good just like people. I got my foot in the stirrup, and before I got my other leg over the cantle, he pitched just enough to throw me right on over and across his back. Papa and Doc Curtis were both saddled up and watching the show. They were trying hard not to smile. I remember Papa telling me, 'If he does that again, take your rope and wrop it good across his withers.'"

The rock house they lived in on the Stevenson ranch had a rock water tank with a hose Rayola used to cool Jug down. "He was one of the few horses we had who loved to be bathed," Aunt Ray said. "Jug would stand and savor every drop from head to tail for as long as I dared to waste the water."

Aunt Rayola was a superior horsewoman who did it all. She roped, branded, helped shoe the horses, and did all of the chores most male ranch workers perform. "A lot of times," she said, "Papa had me ride by myself. Check a fence, doctor wormies. See if the windmill in the back pasture was pumping. Took me a half a day or more, and, oftentimes, your dog Tippy would follow. When he got tired, I would put him behind the saddle and let him ride. Jug never objected."

Tippy was a tough little terrier mix that an old Junction doctor gave me as a puppy. I didn't want to keep him penned at our house while I was at school, so his home became the ranch my grandparents were living on. Tippy would also ride on the front fender of my grandmother's old car when she drove down to the Telegraph Store for groceries and household supplies. He never lost his footing.

There were many rattlesnakes on the Coke Stevenson Ranch during those days, and Tippy developed into a protective rattler hunter and killer. He was always between us and the snake, and our efforts to discourage his rattlesnake killing were to no avail. He found the snake, barking and circling, and waiting for the inevitable strike. When the snake struck and missed, extending its body from the coil, the little terrier mix was on him like jugged lightning. He grabbed the snakes behind their heads and shook them until there was no life left. We never knew how many he killed. It was many until he finally missed. The big rattler got him around his head. The swelling was awful as my grandmother doctored him with potash and whatever country remedy she had at her disposal. There was no vet around Telegraph and the Stevenson ranch in those days. I remember us all crying. Tippy hung on for a day and the better part of another night before his little frame finally succumbed to the venom. I never forgot Tippy. I still have visions of Tippy riding behind Aunt Ray on Brown Jug.

Redbird was a reddish-brown bay, temperamental mare always referred to as my uncle Jimmy's horse. Rayola said the mare was not mean but stubborn. Aunt Ray recalled Mama hitching Redbird to the family's Model-T Ford when the car stalled in the creek crossing. "Redbird did not want to pull," Rayola said. "Mama got in front and tugged on the harness—even laid a few thumps on her rear. Redbird either balked or went backward. So, Mama unhitched her, turned her around facing the Model-T, rehitched her, and it worked. I do not recall what happened to Redbird."

Aunt Ray remembered Buckskin as her childhood horse. He was light gray with black mane and tail. "He was so gentle. He would sit on his haunches and let me and my sister Joyce slide down his back."

Leather Britches was a two-year-old stallion with a chestnut coat and a sorrel-colored mane. When Papa brought him home, Aunt Rayola recalled, Leather Britches was unbroken. She said he was a mixed-breed draft horse, part Percheron, and larger than other horses they had at that time. "When I crawled on him bareback, Papa got really nervous," Rayola said. "He said, 'Watch him.' I remember Papa getting Red Smith to break him. He turned out to be gentle and good-natured. Two things Leather Britches ever put up a fight over were getting his first set of horseshoes and the castration process that would leave him a gelding."

Rayola said:

> The first time he was shod, it was a real man's job. He didn't want his hooves rasped and his frogs picked. [The frog on a horse is the tender inner part of the hooves, and it is important to pick the frog clean when applying new horseshoes.] He snorted and kicked, and Papa and Red first hobbled him and then tied one leg to a tree, and he wound up lying broadside on the ground. How undignified. When he got up, he was wearing four new horseshoes.
>
> When Papa and Red made a gelding out of Leather Britches, that was a feat in itself. I wasn't supposed to watch but I did anyway . . . from a distance. That was another man's job—throwing a big animal like that to the ground and then tying his feet.

Of all the family horses, Pinto, Jug, and Dunny have always remained in my memory. Especially Dunny, the sweetest and most lovable of all the horses in the world as far as I am concerned. Dunny was the first horse I ever crawled on, and long before I was large enough to saddle a horse, I constantly pestered Aunt Ray to "saddle old Dunny." Mama Chenault loved the story and delighted in retelling of the time that Rayola lost her cool. "Would you saddle old Dunny," I whined for what may have been the umpteenth time and counting, causing Ray to shriek in frustration, "No, I will not daddle old Sonny." My grandmother never tired of telling the story.

Of Dunny, Rayola said:

> He was old when Papa bought him. And Papa wouldn't use him to work stock if another horse was available. Dunny babysat all kids. If any of the grandchildren ever said they knew how to ride a horse, it was because they sat on Dunny first. When all of the horses were in the horse trap [a forty-acre pasture used to hold the horses before the workday started], it was my job to bring them out at daylight. One always wore a bell. Most of them were hard to catch. I would

hide the bridle behind my back and tempt them in with an ear of corn. But not Dunny. I remember how easy Dunny was to catch. I could walk up to him, put on the bridle, and then lead him to a stump or fork in a tree where I could climb on bareback and drive the rest of the horses in.

Dunny was patient and tolerant as an old brood hen. One time we were heading home at a pretty good clip. I was probably daydreaming, and Dunny was probably thinking of the bucket of oats he would get when we reached the barn. He made a quick turn around a fence corner, and I wound up underneath him. The minute I left his back, he came to a dead stop. He had his head turned as he watched to see what I would do next. He didn't move an inch until I had crawled back on his back.

Dunny was a good horse to teach you horse things. I learned how to prepare a horse's feet for shoeing by working on his feet. He would patiently let me hold his feet and pull the nails out to remove the shoes that needed replacing. I would dig all of the gunk out from under his hooves and use the pincers and rasp to trim them. Then Papa would form the horseshoes to his feet using anvil and forge.

Papa and I were rounding up sheep one day, and Dunny and I were heading off a sheep through a live oak thicket when a limb raked me out of the saddle, knocking a wasp nest down my collar. There was a swarm, and as I fought to get them out of my shirt, some of them must have gotten under the saddle blanket. It was the only time I ever saw docile old Dunny kick up his heels, pitch, and break wind like a real cavorter.

Dunny's ending was the saddest story I ever heard Aunt Rayola tell. "The day came," she said, "when Papa had to make the decision to sell Dunny. I know it wasn't pleasant for Papa. He just couldn't afford to keep horses that could no longer pay for their oats. I can still see Dunny turning his great head and looking wistfully toward us from the back end of the horse truck until it was out of sight. I never asked, but I know all the horses on that truck were being sold to a glue factory or for dog food. After some forty years I can still see Dunny's face. I never blamed Papa. He did what he had to do."

Mom dressed little Sammy in ruffles at age 2.

THE GREATEST COWBOY

Red Smith died December 20, 1985, at age eighty from natural causes. I was in San Antonio and nobody bothered to call me until Red was already buried in the South Llano River Wooten Cemetery. I wasn't as closely connected with Junction historian and newspaper columnist Frederica Burt Wyatt as I later became, so I got word of Red's passing by word-of-mouth happenstance. The following is part of a tribute to Red I published in *Action Magazine*:

The Junction town marshal might have worn out at least two pistol barrels on Red's head.

He had his own personal cell in the Kimble County Jail where he spent the tail end of most weekends.

The weekdays were spent breaking horses and no Comanche Indian ever lived who could talk horse language better than Red Smith.

I had a personal interest in Red. My father died when I was a baby and Smith was around to offhandedly contribute to my upbringing.

Some of the upstanding townsfolk looked down their noses at Red. They called him a no-good saddle tramp without a direction in life. But I knew better.

Chester (Red) Smith was a flat-belly with hide tougher than corrugated sheet iron. He liked the wind at his back so he had a new direction every time it shifted. His 150-pound frame remained lithe and muscular even as he advanced into his 70s. When young, he had bright red hair. And the kids would all gather on Saturdays to

42

Red Smith (*left*) and Sam. Red, he was my father. He believed in cedar-stick justice: "Don't take any shit from anybody." I loved that cowboy. But the toughest cowboy I ever met and whom I revered also had his flaws: he drank anything he could get his hands on.

watch Red ride his horse into town from whatever ranch he might be working on.

Smith spurred a snot-slinging colt down Junction's main street, knowing full well that he was on a collision course with Marshal Joe Baker.

Smith's home was a saddle. The ground was his bed. He would spit in the devil's eye and charge hell with a bucket of water when he believed he was right. Red went to prison for a crime he didn't commit, and later received a full governor's pardon. But it is said he stayed in Huntsville long enough to make a lasting impression in the big prison rodeo.

A bronc raked him off on a tree limb once. Red landed in one of those giant prickly pear mottes.

I recall his laughter as he shaved off thousands of pear thorns protruding from his leathery hide. It was a dry shave with a straight razor. We were at my grandpa's place on the North Llano River at the time. This was the ranch Stevenson later sold to J. M. Livingston.

"Can't pick 'em all out," Red said. "I'll shave 'em down and the rest will rot out in a few days."

Red died at age eighty, but he never got old. When he was about seventy-five, he was leading a parade through Junction with a broken bone sticking out of his leg. Someone decreed that Smith, the living legend of hard-to-curry cowboys, should serve as grand marshal of the annual horse race and fair parade. In typical fashion, he showed up on a green half-broken colt that was spooked by the noisy crowd. The horse rolled its eyes, chewed at the bit, and jitterbugged nervously on the asphalt. As it attempted to bolt, Red hauled back on the bridle and swatted the two-year-old with his hat.

The horse slipped and fell on Red, shattering his leg just above the ankle. A veterinarian was among the crowd that quickly gathered. "Don't cut that boot off," Smith said. "I have been jailed a thousand times for riding a horse down this street, and I ain't about to miss a chance to do it legal."

And with the broken bone poking over his boot top, Smith triumphantly led the annual parade on that same slobbering colt that fell with him. Red was part horse. We all knew he could train a horse to jump car hoods, and I personally watched him coax his cow pony Blue Boy into the open bed of a pickup truck.

So the thought of Red Smith dying had never occurred to me. The deep draws and high bluffs overlooking the South Llano River don't die. Rocks don't die. The creaking, clanging windmill doesn't die. So what the hell right did Red Smith have dying? When I heard that Red Smith was gone, my first reaction was anger. Red was the clean smell of juniper cedar on a bright morning. He was squeaky leather on a muscled blue pony. It just wasn't fair that he should go. I felt cheated for myself. And I felt cheated for the millions of people who never had the privilege of knowing Red Smith. I cussed as tears flooded my eyes. As was his way, Red didn't let anyone know he was going to die. He just did it. And in accordance with his last-minute instructions, they took him to the obscure little Wooten Cemetery and buried him in a simple pine box.

When I was a kid, Red helped my grandfather stay alive on that drought-stricken range that sustained more screwworm flies than anything else. At that time, Old Shinny, my grandfather, was lease-ranching on the half-dry North Llano River. A lease rancher is the equivalent of a sharecropper, and no row ever hoed could be any harder than a summer of screwworms killing the livestock, followed by a record cold winter that killed what the worms missed.

They hunted for their food that winter. I was just a sprout, but I can remember it was the same winter that Red had the rest of his teeth pulled. The first batch of teeth went when a horse stepped on Red's face. I remember that toothless grin as Red rode out of the snowy half darkness with a buck deer tied behind his saddle. When not hunting for table meat, he had been searching for freezing livestock, and there were actually icicles hanging from the brim of his hat.

Red worked all over, twice riding a horse to California and back, and if he had a family he felt close to, it was my mother's. He came and went, sometimes staying a year or so at a time and working for no more than his board and some Saturday-night drinking money.

When I was attending Sul Ross State College in Alpine, I awoke one snowy winter morning to find Red's dappled gray pony Blue Boy hobbled beside my car. Red was in the back seat sleeping. The movie *Giant* with Elizabeth Taylor and James Dean was being filmed in nearby Marfa. Red had ridden Blue Boy from Junction to Alpine, hoping to land a horse-wrangling job on the movie set. He got the job.

When I was working at the *Express-News* in San Antonio, Red rode his horse to my house on Harriett Street. He rode Blue Boy to my mom's house in Terrell Heights a number of times, and I believe he visited by horseback my uncle Nunelee Chenault, who lived off Flores Street on San Antonio's South Side. They had been friends since childhood. I was starting to drink heavily in those days, and I had no trouble getting Red to join me in San Antonio skull orchards such as the Burnt Orange, the

SWC Club, and the San Jacinto. My wife at the time, Vicky, was kind enough to put Red up, but after we boozed it up for more than a week, she was happy to see the old cowboy ride away.

Red Smith taught me to shoot a rifle. He helped steady the gun when I shot my first deer, an illegal spike on ranch pasture where we had no permission. Red broke off one of the spikes with his boot. "If a game warden stops us, we will just say the broken antler was shot off and that it had three points." Red did not believe we were morally wrong. He taught me how to bridle a horse. He taught me to never hit a woman. He showed me how to dress a deer without breaking the fine membrane that covers the carcass. He taught me how to sharpen an axe. And he taught me to stand for what I believed to be right. I learned how to get drunk all by myself. Although Red and I got hammered a few times together in later life, Red had nothing to do with me getting my head in the jug.

When Red Smith sat on a horse, he looked like a part of the animal. His spurs were equipped with little slick rowels that would do little or no damage to a mount. Red literally slept in his spurs. Except for the prison rodeo, Red stuck to horse training. "I'm a horse breaker," he often said. "Not a bronc stomper."

The people who looked down their noses at Red never saw him work with a horse. My grandfather called Red a good, honest man. The horses knew, too. Red loved children, and I experienced his affection at an early age. When there was money left after one of his weekend sprees, the old cowboy would spend it all on candy that he would pass out to kids who were waiting for it.

In his younger days, Red hired on to help move some heavy ranch and farm equipment that he didn't know was being stolen. He was arrested and sentenced to prison along with the others, and he remained at Huntsville for almost a year before one of the real thieves made a statement that exonerated him.

With his pardon from the governor came a pocketful of cash and a new suit of clothes as compensation for his false imprisonment. I know Red held on to the suit, for I saw him in it at my grandfather's funeral. He used the cash to throw a drunk that lasted more than a year. He loved Shinny. When my grandfather Chenault was near death at my mother's home in San Antonio, Red was there. I have a distinct memory of Red bathing my grandfather's face with a damp cloth. There was a bond between those old cowboys that I cannot explain.

My grandmother was smashing up Smith's food after his remaining teeth were pulled. He never considered wearing dentures, and in short order he was able to gum his way through anything, including corn on the cob and rock candy. The toothless look seemed to match up with Red's other facial architecture. His face suggested he may have looked forty-five when he was born.

Although records show he had only one brief marriage to Dorothy Bohissen of Houston, Red liked the ladies, and there was sometimes a twinkle of contentment in his eye after one of his visits to the dude ranches that dotted the South Llano River. I recall one of my grandmother's comments when Red came dragging in after a night of tomcatting at Henry Bossman's Flying L guest ranch. "My, my," said Mama. "Those city women do have a taste for roughness."

Red did a stint in the Merchant Marine Corps, and Aunt Rayola remembered him showing my grandmother a marine pants-creasing technique he liked.

Junction Eagle columnist and Kimble County historian Frederica Wyatt filled me in on some Red Smith history. He came from a hard-luck family. His mother, Fannie, died when he was fifteen. His father, Monroe, was killed by poison placed in his food by a ranch wife who was trying to kill her husband. Monroe was working with the husband and was an accidental victim. Red's brother John D. was shot to death in a Rocksprings cafe, and a younger brother, James Monroe Smith, was knifed to death on Junction's main street.

I know Red had little in the way of material possessions. He was wealthy in the ways that count. I was thankful to God when Frederica assured me that Red had no pauper's funeral. "Red had a nice funeral," Frederica assured me. "No tent, just the overhead sky as the canopy. It was a beautiful morning, and we all felt a little bit closer to Heaven. I sat there and wondered if anyone had notified you as I know you would have been there had you known."

The late Ramsey Randolph was Red's lifelong friend, and Frederica relayed Randolph's words to me: "Red and I had been friends since we were teenagers. As I walked away from that open grave where Red's body had been placed, I thought unless his friends mark his grave, no one will know a hundred years from now whose body rests in that spot. So my concern led to thirty-five of Red's friends joining together to erect a Georgia granite monument at his grave. It cost us $525."

Graveside services were held in the Wooten Cemetery on Cajac Creek eleven miles southeast of Junction. It was Red's request that he be buried in the valley of the South Llano River in the ranch country he loved. The Reverend Sam Coffey eulogized his friend. Members of the group sang "Amazing Grace" as the grave was filled.

Bennett Boone was later buried beside Red at his own request. Bennett was named after my uncle Bennett Kindrick. I later took my wife Sharon to visit Red's grave. As I looked down toward the river, I recognized the very spot where my dogs once treed a coon. As it always did, the gentle spring breeze was reminding me how much I loved my homeland.

4

LOVER'S LEAP

egend has a young lovesick Indian couple leaping to their deaths from a rugged limestone bluff near my hometown of Junction. Their parents had refused their dream of marriage, so they went hand in hand together over the edge and into the Great Beyond. The craggy cliff is known to this day as Lover's Leap, and the legend of those despairing young Indians has long been part of the magic of my home. An unknown scribe from long ago had this to say: "Knowing their love can never be, the young couple stare at the swirling river far below. One last kiss, and then, holding hands, they leap off the cliff, united forever in death—and legend."

That river below had to be the South Llano, which joins the North Llano by the town of Junction, forming the Main Llano that winds on toward the Gulf of Mexico. Lover's Leap overlooks the annual Junction Easter pageant, which is held in the Lover's Leap Amphitheater, a cleared area beneath the rocky bluff and close to the spot where legend had the young Indians meeting their death.

There are Lover's Leap cliffs with similar legends in three other Texas locales, but the one at Junction has always been the one that inspired the writer J. E. Grinstead to wax poetic in his 1916 magazine *Grinstead's Graphic*:

Thus they stood a single moment,
On that rocky, towering heap;

Then, they named the place forever
As they made the Lover's Leap.

I believe the legend. It was part of my boyhood. I fished the swirling waters of that river below, and I hunted the juniper-covered hills of Kimble County that surround Junction, truly the land of living waters. To this day, when I take Exit 456 off I-10 and start the sloping-road descent north beside the high craig of Lover's Leap, I look down with mist of eye and nostalgic chill upon the prettiest little river valley town in the entire state of Texas. Junction will always be my home.

Spring and then summer were the seasons I loved as a kid growing up in Junction. When the mesquites showed their first traces of green, off came the boots and shoes. The pecan trees in our yard were towering. Their leaves followed the mesquites'. The sweet scent of blooming agarita bushes belongs to Junction and Kimble County. I loved going barefoot during the grade-school years. My feet grew calluses that were tough as a pig snout, enabling me to run with impunity through grass burr and goat head thorn patches that would seriously cripple a city kid.

My father had died before I was a year old. I lived with my mother in the little stucco house my father hand-built. It had a standing-seam metal roof and a fireplace built by master rock mason Oliver Lynn Verlin. There were two bedrooms, a small living and dining room combination with a hardwood floor, and a small kitchen with linoleum flooring. It was a mansion in my eyes, the most beautiful home in the entire world. The flat roof was drained by square metal pipes. The noise they made put me to sleep on many a rainy night, and when Junction got its occasional snow, I could hear the drains making a strange ticking sound. When I heard that sound at night, I bounded out of bed the next morning to play in the mysterious white stuff. I knew the snow would be covering the ground.

Our house also had an adjoining one-bedroom garage apartment, but I couldn't recall any of the tenants. They were mostly working women, none of them staying for any significant length of time.

In the summer months before I was to enter the eighth grade, I prowled the South Llano riverbanks with a fishing rod and a dog. I don't think my mother worried a lot. I had learned to swim at age six. My mother was there, too. I took my first swimming strokes at Flat Rock Crossing, a natural swimming hole at the time on the South Llano River about a mile from our house. At that exact spot, my mother had me baptized by a Baptist preacher. I took to the water much quicker than I took to the preacher. My mother was a natural athlete and a dark-haired country beauty, starring on the Junction High School girls' basketball team and swimming like a Llano riverbank beaver when she was a young girl.

She led me out to the deeper water and held me belly down, supporting me with her hands on my midsection. I had seen her swim and I knew what to do. I started stroking with my arms and kicking my feet. She stepped back, and I was swimming free. I crossed the Flat Rock Crossing deep hole with little effort, and after that day nobody could have kept me out of the river.

With cane poles and later a cheap Montgomery Ward rod and reel, I stalked the fishes of the Llanos, landing an array of perch and catfish that included sun perch and black Rio Grande perch, silvery channel catfish, and blue cats when I was still very young. The heavyweight yellow cats and alligator gar would come later when I was older and strong enough to handle the deep-water throw lines and trotlines, which required a boat.

I can close my eyes and conjure up a South Llano River morning as if a seventy-five-year gap in time did not exist. My spotted terrier mix pup, Tippy, is sniffing the river-bottom humus, checking for gray squirrel scent and maybe some coon sign left over from the night before. The sparkling clear water is gurgling and burbling as it spills over a gravel bar into a pool below, lined by sycamore and water elms. The sun is just beginning to rise on a Kimble County morning, beautiful and inviting as steam slowly rises from the pristine water and lily pads of the South Llano.

Then splat! The cork on my fishing line disappears under the river surface. My breath was like pure oxygen. I had the long-shanked hook baited with earthworms. I had raised and nurtured those worms with liberal helpings of coffee grounds from our kitchen. The cane pole tipped and then bent as a flash of orange appeared just beneath the river surface. It was a sun perch, a big one, maybe a quarter pound or more. My mother deep-fried these fish, cooking them crisp so bones and meat could be consumed safely together. Much like potato chips.

I would have a full stringer of perch, plus a channel cat or two if I was lucky, and the sun would be setting on a happy country boy as Tippy and I made our way home. I wore nothing but cutoff jeans and a shapeless farm boy straw hat that didn't cost more than a couple of dollars. A cacophony of frog and cricket sounds would follow me as I left the river bottom.

The call of a wild gobbler was common. Harmless Texas water snakes would leave their "V" wakes as they glided across the river. And we would see the occasional poisonous copperheads and cottonmouths that bothered no one if they were not messed with.

My back and feet were tanned by the sun. My hide was burnished the color of a burnt stump, but nobody cared. I will forever remember the sounds of the river at night. They were the familiar hoot of a great horned owl, the crazy gabble of a screech owl, the mournful cry of the whippoorwill, the warning pop of a beaver's tail hitting the surface, and the sharp bark of a hunting fox. I loved all of the sounds, even the spooky ones nobody could identify. I have always believed they might have been made by ghost people killed by the Comanche who left their arrow points and kitchen middens on the Llano watersheds for some of us to find.

Animals, both wild and domestic, were a huge part of my childhood. Dogs, cats, burros, pigeons, hamsters, white rats, raccoons, possums, squirrels, feather-legged bantam chickens, bats, snakes, and one beaver were all part of the menagerie that my poor mother managed to tolerate. My mother allowed a small metal shed out behind our house where I raised pigeons and bantam chickens. The beaver's name was Sawdust, and Sawdust had to go when he chewed the leg off a dining room chair. One of two donkeys I kept in the fenced area behind the house was a tough little critter I rode into town from Johnson Fork Creek, a distance of some ten miles. I called him Samson. The wildest pet who enjoyed the most longevity in our house was Possie the pet possum, a nocturnal little creature with a perpetual grin who liked to suck eggs and eat cat food. Possie lived undetected in the house for the better part of six months, emerging at night to dine on the cat's food. My mother finally caught him just before daylight one morning when she got out of bed for some unknown reason. She opened an outside door and the possum was happy to go.

Nobody around Junction in those distant days had ever heard of a golden hamster. I found a hamster ad in a *Fur, Fish, and Game* magazine, and my mother let me order a pair of the little animals. I don't recall what happened to my hamster business.

Those prepubescent years were the happiest I was to enjoy with my mom. She was still trying to accept the death of my father, and the stark reality of our situation was that she didn't know what to do with me. When two large Texas water moccasins escaped from an aquarium tank I had in the garage, my terrified mother wouldn't go near the garage for a month. I guess the snakes high-tailed it for the river. They never came back. But my mother never cracked down on my propensity for collecting wild critters. She basically allowed me to do as I pleased.

My closest childhood friend remained in my life through high school, college, and into adulthood. As I entered my preteens and early teens, I spent a lot of time on the Coke Stevenson Ranch with Rex Thompson Sherry, a powerfully built kid whose father, Rex Sherry, was Coke Stevenson's ranch foreman. Rex Thompson was known only as Tommy Sherry in those days, and his younger brother, Roger, was Bubba.

My maternal grandparents lease-ranched on the Stevenson property several miles from the Stevenson home and ranch worker lodgings. I often found myself hanging out with the Sherry brothers. When we weren't hunting or fishing, we hatched other activities to blunt the boredom, usually in the hottest months of late summer.

One unique game we played and named was called High Pissing. I'm not sure who originated this one, but I do know it became fairly popular with us and some of our associates. The object was simple. We competed to see who could urinate on a dead run and hit the highest mark on the side of a building with our urine stream. We pissed high on the side of a Stevenson ranch stock barn, and we also competed with town friends on the back side of our garage apartment when my mother was away. Tommy Sherry and I excelled at the competition, along with Bubba and town kids, who included Kenneth Stapp and Bob Wallace. We practiced and we perfected our various techniques.

In the competition, we drank all the water we could hold, then waited twenty or thirty minutes before gathering at the designated starting line. We performed individually. When the water was on the verge of bursting our bladders, we unbuttoned our britches, pinched the ends of our peckers tightly with one hand, and then broke into a dead run directly at the barn wall. It was like a cavalry charge with no horse. We knew exactly when to go airborne and when to relax the grip on our tallywhackers. If this was all completed with precision at the apex of our leap, the resulting blast of urine would hit high on the wall, sometimes head high or even higher. Crashing headlong into the wall was no grounds for disqualification. High pissing was not for wusses. The highest piss mark on the wall determined the winner, no matter what happened to the contestant.

While we were largely responsible for invention of the game, the great mountain lion hoax just seemed to naturally fall our way. I don't know who stole the stuffed cougar, a frightening mount that had somehow disappeared from a hunting lodge on one of the South Llano dude ranches, either Lynside or the Flying L. I never was sure which ranch it came from or positive who stole the fearsome-looking feline, a silently snarling menace that seemed ready to pounce on anyone who ventured too close. I was quick to join in the fun with the Sherry brothers when we learned what startling effect the big lion had on night-traveling motorists.

Placed on the side of any number of Junction-area highways and ranch roads, and positioned so that it would be directly facing oncoming vehicles, our stuffed mountain lion proved to be a sensational hoax that would exceed even our wildest dreams. Big cats are rare in Kimble County, but they have always been there. So we had a plausible scare stunt. When the lion appeared in car or truck headlights, the vehicle usually pulled on past before stopping. There were no cell phones in those days, and a nighttime motorist confronted by a snarling mountain lion was more than rattled. Most of them were terrified. After a quick stop, it was a fast dash into town and a telephone where either the town marshal or the sheriff was called.

It didn't take us long to perfect and streamline the hoax. I put small strips of red reflective tape on the mount's glass eyes, and the result was mind-blowing. Never mind that no real mountain lion's eyes would shine red in the night; the reflective tape was the crowning touch.

When one country motorist backed up his pickup and fired what we guessed was a .30-.30 rifle bullet at our cat, we quickly took safety measures. From that point on Tommy Sherry and I took turns driving and positioning the mount. We had a long piece of cotton rope tied to the cat. One of us drove and let the other one out with the cat. When a motorist saw the cougar and started slowing down, the one hiding in the bushes immediately dragged the mount off the road and into the brush. The driver in our team would return to pick the other one and our cat up after the excitement was over.

We waited for days and sometimes weeks between our cougar episodes. Mountain lion reports were flying around Junction for months. We continued the tomfoolery until our poor old mountain lion was a tattered mess of raggedy hide that would no longer frighten anyone. Dragging it through the rocks and brush had taken a toll.

Nobody ever exposed us in official fashion, but Sheriff Van (Rip) Martin did tell me near the end that we had best pull up with the lion foolishness. I think he must have figured it out. Real mountain lions don't have eyeballs that glow like red marbles in a fish bowl.

The cougar pranks and pissing matches were diversions from boredom. I killed deer and wild turkey, but varmint hunting with dogs was my true love. Tommy Sherry's father owned two Treeing Walker bobcat hounds he called Streak and Saddler. They were big, rangy, black-and-white spotted animals with broad muzzles and medium-long ears that were notched and scarred from fighting bobcats. Ranch people all over that area were acquainted with Rex Sherry and his dogs. Bobcats are the most voracious of all predators in Texas sheep and goat country. Streak and Saddler were always welcome on most any of the South Llano River ranches. I was intrigued by the excitement.

Someone would spot a bobcat crossing the road, usually at night as the person drove home from town. Rex would get a call on one of those ancient party-line phones with ringer, crank, and handheld receiver. Sometimes Tommy and I would go along as Rex loaded the dogs into the back of his rusty old pickup truck and headed out. This was not kid's play. This was serious business. We were going out with two celebrated cat hounds, the best in our part of Texas. If there was moisture on the ground, the dogs would quickly pick up the bobcat's trail. The chases would sometimes be short, sometime longer and taking several hours before the dogs had the cat in a tree. If the cat left the tree, the fight would be epic—a snarling, roaring, and screeching donnybrook with the cat's demise happening under the night sky. Usually, though, if the quarry remained in the tree, Rex would dispatch the cat with a .22-caliber rifle bullet, and we would all head for the house.

Inspired by the Rex Sherry hounds, I bought my two Walker hounds, Rock and Ruby. Rock died early, and I kept Ruby until I went off to college, leaving her with a friend who kept her until her death.

We hunted coon, fox, an occasional bobcat, and mostly ringtails. The ringtail cat is a beautiful buff-colored animal with distinctive black-and-white rings on its long tail. In Mexico and some western states it is technically known as a "cacomistle." It is a relative of the fox. When we were growing up, ringtail pelts were being used as imitation mink for coats and other garments. At one time, Leonard Sutton, the Kimble County fur and pecan buyer in Junction, was paying up to ten dollars each for prime ringtail pelts. With dogs and headlights, kids like us could sometimes bag as many as a half-dozen ringtails in a single night. A sixty-dollar fortune for us.

We varmint-hunted at night and on horseback, always in the dead of winter when varmint fur was prime. Junction and Kimble County record some of the coldest winter temperatures in Central Texas. We rode the Stevenson ranch horses bareback for their body warmth. They were a gelding named Star, who was a sorrel with a white star between his eyes, and a mare called Flaxie, who was a flax-colored dun the color of broom straw. I usually rode the mare. Both horses had been broken by my cowboy hero Red Smith, and both of them were as gentle as house kittens. Standard bridle bits were not needed with these horses. They were easily steered with rope hackamores, bridles that required only light pressure on the mount's nose. We had gaps in fences that encircled both the Paint Creek Ranch and the Seven Hundred Springs Ranch, enabling us to hunt on both of these Texas paradises without detection. We crossed onto them from the Stevenson property when the mood struck. There was a spring-fed ditch near the Sherry cow pens. Sometimes we hunted all night, returning to the house in the predawn hours. The irrigation ditch was only a couple of feet wide, but Flaxie had an aversion to getting her feet wet. Instead of wading the ditch, she would stop dead still and then jump the little waterway. By that time of the morning I would be half asleep on the mare's back. When she made her little crow hop, I invariably toppled from her back and into the icy water.

Flaxie would turn and patiently wait for me, the hackamore bridle trailing in the water. Flaxie's eyes said it all: "Come on, dumb shit, let's get on into the barn." When I night-hunted with a dog, it was always with Ruby, a petite hound with black and tan spots on a white body with a sprinkling of blue freckles around her face and muzzle. The people who sold her to me said she had some of the Tennessee July Foxhound blood in her along with some Treeing Walker.

Ruby had the sweetest disposition of any dog I ever owned and a hunting instinct that was a constant threat to her health. She would run over the rocky terrain of the Texas Hill Country until her paws were leaving bloody prints, and then she would run some more. Her big flaw in our part of the country was her disdain for fighting or sitting under a tree. If the quarry—whether coon, fox, or cat—went underground or into a tree, Ruby soon lost interest and went on to chase another critter that would run.

Hound dog men in my neck of the woods were into tree dogs that would fight the quarry. I always heard that true fox hunters in other southern areas were satisfied to sit by a campfire and listen to their dogs. I think Ruby had more July Foxhound blood in her than anyone suspected. I always enjoyed her high-pitched excitement when she was running a trail. It always reminded me of the old foxhound story *The Voice of Bugle Ann*, which was an early-day motion picture.

Ruby didn't have a conventional bay when on a varmint trail. She had a soprano song like no other. Red Smith said she sounded like a squeaky bedspring. There was no calling Ruby off a trail. She ran until she could run no more. If we were hunting anywhere near Junction, Ruby would find her way home. I once took her on a hunt many miles away near the Kimble/Edwards County line. She had run completely out of hearing, and we had returned the twenty-five-mile distance to Junction before the sun came up. No Ruby, but I knew what to do. Later that day around noon, I returned to the ranch we had hunted the night before. There had been a campfire, and I had left my Levi jacket by the fire ashes when we left for home. Ruby was there sleeping on my coat as I had known she would be. One of the hardest decisions of my life was to leave Ruby behind with others when I went off to college at Sul Ross in Alpine. I truly loved the crazy little girl.

ELVIS AND OTHERS

When I graduated from Junction High School in 1953, I had little to show. I lettered in football, basketball, and track and field, no big accomplishment in a small Class A school. From Junction I went to Alpine, where I enrolled in what was then Sul Ross State College. It became Sul Ross University in 1969.

During the two years I spent at Sul Ross I was to meet Elvis Presley, Norman Cash, and Dan Blocker. None of these names meant much of anything to the world back in 1955. Little did any of us suspect that Presley would become the king of rock, that Cash would become an American League batting champion, or that Blocker would emerge as the hulking superstar Hoss Cartwright on the TV series *Bonanza*.

I met Presley at an off-campus café the day before he was to make his West Texas debut at the Alpine High School Auditorium. I don't recall the name of the restaurant, but it was directly across from the Sul Ross campus on Alpine's main drag. Presley was with Scotty Moore and Bill Black, his lead guitarist and upright bass player, respectively. The three of them had been out tacking up flyers promoting the upcoming show. Presley's early recordings on the Sun Records label were just starting to get air play. He was also coming off a successful run on the *Louisiana Hayride* radio show.

I was in the café with Glenn Llewallen, a Sul Ross basketball player. I don't remember which one it was, but Elvis, Scotty, or Bill invited us to at-

As a teenager, I was a defiant rebel and couldn't abide by my mother's fire-and-brimstone beliefs.

tend the upcoming show. Colonel Parker had yet to enter the Elvis Presley picture. Alpine KVLF Radio DJ John Nelson and Memphis promoter Bob Neal booked the show for $250. Elvis, Scotty, and Bill had to make that stretch three ways. The show was to benefit the Alpine Future Farmers of America. The high school furnished the PA.

Llewallen and I did attend the show with Vicky Miller, a senior at Alpine High School who was to become my first wife and the mother of my children. My interest in that first Elvis show started with an attraction I had to guitarist Scotty Moore's quirky rockabilly style. At that time, I had been fooling around with an electric guitar, a misguided folly I soon abandoned when it became more than obvious that I would never become the next Merle Travis or Tommy Emmanuel.

Scotty did not disappoint on that distant night in the Alpine school auditorium, but the main attraction came as an unexpected jolt. Elvis was not decked out in the regal, high-necked gold lamé finery that was to become a part of his bigger-than-life image. He hit that school auditorium stage au naturel Presley, wearing a white T-shirt, jeans, and blue sneakers. It was Memphis magic with the Blue Moon of Kentucky shining somewhere out there with the Marfa Ghost Lights.

It was 1955 and West Texas college girls were all but coming out of their undies in a high school auditorium. Who in the hell told them they could shuck their britches? I had never witnessed anything like it. Presley was doing his pelvic palpitations that no modern-day dick dancer has ever been able to emulate. Moore had the guitar calling from Rockabilly Heaven, and as Kinky Friedman might observe, Bill Black was snortin' and fartin' on the Tennessee upright walking bass.

Petticoats were popular with many young females in those days, voluminous body draperies that were flying like kites as Presley somehow wound up with a marking pen in his hand. With some of the girls yanking petticoats all the way over their heads, Elvis couldn't miss. He signed everything but bare bottoms, and he might have autographed a couple of those in the melee. Just one year after that incredible night, Presley packed San Antonio's Municipal Auditorium with screaming damsels. By this time, he owned three Cadillacs and was on his way to unheard-of world superstardom.

Glenn Llewallen and I had asked Elvis, Scotty, and Bill after the Alpine show to join us for drinks at a popular college skull orchard known as the Bull Beer Parlor. They accepted at first but later declined. They had a show booked for the following night in El Paso, and there was some concern that the old Cadillac they were driving might overheat if they didn't get an early start. They pulled out at daybreak, and I never again laid eyes on the king of rock and roll. Elvis died August 16, 1977; Bill Black died October 21, 1965; Scotty Moore died June 28, 2016.

Norman Cash and I had two things in common. We were both born on November 10, 1934, and both of us liked to play nine-ball pool for money. Baseball and baseball players were foreign to me. We didn't have the sport in the Junction school system, so when I met Norman Cash in the Sul Ross Student Union Building, we were competing with each other on a pool table for a dollar a game. Cash was as country as pig tracks, an easy guy to like and be friends with. He hailed from Justiceburg, a greasy spot in the road that was just down a fence line or two from the West Texas town of Post, population five thousand plus a few more.

We all called Cash the "Justiceburg Flash." I don't think he minded the nickname. I knew Cash was a Sul Ross baseball and football player. He was an All Lone Star Conference running back. What I didn't know was that he was a world-class athlete who would be drafted as a football running back by the Chicago Bears and as a baseball player by the Chicago White Sox. He declined a pro football career to sign with the White Sox, and after a series of trades, he wound up with Detroit.

Also known by friends and fans as "Stormin' Norman," Cash was the American League batting champion in 1961. He was a lefty. At Sul Ross I started watching baseball only because of my friendship with Cash. He drove home runs over the right field fence in Kokernot Field with regularity. An outstanding power hitter, Cash's 377 career home runs were the fourth most by an American League (AL) left-handed hitter when he retired, behind Babe Ruth, Ted Williams, and Lou Gehrig; his 373 home runs with the Tigers rank second in franchise history behind teammate Al Kaline (399). He also led the AL in assists three times and fielding percentage twice; he ranked among the all-time leaders in assists (fourth with 1,317) and double plays (tenth with 1,347) upon his retirement, and was fifth in AL history in games at first base (1,943).

Cash never seemed to take himself seriously. He was the first Detroit Tiger to hit a home run ball out of Tiger Stadium. He was to repeat the feat three more times before his retirement. And he may have been the first major league baseball player to bring a table leg instead of a standard baseball bat to home plate during a game. Nolan Ryan was in the midst of his second no-hitter when Cash walked up with the table leg.

The umpire said, "You can't bat with that."

Cash said, "Why not? I can't hit him anyway."

That was the Norman Cash I knew.

Cash drowned near Beaver Island in Lake Michigan in October 1986. Authorities ruled that he slipped on a wet dock and struck his head, causing him to slide into the water and drown. There were those, though, who believed Cash was murdered. One of the doubters was Detroit Lions football player Alex Karras, a friend and drinking buddy of Cash. Karras was quoted by one of their friends: "They killed him, you know. They hung him over the boat, filled his cowboy boots with water, and let him sink. Gambling debt. He owed the wrong kind of people more than he could pay back. So they killed him."

I hate to think that Stormin' Norman went that way. Toxicology tests showed that Cash was not drunk when he died. He was a powerfully built man, only fifty-one, and with reflexes like a cat. I tend to believe Alex Karras might have been on to something. Norman never returned to Justiceburg as far as I know. I know that he had a wife when he died and that he was buried in Michigan. But you can never get all of the Texas out of a real Texan. Norman Cash was wearing his cowboy boots when he died.

Dan Blocker had finished his Sul Ross football career and was back working on his master's in the dramatic arts when we met. I was working summers at the Sul Ross swimming pool, part-time lifeguard and part-time pool maintenance man. Dan Blocker was a friendly giant who told me he had been teaching drama at Sonora High School. A native of De Kalb , and weighing fourteen pounds at birth, Blocker was the biggest baby ever born in Bowie County. When I met him, he must have weighed 350 or more, and with hair on his back like a West Texas peccary.

I had already heard the Tobe Gober story before I met Blocker. Sul Ross was a rodeo school when I was there, and some of the cowboys on scholarship were enough to scare poop out of the average student of the finer arts. One of the scariest was a big cowboy named Tobe Gober, who wrote with bold black marker in the Sul Ross Student Union men's room: "All Band and Drama Majors are Queer." He signed it Tobe Gober.

I heard the Blocker/Gober confrontation was brutal, but I could never say for sure since I wasn't present. But there were more than a few witnesses who would testify that Blocker dragged the huge bulldogger into the Student Union Building men's room by his hair, then stood over the battered cowboy while Tobe scrubbed the wall clean with soap and water.

Such went the stories in the summer of 1955, a heady and exciting time for students at that West Texas college. Besides Elvis Presley playing the Alpine High School auditorium that year, such stars as Elizabeth Taylor, Rock Hudson, and James Dean were filming the epic movie *Giant* at nearby Marfa.

Many of the stars, including Taylor and Dean, were driving the thirty miles over to Alpine, where they swam in the college pool as townsfolk and students alike gawked.

Dan Blocker was in his element. The movie stars were enthralled. Despite his gigantic size and fifty-gallon oil-drum physique, he was a stunningly graceful diver. With Liz Taylor and her swimming pool hand-maidens-in-waiting, Big Dan did his thing on the three-meter diving board. His massive 350-pound bulk would bend the high board almost to the water before catapulting Blocker skyward. He did graceful flips with twists that never failed to amaze the audience. Little did any of them dream that they were watching the big star of another generation and New Age medium. They were watching big Hoss Cartwright before the prize-winning TV serial *Bonanza* was even a germ in some producer's mind.

The Dan Blocker I remember was the playful giant who would enliven his own awards ceremony with humor not for the faint of stomach. I don't recall exactly what the honor for Blocker was all about, but the ceremony was in the Alpine Holland Hotel banquet room. In the 1950s, many news photographers were still using the Speed Graphic camera with flash bulbs that were cloudy blobs when spent. Blocker somehow picked up one of these discarded bulbs and stuck it in one of his nostrils. It did resemble a giant booger when big Dan faced his audience. "Anybody holding a hand-kerchief," he hollered. And the solemnity of the occasion was no more.

My most vivid memory of Dan Blocker goes back to one late-summer day when I returned to my job at the swimming pool after visiting Junction for more than a week. That pool was without a roof, and my swimsuit had been hanging in the bath house. I slipped it on, and when I made it out to the pool, Dan Blocker was sunning himself on the pool apron.

My suit was stiff from disuse, and I was vaguely aware of some sort of movement on my back when Blocker yelled at me. "Hey, Sam," he said. "You need to be real still. And don't make any sudden moves. There are three big scorpions on your back and you need to dive into the pool." That did it. My back muscles spasmed, and three giant scorpions stung me in unison as I leaped into the pool.

I can still hear Dan Blocker's guffaws. Those damn scorpions almost killed me, and Blocker loved every minute of it. But he liked me. His belly laughter told me so. Dan died May 13, 1972, in a Los Angeles hospital. Cause of death was a pulmonary embolism following gall bladder surgery. It was supposed to be a simple operation, but someone used a dirty knife. I felt like crying when I heard the news.

The English professor's name was Elton Miles. He was a member of the Sul Ross State College faculty in 1955. Miles kept me after class one afternoon to deliver this message: "I know you have been writing theme papers for other students and charging them in the neighborhood of ten dollars. The papers are obviously the work of one writer, and many of them are quite good. But this business is going to stop."

Then Miles asked me what I was majoring in. I told him I had no major. I was taking general courses and drinking a lot of beer. He was a skinny little fellow with a crooked grin and a limp shock of brown hair that kept falling down over one of his eyes. I knew he was plenty smart. I sensed that he liked me. Even when he was dressing me down, he was doing it with his lopsided grin.

"You are accomplishing nothing," Miles said. "You need to transfer out of Sul Ross to a school with a journalism department." He was telling more than suggesting. "Southwest Texas State in San Marcos has a journalism department. Joe Vogel is head of the department and he is my friend. I am going to recommend you to Joe. This is something you really need to do."

The rest is history. I didn't know what journalism really was at the time, but I became a journalist in spite of myself. Vogel was a one-man journalism department with one part-time professor by the name of Box. I never took a course from Box. All of my J school courses were from Vogel. I hit

My first marriage was going to be one of those all-American marriages.
My mom loved Vicky like a daughter.

it big with Vogel. My very first article for the *College Star* was an interview I did with a half-naked female student with hair scorched in a student housing fire just off the main campus. The reporter for the weekly *San Marcos Record* concentrated on the fire, the damage done, and the number of firefighters it took to control the blaze. I wrote about nothing but the half-naked girl with the burnt hair, and Joe Vogel loved my story.

I married my first wife, Vicky Miller, shortly before leaving Sul Ross and Alpine for San Marcos. Vicky had just graduated from Alpine High School. She and Ann Bounds were the two prettiest girls in Alpine High. I pegged Vicky as the most attractive.

After I graduated from Southwest Texas State, my first newspaper job was editor of the *Bay City News*, a small Bay City weekly owned by shrimp boat owner and captain Steve Parsuit. Steve didn't have a printing press, so we got the *Bay City News* printed just a few miles up the road in El Campo at State Senator Culp Krueger's *El Campo Leader-News and Svoboda* (Svoboda was the Czech-language part of the paper). El Campo was and still is rice-farming country with roots going back to the Czech Republic. Before this, the country was known as Czechoslovakia and the language was Czechoslovakian. A number of the old-timers still spoke the language back in the 1950s. I heard it in some stores around Bay City and El Campo. I would write copy and headlines for our paper; then Parsuit's business flunky Chuck Arthur and I would drive it to El Campo for printing.

I fished and drank a lot of beer the three months I was in Bay City, the big event of my Bay City newspaper tenure being the birth of my first child, Grady Michael Kindrick. Grady was born premature on June 26,

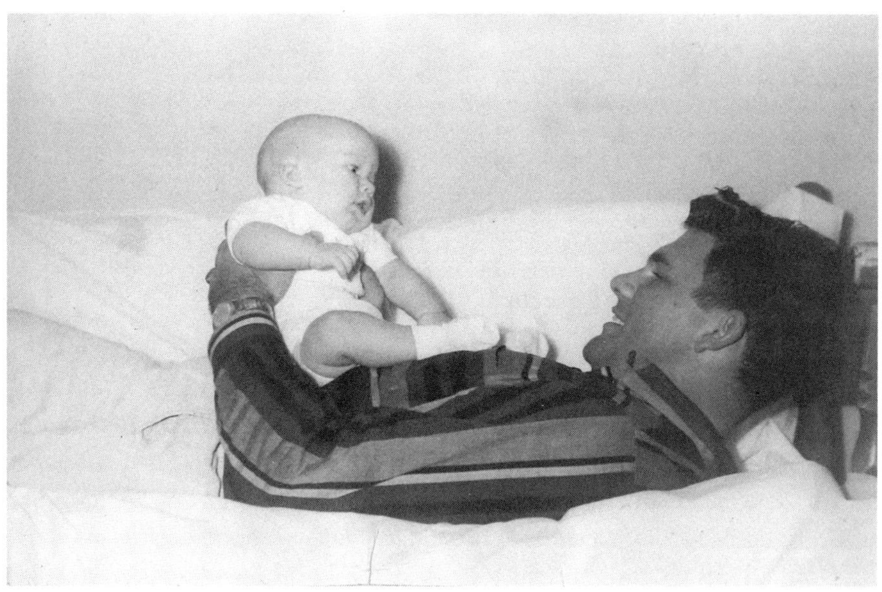

Sam with baby son, Grady, the child named for the father I never knew. Life in Bay City, Texas, was happy in the late 1950s. Decades later, Grady would beg me to "get off the dope."

1957, in Matagorda Regional Medical Center. He weighed three pounds at birth. Within two months, his weight had climbed to that of a normal child of that age. I was making sixty-five dollars a week in Bay City, and when it began looking like the *Bay City News* might have been on shaky ground, I headed for Kerrville to write for Rankin Starkey's *Kerrville Daily News.* The pay at Kerrville was seventy dollars a week.

We rented a little duplex not far from the Junction Highway that ran through Kerrville. Vicky was spoon-feeding baby Grady. We couldn't afford to go anywhere, and our only entertainment in those days was a little black-and-white TV with rabbit ears. We could see snowy forms on the little screen, and the audio was just as bad. Sometimes we tried to watch boxing and wrestling.

The Kerrville job lasted a month because I started out on the wrong foot. Carroll Abbott was Starkey's editor, and I was all ears as Abbott explained that to become successful in the Kerrville newspaper business, a young newsman like me should join the Kerrville Junior Chamber of Commerce. Abbott was a big wheel with the Jaycees. He insisted that this was the only way for a young fellow with any kind of ambition to go.

I didn't know what the hell a Junior Chamber of Commerce was all about, but I wanted to do good, so I told Abbott to sign me up. Abbott then directed me to the city park. The Miss Texas pageant had just been held in the park, and the Jaycees had been tasked with dismantling the stage and catwalk that had supported the beauty contestants.

The Jaycee who seemed to be in charge handed me a clawhammer. "What do I do with this," I asked.

"Start pulling nails out of that catwalk," he said.

"What's the pay?"

"Nothing, of course," he said. "The Junior Chamber of Commerce is a civic organization. We do work like this because we are proud of our city."

I handed him back the hammer and quit the Kerrville Junior Chamber of Commerce on the spot. I never joined anything again.

But my days in Kerrville were already in short number. When Rankin Starkey ordered me to wear a coat and tie to work, I told him I would if he would pay the cleaning bill. He refused, and I was headed to San Angelo the next day for a reporting job with the *San Angelo Standard-Times,* the daily newspaper I grew up reading in my hometown of Junction.

I got the San Angelo job by telephone. I called and asked for the editor, and managing editor Ed Hunter came on the line. I told him I was from Junction, that I had graduated from Southwest Texas State, that I wasn't making enough money in Kerrville, and that I needed to make more than seventy-five dollars a week. Hunter said he could start me at eighty-five dollars a week, and I was rich. I herded Vicky and Grady into our peach-colored 1951 Ford sedan, and we were loaded and rolling into the sand dunes and tumbleweeds of West Texas. I had the world by the tail with a downhill pull. I would make money and history in the metropolis of San Angelo where the Harte-Hanks red rooster was emblazoned on the door of every *Standard-Times* staff car.

I did know that Houston Harte and Bernard Hanks came out of the Missouri School of Journalism at the University of Missouri. They founded the *San Angelo Standard-Times* and branched out with a chain of midsized daily newspapers that included the *Corpus Christi Caller-Times*, the *Greenville Herald*, *Abilene Reporter-News*, and three others that were not Texas papers. Bernard Hanks died during the early going, and Houston Harte kept the Hanks name in respect for Bernard Hanks's widow.

It would be euphemistic to say that Houston Harte Sr. was eccentric. He was that and then some, a compact-sized executive with the stern and craggy features of a pit bull. He had red rooster images on most everything he owned. I never knew the story behind Harte's affinity for the barnyard cocks; I learned quickly, though, that the image of a crowing rooster in red ink was overlaid on the front page of every San Angelo newspaper when it rained an inch or more over three or more counties in the newspaper's circulation area.

The red rooster was emblazoned on the door of every *Standard-Times* staff car. The foyer tile in Harte's San Angelo mansion was red, white, and black, in the giant image of a crowing red rooster. Harte's cufflinks were red roosters, and the newspaper icon was adapted by at least one independently owned drinking joint, the Red Rooster on Concho Street. Harte-Hanks had no interest in the saloon, but most of the *Standard-Times* staff frequented the place.

The one staffer who did not drink in the Red Rooster or anywhere else was farm and ranch editor Elmer Kelton, a serious writer who was raised as a cowboy near Horse Camp on the Five Wells Ranch near Andrews in

The Sam Kindrick family at a San Antonio burger stop: (*left to right*) **daughter Gena, Sam, son Steven, wife Vicky, and son Grady.**

West Texas. Kelton, a graduate of the University of Texas at Austin, is now recognized by many as the top writer of western fiction in America. His story lines were fiction, but Kelton's work was as honest and unfailingly accurate as most pieces of library history.

Elmer had published his first western best seller, *Buffalo Wagons*, when I met him. I was impressed with his humility. He wrote his fiction at night, his newspaper farm and ranch news by day. "It's fine to write western fiction at night," Kelton once told me, "but be sure and hang on to your day job. There ain't a lot of money in it."

He then went on to win every western writer award available. He was voted the best western author in the country by the Western Writers of America. I liked Kelton because of his affable nature. He treated everyone the same and we all loved him. But he always declined when I invited him out drinking. I don't think he even drank alcohol. Kelton died August 22, 2009.

Publisher Houston Harte's office was behind one-way glass. He could sit in his office and view everything going on in the newspaper city room. The outside of the glass was reflective, and new employees were known to fix their hair or squeeze pimples without knowing that the company's chief executive was looking straight out at them.

I had been with the newspaper for about a year, long enough to rate a staff car with a red rooster on the door, when I committed what I thought then was my worst gaffe in San Angelo. I was a general assignments reporter then, covering everything from car wrecks to an occasional murder away from San Angelo and Tom Green County. Each reporter had a designated parking spot in the *Standard-Times* lot. Mine was occupied by a cream-colored Cadillac when I pulled in from an assignment one rainy afternoon. A wooden sign that read "Staff Only" had somehow toppled over. It had a couple of rusty nails protruding from the sign board, and it was caked with West Texas mud.

I picked the sign up and pitched it onto the hood of the Cadillac, mud and nails included. Then I found another parking place for the staff car and went into the newspaper building. I was in the newspaper snack bar when I heard old man Harte screech at Ed Hunter, the managing editor. "Goddamn it Ed, find out right now who put that muddy sign with nails on my Cadillac."

Hunter came to San Angelo from the *Daily Oklahoman* in Oklahoma City. He was a likable professional, but he hadn't been on the job long enough to know that the old newspaper pioneer had a soft spot in his heart for drunks and intemperate kid reporters. Hunter was a little rattled. He seemed to know where to zero in: "Okay, Sam Kindrick, what about this?"

I had to confess. "I thought Mr. Harte had a black Cadillac," I told Hunter. "This one was cream-colored. I put the sign on it because it was in my parking space."

Hunter was as collected as he could possibly be. "Mr. Harte has four Cadillacs," Hunter said. "One is black, one is white, one is blue, and this one is cream-colored. In the future, I think you had best not damage another Cadillac in the *Standard-Times* lot."

Hunter didn't know it at the time that old man Harte had never fired an employee for drinking or booze-related mischief. George Kunkel would go on knee-walking, commode-hugging benders, only to return to his copy desk job with little or no repercussion. I never heard of Houston Harte drinking alcohol or being drunk, but his tolerance for booze-blitzed employees such as Kunkel and sports writer Blondie Cross was a topic of much discussion in high places and some not so high.

Blondie Cross covered high school football for the *San Angelo Standard-Times*, and anyone who knows anything about West Texas knows that high school football is king. Blondie Cross was a big, puffy, albino-looking man with red skin and cloudy eyes. He wrote a *Standard-Times* sports column for years, and half of West Texas believed Cross had supernatural powers when it came to football game predictions. If Blondie predicted a team would win, that team almost always won, and the *Standard-Times* hierarchy ignored or tolerated Cross's penchant for whiskey.

First one and then another young reporter would be dispatched across West Texas to fetch Blondie and bring him home during high school football season. The bosses all knew the score. My first Blondie Cross assignment found me driving to Eldorado, where Blondie supposedly had weather-related car trouble. I found his car in a dry wash with water up to what we called the running boards in those days. The car had stalled but Cross was doing well. He was sitting on top of the car as boiled as an owl. I pulled him down and drove him back to San Angelo. Someone else would retrieve his staff car the next day.

My second child, Steven Howard Kindrick, was born August 27, 1958, in San Angelo's Shannon Hospital. It was shortly after Steve's birth that the word got out. Harte-Hanks was buying the *San Antonio Express-News*. This, to me, was the big time. Houston Harte, we all knew, had long yearned for a flagship daily newspaper in a metropolitan setting. San Antonio was it, and I was determined to go with them. I had little trouble making the transition. Ed Hunter recommended me, and I was subsequently hired by *Express-News* executive editor Charles O. Kilpatrick.

My salary: one hundred dollars a week in 1960. I had arrived.

7

CAPTAIN ALLEE

When I left Sul Ross at Alpine for my final two years of college at Southwest Texas State College in San Marcos (now Texas State University), there followed jumps to newspaper jobs in Bay City, Kerrville, and San Angelo before I landed a general assignments reporter job at the *San Antonio Express-News* in 1960.

I covered three major hurricanes and wrote a daily column for the *Express-News*, but the defining time in my early career came in the beet and onion fields of deep South Texas. I was in Crystal City, a small South Texas town that residents still proclaim to be the "Spinach Capital of the World." It was circa 1970, and the statue of Popeye on the town square belied the explosive atmosphere that was beyond my sense of comprehension at the time. The *Express-News* articles I wrote during and after the Crystal City political phenomena resulted in me being nominated for a Pulitzer Prize. Ironically, the man on the Pulitzer committee who nominated me, Executive Editor Charles Kilpatrick, was to fire me from the newspaper in years to come. Times were crazy in those days.

La Raza Unida had been formed by Chicano activists Jose Angel Gutierrez and Mario Compean, both Mexican American firebrands whose party name translated to National United People's Party. I was in the midst of a political racial takeover as La Raza, with help from the Teamsters Union, fielded their own candidates and trucked South

Texas migrant farmworkers to the polls in an unheard-of takeover of all municipal offices. None of the candidates, including newly elected mayor Juan Cornejo, had better than a fifth-grade education. La Raza had made a statement. La Raza candidates won every municipal office in Crystal City that spring as tensions hummed like a fiddle string about to break. Anglo townspeople were boarding up their houses and leaving town as the governor sent famed and feared Texas Ranger captain Alfred Young Allee in to keep the peace.

As the polls closed and final votes were tabulated, I heard shouts on the streets that made it plain and clear that gringos such as myself were not welcome in Crystal City. I heard a couple of bottles shatter on the street asphalt. They were tossed from moving cars, but I saw no faces. There was an almost-palpable fear in the air. I had rented a motel room from friendly Anglos who had moved to Crystal City from New York State. They had customers and friends with white faces and brown faces. They did not know what was happening. They didn't understand what the racial divide was all about.

For many years the Texas Rangers had been a feared and hated force in the beet fields and the barrios of South Texas. The Mexican American people have charged ranger brutality for years, and while there has no doubt been some justification for the racial prejudice charges, the rangers have proven themselves through the years as the unstoppable crime-fighting machine of Texas.

Joaquin Jackson was the last Texas Ranger to be appointed by Captain Allee. Now the rangers come up through the Texas Department of Public Safety ranks like regular patrolmen. In his book *One Ranger*, Jackson devoted an entire chapter to Captain Allee. In his prime, Captain Allee weighed about two hundred pounds and stood about six feet tall. But Ranger Joaquin Jackson told me there was not a man on the planet who could stand up to Captain Allee.

Joaquin Jackson was my friend. I put him on the cover of my magazine once, and I also wrote about his wife, Shirley, a country music vocalist with a lot of talent. So I believed every one of Jackson's words when he described the ranger captain who gave him his job. "Cap Allee is the most formidable man I have ever met," Jackson said. "I believe him to be totally fearless. You meet him, you know. It is in his eyes. There is no fear. It's the A. Y. Allee presence. Nobody can stand up to it."

Sam, leaning against the *San Antonio Express-News* building. I always had a cigarette in my hand. See those wing-tipped shoes? I was playing it straight in those days. I just turned outlaw little by little.

I was to meet Allee and understand that presence on my first day in Crystal City. He was getting up in years then. Allee called me "newspaper man," but I could sense he meant "newspaper boy." We became friends over the ensuing months, and I believe the tough old ranger captain developed a genuine liking for me. He chewed cigars, but I never saw him spit. He grunted on occasion, and I came to learn that some of his grunts were to emphasize his wishes or meanings.

The streets of Crystal City were almost deserted on election night. There was an eerie quiet when Captain Allee said, "Come on, newspaper man. You can go with me to the election party if you like." Then Allee started walking and I fell in behind him. It seemed like the safest place to be at the time.

The election victory party was being held in a ratty, run-down whiskey bar known as the Veteran's Club. It resembled an ancient army barracks that had long since said good-bye to its original and then peeling paint job. La Raza celebrants had a snoot full when we arrived. They were hooting, hollering, and filling the air with Spanish-language invective that suggested raw danger.

Captain Allee's cowboy boots thumped loudly as we crossed the Veteran's Club flooring toward the bar. It sounded like a drumbeat of doom. When Allee grunted, it was like a combination of grunt and clearing of the throat: "Grrruuump."

The Veteran's Club was crammed with some sinister-looking characters, the shine of alcohol hatred and menace in their eyes. "Grrruuump." He did it before he spoke. Utter quiet. You could have heard a matchstick hit the floor. "I need your attention," Allee said. Not loudly but evenly. "Some of you know who I am. For those who don't, I am Alfred Allee, captain of Texas Rangers. I have been appointed by the governor to see that the law is upheld in Crystal City. I will now take a minute to congratulate you on your election victory tonight. You won fair and square, and I would be the last one to deny you."

Another pause. Another "grrruuump" before Allee finished his speech. "You won this election. But if any one of you tries to take the law into your hands, I will kill you." He grunted again and headed for the door. I fell in behind. No graveyard was ever quieter than the Crystal City Veteran's Club at that moment that night. I was waiting for the bullet to crash into my back as I followed Allee across the floor and out the door.

The next day, I visited the captain at a small temporary office he maintained on Crystal City's main street. I asked about his stunning promise to the party celebrants, and he told me something I will remember for the rest of my life: "You will always be okay, newspaper man, if you say what you mean, mean what you say, and cover the ground that you stand on. Not one of those drunks last night doubted for a minute that I would kill the first one who broke the law and violated the peace."

Allee was over seventy then and not far from retirement. He epitomized the legendary saying, "You got one riot, you need only one ranger." His era was coming to an end, and I think he might have sensed it. After the Crystal City showdown, Allee's antagonists were relentless.

Crystal City mayor Juan Cornejo, a diminutive fellow who might have stood five foot four at the most, flew from Crystal City to San Antonio, where he filed federal assault charges against the ranger captain. If I asked Captain Allee what was going on, his answer never wavered. "You are the newspaper man. You tell me."

He answered a specific question with a straight answer. "Mayor Cornejo has filed a federal assault complaint against you in San Antonio," I told Allee. "What do you say to that?"

That warranted an Allee "grrruuump "and a typical Allee answer. "If I had assaulted the mayor," Allee said with a laconic grin, "he wouldn't have been able to crawl on an airplane and fly to San Antonio to file any complaint. He would have been in a hospital. I didn't assault him. I just picked him up and shook him a little."

Captain Allee died in 1987 at age eighty-two.

The legend of the Texas Rangers has had a good run. Ranger Manuel (Lone Wolf) Gonzaullas tamed the oil-boom towns of Texas; Captain Gully Cowsert of Junction wrecked every carnival that came near him; and Ranger Captain Frank Hamer ended the lives and bloody crime spree of Clyde Barrow and Bonnie Parker. A. Y. Allee was the last of the breed. He averted a race riot in Crystal City. His tormentors danced around him near the end, filing lawsuits and complaints like a bunch of kids poking sticks at a proud but crippled bear.

I was proud to call him friend who was true to his word. He said what he meant, he meant what he said, and he always covered the ground that he stood on.

HURRICANE BEULAH

My transition from San Angelo to the *San Antonio Express-News* was seamless, partially because I was already familiar with the Harte-Hanks way of gathering and printing the news and partially because I wasn't terrified of Houston Harte Sr. Strange as it may seem, old man Houston Harte took a shine to me after I pitched the big muddy sign on the hood of his Cadillac.

Executive Editor Charlie Kilpatrick hired me after a short telephone conversation and a brief meeting. I was soon to learn that Kilpatrick was a frightened executive who bent and turned with the winds of company politics. Kilpatrick knew I was coming in from the Harte-Hanks home base of San Angelo, and he was taking no chances.

I hadn't been on the job a month when Harte Senior walked into the *Express-News* city room and yelled, "Where is the kid who worked for us in San Angelo?"

My desk was in the back of the city room next to the sports department. When I said "Here," the old man hustled right back and took a seat on the side of my desk.

"Well," he said. "How do you like it here?"

When I said I liked the new job, the millionaire publisher asked, "What do you think we need to do to make the paper better?"

"Stop running shinplasters," I told him.

"Shinplasters?"

"Yes, sir, shinplasters."

I explained the shinplaster, a derogatory term I had picked up in the paper's editorial department. Advertising copy that is disguised as news, I told him. He frowned and had me repeat the bit about shinplasters.

"I didn't know we were doing that," Houston Harte said. "We will stop it today." And stop it he did.

This had a profound effect on the entire editorial staff, all of them older and more experienced than me. It is hard to believe that the executive editor of a daily newspaper in a metropolitan market would fear a cub reporter. But I honestly believed that Kilpatrick was afraid of me from that day forward and as long as the Hartes owned the *Express-News*.

Dan Cook was the *Evening News* sports editor and columnist when I arrived. Cook was a great writing talent and the most popular sports writer in the city. Of Charlie Kilpatrick's unctuous propensity to please his superiors, I heard Cook say, "If a chicken farmer bought the newspaper, Charlie would show up for work wearing a feather suit."

Cook and I became friends and drinking companions, as did company artist Bob Dale. When referring to the rival *San Antonio Light*, Cook was wont to say of certain *Light* reporters: "I could swallow a bottle of ink and piss a better story than any of those hacks."

Front-page *Evening News* columnist Paul Thompson, a recovered alcoholic, became my friend and mentor. I also worked with legendary photographer Bill Goodspeed, who was nearing the end of his career when I arrived on the scene, but I had heard about his pigeon loft on the top floor of the newspaper building. In the 1940s and 1950s, Goodspeed used homing pigeons to fly his football game film back to their newspaper home. The rival *San Antonio Light* and other Texas newspapers could not compete. Goodspeed would have film flown home, processed, and ready for print before any other newspaper could even hit the streets. I sold an article on Goodspeed to *Editor and Publisher Magazine*, a national trades publication.

I was the *Express-News* top general assignments reporter early in my career, a time when my third child and daughter, Gena Gay Kindrick, was born. She was delivered without complication in San Antonio's downtown Baptist Hospital on October 20, 1963.

Most of the major story assignments were falling my way as I worked with three photographers, Goodspeed, Johnny Tarsikes, and Jose Barrera. Tarsikes burned up a company Chevrolet as we raced to Austin. Infamous University of Texas Tower sniper Charles Joseph Whitman was picking pedestrians off like fish in a barrel.

Then came the disaster of nature that nobody could ever forget. I had just returned home from a night of fishing on Canyon Lake when I got the call. The day was Tuesday, September 19, 1967. It was Ken Kennamer, city editor of the *Morning Express* and my immediate superior in the newspaper's chain of command. Unusual, I thought, to get a morning call from Kennamer. We both worked night shifts on the *Morning Express*. "Pack enough clothes to last several days," Kennamer said. "Bring rain gear. Rubber boots if you have them. The storm is bearing down on Brownsville, and that's where you are going. You will be riding with Joe. Expense money will be waiting when you get to the office."

Joe was Jose Barrera, one of the young photographers for the *Express-News*. The storm Kennamer referred to was Hurricane Beulah, one of the biggest and most deadly hurricanes to ever hit the Texas Gulf Coast. I was a greenhorn reporter who had never heard of a category 5 hurricane. Photographer Joe Barrera was equally inexperienced. I met him at the *Express-News* city room, and we were off to cover the hurricane, which would pack 160-mile-per-hour winds, dump rain bombs that would total twenty-five inches, and kill fifty-eight people, fifteen of them Texans.

I covered three major hurricanes while working at the *Express-News*— Carla, Celia, and Beulah. Big bad Beulah was the first and the most destructive. Weather experts, law enforcement officials, and first responders all agreed that Beulah probably packed more than a few tornadoes close to the hurricane's eye.

Joe Barrera and I started out in high spirits, like a couple of kids embarking on a Boy Scout adventure. We had never experienced wind that can turn your mouth wrong side out or broken power lines spewing high-voltage death in the dark. Who would ever believe that hurricane-force winds and heavy rain can somehow bring six-foot rattlesnakes up out of their dens and onto city streets, writhing and buzzing their deadly song? And only those who have suffered a shotgun charge of buckshot could imagine the searing pain of rooftop pea gravel driven by the ungodly winds of a major hurricane.

Joe Barrera and I were babies heading for our baptism of fire in the Rio Grande Valley. Joe drove. I noticed the stream of cars coming our way. We seemed to be the only ones heading down into the Valley. We reached Brownsville at dusk. It took us longer than we had anticipated to cover the 250 miles. We were told the Fort Brown Motel was the place to stay, but we found a no-vacancy sign on the entrance. Everything else in town was taken. Media people had filled the Fort Brown, including a reporter/photographer team from the *Dallas Morning News* and award-winning *San Antonio Light* photographer Gilbert Barrera (no relation to our Joe Barrera).

Joe and I had about despaired of finding shelter when help appeared behind a badge. It was a Cameron County deputy sheriff who told us to head for the courthouse. There were no beds available, but the sandstone courthouse, which was built in 1912, was open for us and some others fortunate enough to run into the helpful deputy. "There ain't any building stronger or safer than a Texas courthouse," said the deputy. "They will be standing when nothing else is." The deputy knew of which he spoke. Most of the Fort Brown Motel was wrecked by the storm, and there was little else left standing in the town. Only the majestic Cameron County Courthouse took the big wind hit with no damage done.

I will never forget the early-morning hours of September 20, 1967. We knew Beulah was coming. The Coast Guard had radioed ahead. The air had a waxy feel, and there was an eerie yellow hue to the sky. The Devil had to sit this one out. This morning belonged to the big bad bitch called Beulah. She roared across Boca Chica Pass with unrelenting fury. She screamed like a runaway freight train with no engineer. Power lines were snapping in the darkness, showering Brownsville with deadly white and blue ribbons of electricity. Great sheets of roofing metal were windmilling through the air like airborne guillotines, any one of them capable of removing a human head. This was hell on the Texas coast, and it would get worse long before the people of Brownsville would recover from Hurricane Beulah.

It was raining bathtubs when the photographer and I ventured out to view and photograph the aftermath. One big rattlesnake buzzed at our approach, and we saw several smaller ones as we made our way around live power lines that were snapping and popping. I learned later that intense rainwater flooding their underground dens drove the snakes above ground and often onto downtown streets.

Our *San Antonio Express-News* staff car was a white Chevy II, and we were preparing to drive out and survey the damage when *San Antonio Light* photographer Gil Barrera flagged us down. I knew Gil Barrera to be an award-winning photographer whose work had graced the cover of *Life* magazine. Gil was the younger brother of ace criminal defense attorney and district judge Roy Barrera. The younger Barrera had been staying in the Fort Brown Motel when a two-by-four timber was driven through the windshield of his staff vehicle. He came down to Brownsville with a *Light* reporter, but the two of them had been separated in the storm. He asked if he could ride with us that morning, and I said, "Hop in."

In those days, the *San Antonio Express* and the *San Antonio Light* employees were spirited competitors and often bitter enemies. But my relationship with Gil Barrera had always been one of professional respect and admiration. With other editorial employees from both newspapers, we often drank beer together at the Melody Room Lounge on Avenue E, about a half block from both papers. And privately we had lamented in the past that we did not work together for the same publication.

Joe Barrera was quiet when Gil crawled into the back seat. I knew Joe was intimidated by the presence of the older and more accomplished photographer, but Gil's naturally humble demeanor belied his genius with a camera. He wore horn-rimmed glasses that were seemingly always broken and patched together with scotch tape. "I'll just ride along and snap a few pictures when I'm not getting in anybody's way," he said. I knew that was bullshit. I was already feeling nervous.

Gil Barrera was carrying what we considered to be a little-bitty new-fangled 35-millimeter camera. He also had a ragged rain poncho he held wadded up in one hand. Joe shot a number of photographs as we worked our way through the wind wreckage that was Brownsville. He shot an upended car, downed power poles, wrecked storefronts, and other damage. Street signs were twisted like pretzels, further indication that tornadoes were probably in the mix.

Gil Barrera sat quietly in the back seat while we worked our way through Brownsville and out onto the highway leading to Port Lavaca. He had not said a word or taken a photograph. The rain was a solid sheet.

Then Gil Barrera spoke to Joe Barrera. "Hey, Joe, would you mind letting me out here for a minute or two?"

Gil had the old poncho over his head when he crawled out of the car. He headed straight to a highway sign that had been bent down by the wind, almost level with the ground. I think it read "Port Lavaca 20 Miles." Nothing different from many other similar signs in the same condition. We had been passing them all morning. They were barely visible through the curtain of water. I suspected something might be happening that foretold nothing good for the *Express-News*.

Gil Barrera was my friend and competitor, but to be scooped by the *San Antonio Light* was a horrible fate to contemplate. At this point, I was driving the car. Joe was shooting the *Express-News* photos. "Find out what Gil is doing out there by that sign," I hollered at Joe. The rain was pouring.

"He's shooting the sign," Joe said.

"We have been passing signs like that all morning," I yelled at Joe. "You better get over there."

Gil reappeared. He seemed relaxed. Jovial. Deep in my bowels I knew that the greatest news photographer in the country wasn't taking pictures of a Port Lavaca road sign. "Thanks," Gil said. "I really appreciate you guys letting me ride along."

Oh, shit. I thought it but said no more. We found couriers to deliver storm film to the *Express* city room. Gil Barrera did also. We found out the next morning when issues of both papers hit the streets. My greatest fear bloomed into horrifying reality.

Joe Barrera had a hellacious photo of hurricane wreckage that appeared on the front page of the *Express-News*. I don't even know what it was. But I will never forget the photograph that Gil Barrera killed us with.

Gil had one simple photo that said it all. The photograph was six columns wide, engulfing the entire cover page of the *San Antonio Light*. The photograph pictured a tiny chihuahua dog and a large rat. They were wet and bedraggled as they snuggled together, cheek to cheek and paw to foot, shivering and exchanging body warmth with all four eyes tightly shut. I think the headline said: "Strange Bedfellows in the Eye of a Storm." I didn't say anything about it to Joe. He was hurting enough. And I was part of it, too. Maybe I should have tackled Gil in the rain. It didn't feel good. That's for sure. But I later told Joe we had nothing to be ashamed of. We got beat by the best in the business.

9

SUGARLAND EXPRESS

When I met Steven Spielberg, my head was falling off my shoulders and rolling around my feet. It was spring of 1974 in Floresville, Texas. I was hungover bad and wishing I had never heard of Spielberg or casting director Shari Rhodes. The filming of *Sugarland Express* with Goldie Hawn and Ben Johnson had begun. I have a speaking part in the movie. This was Spielberg's first gig as a director. He had somehow persuaded coproducers Richard Zanuck and David Brown to foot the production bill.

I was still with the *Express-News* during those times, and my drinking was starting to escalate. I had the shakes that morning in Floresville. I was hurting so bad that my hair hurt. I am the Texas newspaperman in the film who tries to interview a howling baby Langston. I will get into the story line and other details later. There are tidbits here of human interest, like Goldie getting her drivers so stoned on weed they never got her to the movie set on time or the fit she pitched when some of us hauled her to Luckenbach. Suffice it to say that Goldie Hawn did not care for Luckenbach, but more on all of this later.

What I remember most about Steven Spielberg and the *Sugarland Express* filming was my miserable hungover condition and Spielberg's torturous obsession for detail. He achieved it through mind-rattling repetition, bolstered by a fetching ability to reach the hearts and souls of veteran film stars.

It all started for me in the Gunter Hotel coffee shop where I met casting director Shari Rhodes. I'm not sure how this meeting came about, but I think it may have been arranged by my friend Big John Hamilton, owner of Big John's Steak House and a movie actor himself who appeared in several John Wayne movies.

Guich Koock may have been with me that morning. He did wind up with a part in the movie. Koock had partnered with Hondo Crouch to buy the town of Luckenbach, and the two of them were popping up all over the burgeoning San Antonio and South Texas entertainment map. In *Sugarland*, Guich played a Louisiana highway patrolman. Shari Rhodes was a delight. Even with the hangover I took to her immediately. "How would you like to play a part in our film?" Shari Rhodes laughed. "You look like a movie star in the making."

I didn't have any idea what *Sugarland Express* was all about, but I agreed to give it a try. Shari had me sign a bunch of papers, and two mornings later I met her and other people from Universal Pictures back at the Gunter Hotel. It was five o'clock in the morning, and we were loaded in a van and headed for filming in Floresville. Shari was with us. I had no idea of her stature in the film industry. She was laughing and cutting up with me like we had been friends for ages. Who would have suspected that she would work in films like *Jaws* and *Close Encounters of the Third Kind* and many other films? I think she may have directed a few movies herself. Years later I was to learn that Shari Rhodes died from breast cancer in 2009.

In addition to me, Shari, the van driver, and maybe a couple more, there was Louise Latham, a veteran Hollywood character actress whom I recognized immediately but had no inkling as to her name. The supporting actors and actresses like Louise Latham are the true talents who keep the Hollywood star ship afloat. You see them in a film and there is immediate recognition, but their names are but a meaningless string of letters among the film credits. Like Shari Rhodes, Louise Latham proved to be an affable, down-to-earth, and engaging lady of grace with a ready sense of humor.

I had been drinking most of the night and early morning in San Antonio's downtown Commander's Room, an after-hours nightclub that sometimes stayed open until daylight. Louise must have sensed that I wasn't quite right in the head and nervous system. "Are you feeling all right?"

I didn't want to tell her I was experiencing a monumental hangover. "It's early for me," I said.

**Newspaperman Sam in the early 1970s. I was probably
hung over bad. Alcohol did a number on me. That was
my perception of what a newspaperman looked like,
and they were all drunks. I'd lost my illusions.**

Latham seemed to understand. "This is just the way for us people who
work in films," she said. "The public has no idea. The reason we are up at
these ungodly hours is all about time and money. When we are on location away from the Hollywood studios, it costs a tremendous amount of
money to pay everyone involved and cover the huge production expense.
We are up at dawn because we utilize every minute of real daylight we
have available. Daylight is like pure gold in the film industry. When on
location, we go from first light until dark."

The setting in Floresville where my scene was filmed was one of those
old country-style houses with a wide front porch, wide concrete steps,
and a long concrete sidewalk that led from the street to the porch. I recall lying down in the shade of a tree, waiting for instructions. Finally I
was up and facing the director. I had donned a dark red and black sport

coat that was almost new. I owned only two sport coats. I was ready for my debut on the silver screen when Spielberg called out to Shari Rhodes. "Take this guy to the wardrobe trailer and have them outfit him in a gold coat," Spielberg told Shari.

Turning to me, the director explained: "Nothing against your red coat, but gold fits your dark coloring. We want you to look your best for this scene. I know you will do fine."

Steven Spielberg is one of the greatest and most liked directors in Hollywood.

We saw the Spielberg genius early with *Sugarland*. The world saw it one short year after *Sugarland* when he broke the record bank with *Jaws*. Spielberg was a fuzzy-cheeked twenty-eight years of age when *Sugarland* was filmed, yet he held some sort of hypnotic magic over his veteran actors and actresses, grizzled pro Ben Johnson being a prime example. Over and over and over again, in one scene, Spielberg coaxed Johnson into jumping out of the same pickup truck. Slamming on the brakes, Ben jumped from the vehicle. Spielberg the kid director was congratulating Johnson when his feet hit the street. "Great job, Ben," Spielberg gushed. "An incredible scene. Let's do it once more, please sir."

Johnson jumped out of the truck again. "Fantastic, Ben," Spielberg bubbled. "What an actor you are. I would like to see this at one more angle. Please do it for me again, Ben." Johnson jumped out of the truck yet again. "Incredible, Ben. I don't believe I have ever seen anything better." Spielberg was relentless.

I don't know how many times Ben Johnson jumped out of the truck with Spielberg rooting him on. Nobody was keeping count. And I can't say how many times the director had me and other faux newspaper reporters and TV cameramen walk up the sidewalk to the front porch of that old house in Floresville.

Spielberg also wrote *Sugarland Express*, the story based on a true Texas tale of comedic madness that started when Lou Jean Poplin talks husband, Clovis Michael Poplin, into breaking out of a low-security prison to go after their two-year-old son, Langston, who is in foster care. Adding to the absurdity of it all was the fact that Clovis was only four months short of release from the pre-release prison farm when Lou Jean talked him into the jail break.

The slow-motion and ever-growing chase that ensued, with over two hundred cop cars, rubberneck spectators, gun nuts, and self-anointed honky-tonk heroes, was a carnival on wheels with a light show the likes of which Hollywood had never known before. Clovis and Lou Jean were crossing South Texas to retrieve their son from foster parents in what was actually Floresville. They had a kidnapped highway patrolman in tow. Adding to the insanity of it all was a Boy Scout troop Spielberg had out directing traffic.

Goldie Hawn played Lou Jean Poplin. Her husband, Michael, was played by William Atherton. The zany plot has Lou Jean and Michael kidnapping Highway Patrolman Maxwell Slide, who is portrayed by Michael Sacks. The baby Langston was portrayed by producer Zanuck's two-year-old son, Harrison. Louise Latham played Mrs. Looby, the foster mother. The foster father was played by Merrill Connally, Governor John Connally's brother. Ben Johnson plays DPS Captain Harlin Tanner, and it was Captain Tanner who led the procession of lawmen and weirdos.

The news crew arrived first at the Floresville house where Langston was being fostered. The script called for us news people to march down the sidewalk, up the flight of steps, and onto the porch where we are met by Mrs. Looby and Merrill Connally, who is holding Baby Langston. While this may sound simple, it was not. I think there were five of us in the entourage of news people. I know that country singer Dale Jackson was holding a giant TV sound camera. The others may have been holding notebooks. I was the only one of the bunch with a speaking part.

Here was the rub. After we completed our advance down the sidewalk and up on the porch, Spielberg insisted that we all land in exactly the same spot. He also insisted that none of us look down at our feet as we advanced on the house and stopped on the porch. Here is where the operation got maddeningly tricky. Spielberg got down on his knees and placed chalk X marks on the exact spots where he wanted us to land. We had to repeat that advance maneuver over and over and over again, counting the exact number of steps from the street to our exact designated landing spots on the porch. Not until all of us were able to count our steps and land squarely on our designated porch positions in complete unison did the filming proceed.

It was late afternoon before we got to the grand climax, an irate foster mother meeting the encroachment of a bunch of news yo-yos trespassing on her porch. By this time everyone was irritable, restless, and discontent. Especially Harrison Zanuck, the Baby Langston who was the object of it all. He was holding soda crackers slathered in grape jelly because his father said that was the only goodie he would respond to. And producer Zanuck was there overseeing his baby.

I was leading the newspeople onslaught, so it was me whom the infuriated foster mother lit into.

"I know why you people are here," hissed Mrs. Looby. "You are not welcome here and I will have to ask you to leave."

Here is where I saw the great actress in action, eyes narrowed in slits of hate. Louise Latham was earning her pay. She was scary. She was living the life of a foster mother in danger of losing her baby. Mrs. Looby did not resemble in any way the Louise Latham that I rode with to Floresville. I had my lines down. "But, ma'am, we just want to talk to the little child." Then I hollered the kickers: "Langston, do you know who your real mother is? Could you wave bye bye to your real father?"

At this point, someone hollered "Cut." Baby Langston had smeared his grape jelly cracker across his foster father's shirt and coat front.

When my lines were repeated the next time, Harrison Zanuck broke into an ear-splitting scream, flinging one of his crackers at me. "You are scaring the child with your voice," a bystander said.

Daddy Zanuck broke in at this point. "This is exactly how we want him to react, like a frightened two-year-old."

Earlier movie reviews failed to give Goldie Hawn her just due because they didn't know Goldie. The *Hollywood Reporter* said of Spielberg's *Sugarland Express*: "The fledgling filmmaker often fails to keep a tight enough rein on Hawn. Too often she breaks into her *Laugh-in* giggle and bubble-headed blonde routine, destroying the image of a distraught driven mother."

When *Sugarland* was filmed, Goldie was only a few months removed from a go-go dancer job in a cheap saloon. When members of the *Sugarland* cast took her for a visit to Luckenbach, Goldie turned up her nose and started bitching and complaining about "the nasty place" until Ben Johnson told her to shut up. "If you don't like it here," Johnson told Goldie, "you can hitchhike back to San Antonio." And that was it. Johnson

"Preacher Sam." I was cast in an independent film that was never completed or distributed, *The Adventures of Jody Shannon*.

knew how to handle the petulant kid, and Spielberg knew what he was doing when he signed her on. Goldie fit the Lou Jean Poplin part like a kid leather glove.

Sugarland Express concluded my movie career, although I did have a significant part in an independent production that never made it off the cutting-room floor: *The Adventures of Jody Shannon*, filmed in Brackettville, and again I was recommended for the part by John Hamilton.

Preacher Sam with saloon girls. The movie set was in Brackettville, Texas.
I have vague memories of seeing the daily film rushes. Johnny Cash's
former brother-in-law, Ray Liberto, played the piano music for the scenes.

In this one I played a hypocritical dice-shooting, circuit-riding Preacher Sam with a whiskey flask protruding from a hip pocket. I rode a white mule and preached hellfire and damnation to a bunch of saloon girls in the main scene. Playing piano in the saloon was Wild Man Ray Liberto, former brother-in-law of Johnny Cash.

This ill-fated production was financed by a group of San Antonio dentists. It was produced as a children's film, but funding was withdrawn when the dentists decreed that it was unfit for kid consumption. The Preacher Sam saloon sermon and a fight among a bunch of buffalo hunters were the two scenes deemed too rough for kids. And these were the two scenes the kids went wild over when showed some raw rushes of the film.

10

MADALYN AND REVEREND BOB

Famed atheist Madalyn Murray O'Hair sashayed into the *San Antonio Express-News* city room like she owned the place. It was summertime, and I will swear that I could smell her body odor. I had been assigned the job of interviewing the most hated woman in America, who a few years earlier had filed the suit in a Baltimore federal court that resulted in prayer being banned from American public schools.

To this day, I cannot recall much about the gist of that interview. What always stuck in my memory was Madalyn's foul mouth and her hairy armpits. She was wearing some sort of flip-flop sandals and one of those frowsy house dresses of a gauzy material that was almost semitransparent. It was transparent enough to make you look in another direction to avoid Madalyn's folds of flab.

That was in the late 1960s, and most of us were getting accustomed to the Austin-area snuff queens who were expressing their independence by refusing to shave their legs and armpits. A snuff queen of that day was described as a woman who would snuff up your cocaine, then run away without delivering any sex. Madalyn, however, was an extreme example of the female liberation movement. When she reached up to scratch her head, I was repulsed by a mass of armpit hair that reminded me of a black wasp nest, one of those big nasty masses of crawling insects that I used to see on the clay bluffs of the Main Llano River in Kimble County. I shied back as I would from a coiled rattlesnake.

The city room was a large area dotted with desks and open to other departments. My desk was in the wide open, and I recall Madalyn's presence drawing a small gathering of onlookers. I believe that sports editor Dan Cook was looking on as were company artist Bob Dale and a few others. None of us were shy about or sensitive to salty talk, and I was prone to use more cuss words than my mother would have sanctioned, but Madalyn Murray O'Hair delighted in the shock effect produced by her toilet mouth.

When I asked about her new husband, Richard O'Hair, who was not present for the interview, Madalyn rocked us back on our heels when she described Richard. "He's an ex-marine with a hot pair of balls and a prick that stays harder than a fireplace poker," Madalyn said with a leer. "My kind of man. Always ready for action." I believe that Dan Cook and I both blushed red. We were not prepared for anything like the world-famous atheist. She delighted in shocking and embarrassing the shrinking violets and square Johns of this world, and she knew how to do it.

I was never to see O'Hair after that meeting, but I followed her exploits in print, on radio, and on TV, and this included some of the thirty-eight television debates in thirty-eight cities she had with Reverend Bob Harrington, the flamboyant preacher from New Orleans who was then known all over the country as the "Chaplain of Bourbon Street." Never did I dream at the time that Harrington would work his way into San Antonio and the St. Mary's Street strip joint where we would meet for the first time or that we would forge a friendship that would last until Harrington's death on July 4, 2017, in Stigler, Oklahoma, where he had been living with daughter Mitzi. Bob died at age eighty-nine.

Harrington and O'Hair were polar opposites, but they formed an unlikely duo as they debated the existence of God on the *Phil Donahue Show*. Madalyn was as sharp as she was profane, and the big boisterous preacher was the showman's showman—two hundred pounds and then some with a curly mane of graying locks and sequined suits with Bourbon Street lamp poles on the coats. He was a handsome specimen with a glib tongue and an eye for the spectacular.

I recall one episode when O'Hair asked Harrington: "Do you mean to tell us that you actually believe all of the dead people are going to come up out of the ground on some kind of judgment day and walk around stinking up the whole country? We've already got a population explosion. What are we going to do with them all?"

Harrington had a comeback for anything O'Hair tossed at him. When she asked him why he believed in God, Harrington said, "I believe in God because I want to." Of O'Hair, he said, "Madalyn O'Hair knows the Bible. She has studied it page by page, and I will concede that she knows the scriptures better than I ever have or ever will. But there is one great difference—I know the author."

By the late 1960s, I was drinking nightly in downtown after-hours clubs, the Commander's Room on Main Avenue and the Navy Club on Pecan Street. Phil Sfair owned and operated the Navy Club, while his younger brothers, Mike and George, held forth in the Commander's Room. Both clubs managed to stay open after the legal closing deadlines, strictly because of the political connections enjoyed by the owners. Police officials and members of the judiciary who frequented both watering holes ranged from police lieutenants to federal judges. I was to become a close personal friend of Mike Sfair.

Another downtown club operator who seemed to enjoy a measure of immunity from the law was Guy Linton, who with wife, Evelyn, owned and operated the first real strip joint on the San Antonio scene. When she was younger, Evelyn taught the girls how to dance. This club was known all over the state as the Green Gate, a burlesque club or cabaret. The Green Gate dancers wore nothing but pasties and skimpy G-strings. That was tantamount to buck naked in 1968. A sizable number of us who drank regularly in the Sfair clubs paid occasional visits to the Green Gate, a fact that was known by the Lintons.

Never in a million years would I have dreamed of meeting a New Orleans preacher on the Green Gate stage, but that is where I met the Chaplain of Bourbon Street. The year was 1968. Guy and Evelyn Linton publicly announced that they were closing the Green Gate forever, and Bob delivered a hellfire-and-brimstone sermon that traumatized the lead dancer, a busty little blonde who danced under the pseudonym "Candy Cane." As Reverend Bob's voice thundered on the failings of the flesh, I will swear that poor little Candy was trying to cover her tits with a bar towel.

A small part of San Antonio history was made that night, and the entire show was set up from start to finish. I was writing a daily column for the *San Antonio Express* when Evelyn Linton called me to announce that she and Guy had found Jesus Christ through a New Orleans preacher by the name of Bob Harrington. They were turning their lives over to the Lord, and the official announcement would be made directly after a Bob Harrington sermon that would follow the final dance show at the Green Gate.

History verified that the Lintons were serious about their conversion to Christianity, but Guy and Evelyn were lifetime show people, and with the flashiest preacher on the planet, they wanted San Antonio and the world to know that they were officially going out of the skin and sin trade. The Lintons met Bob Harrington when he preached a revival sermon at the Castle Hills Baptist Church. Castle Hills is an independent municipality completely surrounded by the City of San Antonio. The Lintons said that Harrington led them to the Lord, and Evelyn said they all wanted me to write an article about their conversion to Christianity and their decision to shut down the Green Gate forever.

"We have served our last drink of alcohol at the Green Gate," Evelyn told me. I meant it when I told her that I would not cover Harrington's sermon without a beer. She and Guy really wanted the publicity. "Okay," she said with reluctance, "but your beer will be the last one we will ever serve at the Green Gate. And it will be free."

She was true to her word. I drank the last beer ever consumed at the Green Gate. It was a Lone Star. And let the record reflect that Guy and Evelyn Linton remained loyal Christians and faithful members of the Castle Hills Baptist Church until their deaths. When they closed the Green Gate, the Lintons left a sign on the door that read: "Closed Forever, See You In Church."

Unfortunately, my world-renowned minister friend had a major slip on life's slippery and temptation-fraught highway in later years, but he had found his way back to the Lord before his death in Oklahoma.

To my knowledge, Bob had no contact with Madalyn Murray O'Hair after their ballyhooed series of television debates. Madalyn, who founded American Atheists, was murdered in Austin along with one of her two sons, Jon Garth Murray, and granddaughter Robin Murray O'Hair, by ex-con David Waters, a former employee of American Atheists. After his arrest, conviction, and confession, Waters led authorities to the shallow grave in Real County where he had stacked the dismembered and partially burned bodies like cord wood. He told authorities he chopped up the bodies with an electric circular hand saw.

O'Hair's elder son, William J. Murray, disavowed his mother as evil and became a Baptist preacher.

Larry Flynt, founder and publisher of *Hustler Magazine*, was at one time a big contributor to American Atheists. And I can recall Bob Harrington once telling me that he was working to convert Flynt to Christianity: "I've got him just about ready to take the leap. He is almost ready to turn his life over to Jesus Christ. You will really have a big story to write when this happens." But that is all I could recall on the subject of Flynt. Harrington never mentioned him to me again.

In later years after I had left the *Express-News* and established *Action Magazine*, and after a World Championship Menudo Cookoff I promoted with Willie Nelson and some thirty other bands, I had Harrington preach at what we called Sam Kindrick's Outdoor Revival and Music Extravaganza. Bob and I had become friends after the Green Gate closing, and he jumped at my suggestion for the preaching and music show, which was held on the San Antonio River south of the city on private ranchland.

Gary P. Nunn and the Lost Gonzo Band headlined this one with stellar performances by Dub Robinson and the Drug Store Cowboys, including Randy Toman and Robert (Cotton) Payne. Jerry Jeff Walker was supposed to play with Nunn and the Lost Gonzos, but he failed to show. "I can recall that we had some electrical problems with the equipment," Robinson said. "But we wound up having a hell of a show. I will never forget the great time we had."

Harrington became a well-known evangelist during the 1960s and 1970s following his conversion to Christianity at age thirty in his hometown of Sweet Water, Alabama. He was a popular guest on national television shows, including *Phil Donahue, Merv Griffin*, and the *Tonight Show*, due to his one-liners and unconventional religious wit. Bob met Madalyn Murray O'Hair in the early 1970s. He also had a picture of himself with famed evangelist Billy Graham.

In 1960, after only a few years of preaching throughout the South on flatbed trailers and in tents, Harrington moved to New Orleans Baptist Theological Seminary (NOBTS) with his wife, Joyce, and daughters, Rhonda and Mitzi.

During his time in the seminary, Harrington served as assistant pastor of First Baptist Church of New Orleans with J. D. Grey and continued his ministry as an itinerant evangelist. In a chapel service, NOBTS president Leo Edleman said, "Wherever there is a pocket of sin, there is a mission field, and the nearest Christian to it is a missionary." According to Harrington, "The nearest pocket of sin was Bourbon Street."

Harrington immediately began a street ministry armed with a microphone and a Bible. Several months later deacons at First Baptist New Orleans loaned him enough money for a few months' rent to open a chapel on Bourbon Street in the heart of the French Quarter. Harrington began witnessing and preaching to whores, bums, and pimps in the bars and strip clubs of Bourbon Street. In 1962, New Orleans mayor Victor Schiro proclaimed him the "Chaplain of Bourbon Street."

Harrington's street ministry message was bold and simple. "God loves you just as you are. He knows you are a sinner and wants to save you. Don't figure it out. Faith it out!" Before long his unorthodox story reached Doubleday Publishing. *The Chaplain of Bourbon Street*, written by Harrington with Walter Wagner, was published in 1969. Harrington went on to publish seven more books and released more than thirty record albums. The sermon album *Laughter, Truth and Music* was released in 1965, and Harrington was presented with a gold album for more than one million dollars in sales worldwide. Later he received a second gold album for *Chaplain of Bourbon Street*, a recording of his first television show.

Prior to our outdoor revival and music extravaganza, Bob told me he was planning a new album titled *Bob Harrington Goes Country*. I never knew what happened to this project. I had heard that Harrington had gone back to his old wicked ways. I called him at his daughter's home in Oklahoma shortly before his death, and he told me the same thing he had told a writer for *SBC Life*, official publication for the Southern Baptist Convention. "The devil threw me a pass and I caught it and ran for defeat," Bob said. "All of my fame and glory caught up with me."

In the November 2000 issue of *SBC Life*, Harrington shared his past struggles in the article "Chastened Chaplain: A Forthright Account of Failure and Renewal." In the article, he referred to the "pass" that Satan threw him during the height of his success as "pride, arrogance, self-centeredness and stubbornness." His first marriage ended as well as his ministry on Bourbon Street in 1977. He married again and moved to Florida but later divorced. During the 1980s and 1990s, Harrington was a popular motivational speaker, primarily with car dealerships and real estate companies.

One evening in 1995 in his hotel room, he was robbed and nearly beaten to death. Harrington said that during that time "the phone rang and it was Rex Humbard [longtime pastor of the Cathedral of Tomorrow in Akron, Ohio, where Harrington had preached many times], my old friend. He said it was time for me to come back to the Lord and I did." After divorce and bankruptcy, Harrington recalled being at the bottom, which he said "is right where God can use you!" Harrington began a restoration period and moved back to New Orleans.

In 1998, Bob married Rebecca Harris Birdwell and moved to Mansfield, Texas, where he continued preaching. Rebecca died of a heart attack in 2010. That same year, Bob moved to be near his younger daughter, Mitzi Woodson, and her husband, Steve, in Stigler, Oklahoma. He faithfully attended the First Baptist Church in Stigler. When I called him at Mitzi's home, Harrington pretty much reiterated what he had told the Baptist press about his ignominious fall from grace: "Three things got me: fame, finance, and frolic. I was going strong with my little radio program there. Then after the mayor named me Chaplain of Bourbon Street, the governor of Louisiana named me Ambassador of Goodwill to America."

Bob said, "The 'kingdom of thingdom' started to replace the Kingdom of God."

His national TV debates with Madalyn Murray O'Hair started his climb to "thingdom."

The money started rolling in, Harrington said, and following the fame and finance came the frolic. "All those things—fame, finance, and frolic—led me to catch a pass that Satan threw at the peak of my success," Harrington said. "And that pass—I caught that sucker, and ran for defeat. When you break that pass down, P. A. S. S., it's pride, arrogance, self-centeredness, and stubbornness. That stole my first love away from me, and that's when I fell."

The frolic, Harrington said, finally finished him off. "After a while you get those Bathshebas, Delilahs, and Jezebels out there in the church world, not the Bourbon Street world. Those in the Bourbon Street world didn't bother me. I knew about this kind of temptation. It was those

Rev. Bob Harrington, the Chaplain of Bourbon Street, preaches at Sam Kindrick's Outdoor Revival and Music Extravaganza. Sam is in the background.

sweet little ol' church members that got to me. They start telling you how nice and neat and handsome you are, how big and strong you are. Your wife isn't telling you that anymore because she knows what you are turning into."

When I called him, Mitzi answered the phone. Bob must have mentioned my old drinking problem to her because she asked me about it. She yelled out at Bob: "It's Sam Kindrick from Texas, Daddy; he has quit drinking."

I heard Bob call out in the background: "Praise the Lord; it sure is fun being saved!"

Harrington had told his daughters exactly how he wanted his tombstone to read. They followed through after his death. The red granite grave marker in Sweet Water is more than impressive. It features a full-length likeness of Bob with Bible in hand and standing under a Bourbon Street lamp pole. It reads exactly as he directed:

> Robert Leonard Harrington
> Bob Harrington
> The Chaplain of Bourbon Street
> Born: September 2, 1927
> Died: He Didn't
> Transferred to Heaven: July 4, 2017

DANGEROUSLY ANTISOCIAL

A typical day at the *Express-News* when my drinking was really starting to kick in began with me arriving at the Melody Room Lounge on Third Street, just across from the paper, around noon. I recall drinking two or maybe three beers just to quiet my nerves. My hands were shaking slightly then, my guts were shaking inside, sweat was beading and dripping from both hands and feet, and I found it all but impossible to type on my old manual Royal typewriter without the calming beers.

After settling slightly, I managed to write what I needed to write before leaving the newspaper for more drinking at downtown clubs that included the Flamingo Lounge, Black Fox, San Jacinto Club, Burnt Orange Club, and Southwest Conference Club. Sometimes I took a break to eat; sometimes I just drank. I usually stuck with beer until I couldn't hold anymore. Then it was to Jack Daniels bourbon and water and later just Jack Black on the rocks. Sometimes I drank vodka, but never scotch if there was anything else available.

My excuse for all but living in these bars was that I needed this environment to meet the colorful characters who paraded through my written copy. When the clubs closed at the legal alcohol deadline of 2:00 a.m., I headed straight for San Antonio's infamous after-hours joints— Al Paesano's Holiday Club, Phil Sfair's Navy Club, and Mike and George Sfair's Commander's Room on downtown Main Avenue where I did most of my heavy drinking damage. Before the club became the Commander's Room, it was the Dragon Lady and then the Rickshaw, operated by Johnny Jowdy and his wife, Bea. These clubs operated after hours under what we were always told was a federal charter arranged by District Judge Solomon Casseb. These were ostensibly "private clubs" where dues-paying members kept liquor in private lockers and paid for drinks mixed by the club bartenders. To some extent this started as the protocol, but all of the clubs wound up being open bars serving every mixed drink imaginable.

We all learned years later when the after-hours clubs were all closed down that the "federal charter" was nonexistent. It was not uncommon for me to stagger out of the Commander's Room with the rising sun in my face. Mike Sfair was an enormously popular figure among policemen, attorneys, judges, and politicians. Large, dark, and handsome, Sfair was a member of San Antonio's sizable Lebanese American community who had aspired to be a policeman. When he graduated at the very top of his San Antonio Police Academy class, Mike and brother George were already attracting swarms of policemen and others to the club.

Then the inevitable hammer of municipal authority fell on Mike. The city manager got involved, and the San Antonio Police Department's top brass ruled that Sfair could not serve as a policeman while operating a nightclub. He was forced to make the decision, the cop shop or the Commander's Room. Sfair chose the more lucrative nightclub operation, and his Commander's Room was almost immediately filled with policemen and other public figures who sympathized with him, as well as a number of media people who included those involved in television and radio and reporters and editors from both the *San Antonio Express-News* and the *San Antonio Light*.

Mike Sfair knew how to take care of us. Some of the patrons kept bottles in lockers behind the bar, but for the most part it was an open bar that served reduced-price drinks to most of the patrons, with some police brass, judges, and newspaper figures like me drinking free. We were the people who could hurt an illegal after-hours drinking emporium, and operators like Mike and George Sfair knew it.

When I hit the Commander's Room, it was usually after all other drinking joints were legally closed, and I would be half drunk when I entered the door. I wasn't making much more than $150 a week with the

Sam in fur coat and goggles: persona unleashed. It was a beaver coat that Bobby Thomas, "Kid Death," had come up with. I traded him a bunch of meth for it.

newspaper in those days, hardly enough to sustain after-hours drinking of any kind of name-brand liquor, so the Jack Daniels bourbon was not mentioned when I ordered free whiskey from bartenders Wooten and Shaw. Some of us low-income newspaper reporters referred to the cheap-grade bourbon as "Old Tennis Shoe," but we swigged it down nevertheless, me until I was blind drunk and lurching as I left the drinkery.

Charges of driving while intoxicated were rare in San Antonio in the 1960s and 1970s, and if you knew the right individuals, they were almost nonexistent. No policeman would bust a drunk leaving one of the after-hours clubs if he could possibly avoid it. I was stopped many times by policemen who let me go when they realized I was a newspaper reporter. On a few occasions, the patrolman would follow me home to ensure that I arrived in one piece, and when my Ford hit another vehicle at slow speed at four o'clock in the morning as I pulled away from a curb next to the Commander's Room, the investigating patrolman called a wrecker before driving me home in his squad car. No charges of any kind were filed.

After leaving the Commander's Room on some mornings, and headed for my home on Harriett Street between San Pedro and McCullough Avenues, it was not uncommon for me to pull into the Blue Room on San Pedro for one final drink. The Blue Room was the jittery alcoholic's morning oasis, a dump owned by Wynn Little, who opened promptly at 7:00 a.m.

I will never forget those sad Blue Room mornings, which were marked by tendrils of cigarette smoke curling slowly from butts smoldering all over the sidewalk. The men and women suffering alcohol withdrawal were sitting in their cars, smoking furiously, and waiting for the Blue Room doors to open for the medicine that would be available in the bar. They called this medicine Seagram's, Johnny Walker Red, Smirnoff, and Jack Black. The slaves to this juice were the losers I surrounded myself with. I was trying hard to become one of them and had no idea why.

When I reached home on these awful mornings, I had a gallon jug of water I kept under the bed. The alcohol consumption had dehydrated me, and I would swig copious amounts of the water. My skin was scaly and my face was puffed. I weighed 160 pounds, but my face suggested a 200-pounder. The bloated image on the cover of my first book tells the tale. I remember the look. It said my guts are on fire and I know there is nothing I can do about it. What the hell is wrong? The best-recognized recovery guide of the alcoholic calls the condition "powerlessness." I'm sure that I could smell the fire and brimstone. I was that close. But not close enough to alter my drunken regimen. I was living my lie by then. I will quit drinking, by God, when I am ready.

By this point, my marriage was a sham. My poor wife had no idea what to do, and my kids were at loose ends. Alcohol drove the wagon for those 1960s and early 1970s. Somehow I functioned. Barely at times. When my alcohol level reached a certain point, my personality proceeded to deteriorate. Nobody wanted near me. Mike Sfair finally barred me from the Commander's Room when I hit a state representative by the name of Stanford Smith in the mouth. It was an ugly scene, rolling on the floor through the blood, puke, and broken cocktail glass. I had a toilet mouth in those days. If I didn't like your wife, it would not have been uncommon for me to call her a douche bag or worse, unmindful of the repercussions that were sure to follow. It would get much worse before it would ever get better.

My drinking was in full bloom during my last years with the *Express-News*. This was during the mid-1970s when I was nearing my alcoholic rock bottom. After I started writing a daily column with hours of my own choosing, I continued to arrive around the same time at the *Express-News* building at San Antonio's Avenue E and Third Street.

For medicinal reasons known by every chronic alcoholic, I swung into the Melody Room Lounge for my customary two and sometimes three bottles of beer to quell my morning jitters. Josie, the day bartender, had the cap popped on the first one before I got settled on the bar stool. She understood my needs, and the second beer was open and sitting on the bar as I finished the first.

I chugged these beers fast before heading for the third-floor city room to pick up a reporting assignment or to start writing either news articles or my general-interest column. Sometimes I failed to keep the first beers down. There would come the usual dry heaves, which I would stop with another beer. In those days, I worked on a manual Royal typewriter with an inked ribbon, a vital instrument that transferred my thoughts to copy paper when my hands didn't shake uncontrollably. That is where the beer came into play. Without the sudden infusion of alcohol, the shakes made it impossible for me to type readable copy.

A real alcoholic knows this debilitating condition. Trembling hands are a visible part of the shakes known by every true alcoholic, but the internal shakes are far worse. The nervous system seems to short out; armpits drip sweat. It's too early in the day to start on the hard liquor, and no real practicing alcoholic will recognize the horror for what it is. Denial is not a river in Egypt, and those screaming internal shakes are real. I always called them the gut jerks. The only way to make them subside is to add more alcohol.

I never drank on the newspaper property, although I grabbed an occasional beer while on a reporting assignment. The heavy daytime drinking started when I began writing the daily column. The title of the column was "Offbeat," and many of the characters I wrote about were regular denizens of San Antonio's nightclub scene. The newspaper editors didn't question my whereabouts as long as I turned in the column by a late-evening deadline. While working on the column, I was working my way toward the hard booze that I usually started a few hours after sundown. Before I could eat something and get on to bourbon, vodka, or gin, the dry heaves were a part of my day. I did eat on a regular basis, and a doctor told me this was the reason I never developed liver cirrhosis. When I started spitting up blood, I went to a doctor for treatment of what I thought were bleeding ulcers, but there was no internal bleeding. I had dry heaved so hard that blood vessels in my neck were ruptured and leaking profusely.

Mike Sfair and I became close friends during my earlier drinking days. We often met at his house on weekends to watch the Dallas Cowboys on TV, and in 1968 we took our young daughters to HemisFair. The night our relationship ended was a traumatic experience for me. Mike had a hint of a tear in his eye and a catch in his voice when he told me good-bye. "This really hurts me, Sam, but you can't be in this club anymore. Your language was bad enough, but now this violent behavior is too much. I'm sorry, but you have to go."

Ugly scenes like the Smith imbroglio became alarmingly frequent. My personality deteriorated after only a few drinks. Was I losing my mind? Did the poor innocent square John sitting down the bar from me ever expect my venomous approach: "Do I owe you money or something?"

"Why, no, sir. I don't believe I have ever met you."

"If I don't owe you money, motherfucker, then why in hell are you staring at me?"

Only a deranged and angry loser would push a total stranger in such fashion. I had two resentments: I hated me and I hated you. In later years I was to learn more about such troubling outbursts that seemed to dog my trail with alarming regularity. I found myself on page 21 of a world-renowned hardbound book about alcoholism. Regarding "the real alcoholic," the book is explicit:

> But what about the real alcoholic? He may start off as a moderate drinker; he may or may not become a continuous hard drinker; but at some stage of his drinking career, he begins to lose all control of his liquor consumption, once he starts to drink. Here is the fellow who has been puzzling you, especially in his lack of control. He does absurd, incredible, tragic things while drinking. He is a real Dr. Jekyll and Mr. Hyde. He is seldom mildly intoxicated. He is always more or less insanely drunk. His disposition while drinking resembles his normal nature but little. He may be one of the finest fellows in the world. Yet let him drink for a day, and he frequently becomes dangerously anti-social.

When living alone in my tarpaper Bulverde shack, I was threatened in a telephone call by a redneck racist neighbor who objected to a black male friend who visited me on occasion. I should have reported him to the sheriff's department. Instead, I loaded my shotgun and blew the television antenna off his house while he and his wife were having dinner.

Yes, I had to concede to my innermost self, I came under the heading of dangerously antisocial. It was hard for many to comprehend, but I maintained rough and varied versions of this alcoholic insanity routine until after I had parted company with the *San Antonio Express-News*.

12

THE WORLD'S FAIR

My involvement with San Antonio's world fair—HemisFair '68—actually started in 1967 when a group of businesspeople sent me to Montreal for the purpose of selling San Antonio and our upcoming fair to a film company from the Czech Republic. Expo 67, the world's fair in Montreal, had just ended.

This venture was almost as crazy as it sounds, and the outcome is still beyond my comprehension. There were others from San Antonio involved, but I saw only the Czech film executive who represented the two productions—film shows titled *Laterna Magika* (The magic lantern) and *Keno Automat*. No communist countries were invited to participate in HemisFair, but these film productions were independently owned and produced by citizens of the Czech Republic.

I was still with the *San Antonio Express-News* at the time. It was late September 1967, and I was wearing a paper-thin sports coat when I climbed off an Air Canada plane that brought me to Montreal from New York City. It was snowing lightly and I was shivering. I thought I might freeze to death.

My involvement was not financed by the newspaper but by a San Antonio business amalgamation headed by R. Jay Cassell, who was a mover and shaker on the San Antonio business scene at that time. Imagine the hick from Junction checking into Montreal's Chateau Champlain Hotel, billed then as elite and among the most expensive hotels in the world. The Chateau Champlain builder had sworn to construct a hotel that would make Conrad Hilton structures look like chicken coops by comparison. This giant of chrome, glass, and steel then towered forty stories above the St. Lawrence River and the city of Montreal, Quebec, and night lights shimmering over the water were breathtaking.

I did not recall the Czech Republic guy's name, but I do know that he liked me. It was his idea, but I didn't resist when he took me to a wild joint with half-naked women and two bands blaring at the same time. I told him stories of Texas cowboys, menudo, whores, and chicken fights, the specific narratives including fuckers, fighters, wild horse riders, and windmill hands like the indomitable Hunger brothers of Junction and Kimble County, and we drank Canadian Club Whisky until both of us were just short of knee-walking slobbering drunk. "Ah, yas," I recall him saying. "Big fun in Texas, yah?"

My friend finally loaded me into a cab, and we were headed back to the Chateau Champlain Hotel as the sun rose over the beautiful St. Lawrence River. My Czech friend signed a contract the next day to bring both of his productions to San Antonio. *Keno Automat* and *Laterna Magika* were two of the greatest and most successful attractions at HemisFair '68.

On weekends, I had a sideline job in the HemisFair Press Center, a building that also housed an office for Governor John Connally and the Arkansas Pavilion, the only exhibit not representing a country. Highlights of the Arkansas Pavilion were two spectacular female spawns of the Ozarks named Glenda Brown and Sherry Worsham. One look at these two, and you knew precisely why they were chosen to represent Arkansas. And right across the fair walkway was the House of Sir John Falstaff, the largest and busiest saloon on the fairgrounds and my second home until HemisFair '68 was over.

On occasion, my HemisFair job called for me to chauffeur dignitaries and various VIPs around the grounds in a golf cart. I soon learned this was not my calling when I met Canadian actor Lorne Greene, who played Ben Cartwright in the TV series *Bonanza*. Greene was unimpressed when I told him I knew Dan Blocker, the undisputed star of the series whom I had met when I attended Sul Ross State University. I'm sure he must have been jealous of his TV son Hoss. He looked at me as if viewing an insect. "Sure, sure," I recall Greene saying. "Everyone in Texas knows Dan Blocker."

Dallas Cowboys quarterback Don Meredith was my favorite HemisFair passenger. Dandy Don was a hoot, and I have never forgotten that day I spent with him. "Look at my arm," he said, putting his forearm alongside mine. "Not much bigger than yours, right. That's why I have got to get out of pro football. I need to get out before someone kills me."

Those were the hard early years when the Cowboys lacked adequate frontline protection for the quarterback. Meredith was being pounded without mercy on almost every football Sunday. Don was six foot three, and his forearm was a damn sight bigger than mine, but he was making his point. "You can plainly see that I don't have any business playing out there and being assaulted by animals like Dick Butkus and Alex Karras." Meredith was always the showman. He described his lowest point in pro football with a grin: "You are five touchdowns behind in the fourth quarter in the Cotton Bowl, it's raining and freezing cold, and the Cowboys fans are throwing cabbages. It don't get any worse than that."

Of all the celebrities I was to meet during HemisFair, iconic western actor Chill Wills was the one who seemed always to be around the most. Wills and San Antonio restaurant owner and part-time actor John Hamilton had both worked in John Wayne movies, the most noteworthy being the epic 1960 film *The Alamo*. Hamilton owned Big John's Steak House just off Austin Highway in San Antonio, a popular eatery and watering hole frequented by actors, sports figures, politicians, gamblers, musicians, a few police characters, and a scattering of media people. Wills stayed with Hamilton throughout almost all of HemisFair, and I drank with him on many weekend evenings at the Falstaff saloon.

I recall a telephone call I got from John Hamilton at about five o'clock one morning. He and Chill had been drinking all night, and I could hear Chill's gravel voice in the background. "Is that Sam?"

"Yes," John replied. And then said to me: "Chill wants permission to use that saying of yours, the one where you described some politician as having a face that resembled hammered shit."

I told Hamilton I had no patent on the expression. Then Chill Wills took the phone: "I know that saying must be an original, and I would sure like to use it with your permission. I am thinking of a Hollywood jerk right now that has a face that looks like hammered shit." I told Wills to be my guest and that made him happy. Hamilton said Wills then passed out with a smile on his face.

During HemisFair '68 and in months and years to follow, I was beginning to realize that my alcohol consumption was escalating. I told myself that I could handle it, but I never did. At the morning *San Antonio Express* I was on the evening shift, starting my day at 1:00 p.m. The *Evening News* guys started in the early mornings. By the early 1970s I had worked my way into a daily column called "Offbeat," and the *San Antonio Express-News* eventually published a paperback book for me titled *The Best of Sam Kindrick: Secret Life and Hard Times of a Cedar Chopper.*

My subjects for "Offbeat" were just that, offbeat characters, many of whom also became friends. They included bookmakers Jack Hanratty and Tony Salinas, Madam Theresa Brown, and notorious shotgun-packing pimp and drug dealer Arthur Harry (Bunny) Eckert.

Hanratty, who was on the San Quentin prison fire department with Vegas casino operator Benny Binion, later sent me to Vegas to cover Binion's first World Championship Poker Tournament. I sat with Jack as he was dying from brain cancer, and I was a pallbearer at Jack's funeral. The "old alligator," as many of us called him, inadvertently named this book. "You are the outlaw journalist," Jack said. And he crowned me with that appellation several years before my drug busts, jail time, and some of the darkest days of my life. Jack seemed to know. I was the outlaw journalist even before I was to really live up to the title.

My introduction to country music started when I was a kid in Junction. We had country music dances during quarter horse race meets every summer, and one of the most popular bands to play these events was the Texas Top Hands out of San Antonio. Ray Sczepanik was a kid member of that group in 1953, and he was still leading the band at this writing.

Hank Williams was the first musician to impact my life. He died in 1953, my senior year at Junction High School. I never got to meet him, but I did see him once at Cherry Springs Dance Hall, the historic tavern sixteen miles north of Fredericksburg. I wasn't old enough to get in, but I could see and hear Hank through an open window. I heard "Cheating Heart" and "Kawliga." I was a Hank fan for life. When Hank Williams died, people in Junction and Kimble County pulled to the sides of the road and turned on their car and truck lights. It was a phenomenon I couldn't understand but one I could appreciate.

Years later, I watched women on Chicago's Navy Pier climbing wire netting like monkeys, all trying to get at the new Texas superstar known as Willie Nelson. I know; I was there in the gigantic entertainment complex. Willie and band were getting set to mount the stage. Looking up at the females clinging to the wire, we just stood there for a few seconds. "Did you ever dream it would come to this?" I asked Willie.

"Shit, no," said the Redheaded Stranger.

Paul English was on his drum kit, and the downbeat rolled out over Lake Michigan. "Whiskey river take my mind, whiskey river don't run dry." Imagine two thousand female monkeys, all screaming and screeching together. It was a phenomenon I couldn't understand, but I have always been able to appreciate it.

This little redheaded guy who sounded off-key but wasn't off-key had the rare ability to paint a picture with words. I sensed the greatness before I was able to articulate it. It was in the mid-1960s, a time when my alcoholism was becoming more than obvious. Johnny Bush was big then with his Bandoleros Band, and I was enjoying some ill-fated success as a columnist with the *San Antonio Express-News*.

Larry Trader introduced me to Willie. Trader was a local character and golf hustler with an engaging personality who had an uncanny ability to ingratiate himself with some country musicians. I knew that Trader had booked Ray Price for some shows in the San Antonio area. I also knew that Nelson and Johnny Bush had both worked for Price before forming their own bands. Bush was Price's drummer. Nelson was the lead guitar, and he may have played some bass guitar. The regular bass player with Price's Cherokee Cowboys was Darrell McCall.

Willie was smoking a joint when we met. He offered me a hit, and I took a drag just to be sociable. Alcohol was my drug of choice at the time. I had little interest in marijuana. The hard drugs would come later. A hectic, crazy, and life-changing phase was about to begin: the country music years with some of the greatest country musicians who ever lived.

When Johnny Bush lost his soaring tenor voice to something called spasmodic dysphonia, I was there to ask what would he do? Bush had tears in his eyes as he croaked with his broken voice: "Sing. I have got to sing." I was there to celebrate and write about his amazing recovery, thanks to Dr. Blake Simpson, who brought Bush's voice back with Botox injections to his vocal cords. Johnny was packing country dance venues right up to his death.

Hank Thompson *(left)*, **Sam** *(center)*, **and Johnny Bush. I was pals with many of country music's greats, and Johnny Bush was among my closest friends.**

Among this cadre of close musician friends are Darrell McCall and his wife, Mona, a French-Canadian beauty and songbird who put her own music career on hold to birth and raise daughter, Guyanne, and son, Cody. Mona and Darrell have since started working together. Darrell's powerful voice with the naturally built-in vibrato is legendary in Texas. When the McCalls lived in San Antonio for a brief stretch, I hung out at their house, and we have remained close friends since. Of McCall, Bush, and Nelson, Ray Price was often heard to say that his entire band left him to become individual stars on their own.

Kinky Friedman and his Texas Jew Boys Band never fit the country music mold, but Kinky never fit any mold. He is musician, comedian, songwriter, unsuccessful gubernatorial candidate, author of detective novels, and a supreme spoof artist who gets serious only when it comes to homeless animals. The Kinkster and I hit it off from the get-go, and I was to even sing with the band at Sam Ballow's Bits and Pieces Club on such select numbers as "They Ain't Making Jews like Jesus Anymore" and "Asshole from El Paso."

A close friend of both Bob Dylan and Willie Nelson, Kinky has long been king of the one-liner: "Computers are tools of the devil," and "You can lead a politician to water but you can't make him think." Proceeds from the first *Action Magazine* anniversary show at Texas Pride Barbecue went to the Utopia Animal Rescue Ranch Friedman founded. When he dies and arrives in heaven, Kinky believes he will be greeted by every dog and cat he has ever owned.

Just a few of the other musicians I have bonded with include Gary Stewart, Alex Harvey, Sylvia Leal Kirk, Ruben V, and Jimmy Spacek. Sylvia possesses the finest set of female pipes that ever sang lyrics from a San Antonio stage. I have always said that nobody sings like Sylvia. Florida-based recording artist Gary Stewart and I became friends when Russell and Randy Toman were backing him up. We were all floored when Gary ended his own life.

Two of the hottest guitars in Texas belong to San Antonio pickers Ruben V and Jimmy Spacek. Jimmy's blues have long been considered a staple of San Antonio's South Side, while Ruben brought his galloping guitar to San Antonio from the Rio Grande Valley. The two are friends who often perform together. I met songwriter great Alex Harvey in the early 1970s shortly after he wrote such monster hits as "Ruben James" and "Delta Dawn." We rekindled our friendship when Harvey and his wife returned to play *Action Magazine*'s forty-first anniversary show at Texas Pride Barbecue.

Claude (Butch) Morgan was forming his Buckboard Boogie Boys group shortly after Hank Williams Jr. almost lost his life in a Montana hunting fall. Three of Hank's band members found their way to San Antonio, where they joined up with Morgan: fiddler Ron Knuth, bassist Larry Patton, and drummer Larry Roberson. All of them became my good friends.

Almost all of these musicians, including Augie Meyers, played on our three anniversary shows. The Augie Meyers chapter can be found later in this book. There have been scores of musician friends who have crossed trails with me over the years: too many to recount, yet most of whom impacted my life in one way or another. I am grateful to them all.

When I was a cub reporter with the *San Angelo Standard-Times* in West Texas, I learned a basic truth about people that set the tone for my life as a professional writer. Not all readers demand a conventional winner, and the Norman Rockwell myth has never applied to the vast majority of us.

Tom Steph was the San Angelo city editor who launched me into a world of characters who have included the hustlers and the hustled. Steph came to the San Angelo newspaper from the *Daily Oklahoman* in Oklahoma City, and I never forgot what he taught me. "Be different," Steph said. "Write your articles about the losers and the off-color characters of this world. Steinbeck did it; Erskine Caldwell did it. People get sick of hearing about the winners. There is a little loser in all of us, and we can all identify. So many of us are a little odd, a little off-whack, a little removed from the beaten path."

A year after that, I had transferred to the *San Antonio Express-News*, where I started as a general assignment reporter. My first opportunity to put Tom Steph's visionary advice into newspaper print was soon to happen. The San Antonio Livestock Show and Rodeo was in full swing, and the city editor had suggested that I try to interview world all-around champion cowboy Jim Shoulders for a feature article. Before heading for the rodeo grounds, I stopped off at the Melody Room Lounge, a drinking dump on Third Street directly across from the newspaper building. There were a couple of cheap hotels in the immediate area, and this is where I met Robert (Coyote) Perry, a little-known Choctaw rodeo performer and stock pen manure scooper who followed the rodeo tour, entering both bull riding and saddle bronc riding events.

We were shooting nine-ball pool when a cowboy friend of Perry's introduced him.

"This is Coyote Perry," said the cowboy. "He is the losingest cowboy on the rodeo circuit. Some call him Wolf Perry, but to most of us he is Coyote Perry. He gets his name from the coyote yips and howls that come out of his mouth every time he is thrown by a bronc or a bull. When Coyote Perry hits the arena turf, they can hear his howling all the way to Tulsa."

Jim Shoulders was forgotten. Coyote Perry had captured my imagination. Coyote Perry was built like a sawed-off telephone pole, a swarthy competitor who did his best. I soon learned that Perry's rodeo winnings were from scant to nonexistent, and he earned most of the money used to get him from rodeo to rodeo by shoveling manure out of the arenas and stock barns. Sometimes he slept in the barns, sometimes in cheap hotels like the one near the *Express-News*.

When asked about his situation, Perry said, "Heck, who says I'm the losingest? I won eighth place in bull riding at Cheyenne one time, and I placed fifth in saddle bronc at Pendleton. I guess it was a year or so back." I asked Perry why he fought it with the professional rodeo circuit. "I rodeo because I have a bad back," he said without blinking. "I think I have one of them slipped disc doohickeys or something like that. Rodeoing beats hell out of riding a Farmall tractor on the reservation from daylight till dark. It was killing my back."

I asked Perry if being thrown and maybe stomped on by a Brahman bull wouldn't be equally or more painful than the tractor. He had a simple answer: "Being thrown and stomped on only hurts for a little while. Riding that tractor hurt from daylight till dark." I left him in the Melody Room to return to the newspaper city room where I wrote about Coyote Perry, the losingest cowboy on the professional rodeo tour. The wire services picked up on the article, and, within hours, Coyote Perry was featured in newspapers all over the United States, as well as the front cover of the *London Times*.

Tom Steph was right. The losers have a place, too. And many of the off-plumb winners might look like losers through the lens of proper society. I had found my way with that segment of humanity that has produced many of my friends and subjects of my writing. People are continually asking me about the rapport I have enjoyed with many of the subjects. I guess it came naturally for me, and I answer most questions as candidly as possible. How in the hell did I talk world-renowned pool hustler Minnesota Fats into wearing a Santa Claus suit for a picture shoot? Simple. I asked him and he jumped into the suit.

My entire life as a writer has included subjects Hank Williams might have described as fractured stars from "the world's mighty gallery of pictures": some famous and some infamous, the characters who have made my world go around.

San Antonio's El Tropicano Hotel was a favorite meeting spot and interview site for me when I was working at the daily newspaper. It was only a few blocks from the *Express-News* building and just across the street from the old Municipal Auditorium where many big-name country music acts were performing. I met Dolly Parton in the El Tropicano coffee shop. She was with Willie Nelson. The three of us ordered something to eat, and I couldn't remember much of anything that was said except for one crack Dolly made when she caught me staring at her chest. "I know what you are thinking," Dolly said to me. "You are wondering if my boobs are real."

The blood rushed to my face as Dolly burst into laughter.

"They are all mine," she cackled. "Nobody else would have them."

The El Tropicano was where country music great Johnny Rodriguez and I first met. To this very day, Rodriguez blames me for hanging the "goat rustler" tag on him, an appellation that will probably follow him to the grave. "I remember," Rodriguez said. "I had just got out of jail. Me and you and Happy and Joaquin all met at the El Tropicano Hotel in San Antonio. You wrote a story for the paper about the goat rustler from Sabinal, and that did it. I became known as a goat rustler all over the world."

Many older country music fans can recall the improbable rise of Johnny Rodriguez, and I will admit that calling him a goat rustler was a stretch. Rodriguez and some other beered-up youngsters had grabbed what they assumed to be someone's goat that had strayed. They were preparing to kill and barbecue the goat, which turned out to be a livestock show champion, when the law arrived.

Johnny went to the Uvalde County Jail, and he was sitting in his cell with a guitar and singing country tunes he had written when Texas Ranger Joaquin Jackson heard him. Joaquin's wife, Shirley, was a country music recording artist. The ranger recognized the raw talent, and he was soon to introduce Johnny to Brackettville promoter Happy Shahan. My Johnny Rodriguez interview may have originated in the newspaper city room. I'm not sure. I do know it occurred in the El Tropicano coffee shop. The idea behind it all was to introduce the next country music star to South Texas. Jackson and Shahan did all the talking. I don't think Johnny said a word.

In later years, I was hauling Rodriguez to substance abuse recovery meetings while Alan Brown was successfully defending him on a murder charge. Another long story. Attorney Alan Brown once said of my friendship with Johnny Rodriguez and Bobby Thomas: "You are Bobby's friend, and being a friend to Bobby Thomas is not easy. The same goes for Johnny, but you remain his friend."

I realize that I would never have fit well in polite society, so I chose that other fork in the road that included booze, drugs, hustlers, felony charges and jail, pitfalls and pratfalls, and some of the most interesting and talented people this world has ever known. Alex Harvey wrote hits like "Delta Dawn" and "Ruben James," and he offered me this bit of encouragement as I entered my mid-eighties and started on this book. "It ain't the number of years you have that is important; it's still all about how high you can jump."

In the early 1970s I was drinking hard but enjoying some measure of success. The *Express-News* had published my first book, basically a compilation of short articles and columns I had written for the newspaper. The paper paid for twenty thousand copies of the book, and the deal called for the paper recouping all printing expenses before I was to share in the profits.

Sales of the book were going at a brisk clip, one of the big reasons being television promotions by US Representative Henry B. Gonzalez. Henry liked me. His 20th Congressional District covered a large area of San Antonio and Bexar County, and I know that some of those books sold simply because Democrat Henry strongly suggested that people should buy it. During this era both the *Express-News* and KENS 5 TV were owned by Harte-Hanks, so I had unlimited newspaper and television exposure for the book. I didn't realize much money from book sales, but more on that later.

My early friendship with Willie Nelson was starting to grow. Nelson was playing John T. Floore Country Store in Helotes on a regular basis, and my understanding at the time was that Willie needed these regular gigs to pay off his gambling debts. I do know that Nelson liked to play poker for money, and he also loved to play golf. It was the game of golf that first tied Willie to San Antonio golf hustler and caddy Larry Trader.

Larry Trader had carried the golf bags for pro golfer Tommy (Thunder) Bolt, and he was a friend of Lee Trevino, the El Paso hustler who became the greatest Hispanic golfer of all time. Larry's brother Bobby Trader was another scratch golfer who had played on the University of Houston golf team. At that time, Nelson was letting Larry handle some of his bookings at John T. Floore Country Store. Old man John T. had taken a liking to me, and I had the run of Floore's when Willie was playing the big outdoor patio during spring and summer months.

I first played golf with Nelson and Larry Trader when Willie was hanging out at an abandoned country club in Bandera. He had an eye to buy the Bandera club but scrapped that idea and moved to Austin when the redneck culture around Bandera started rubbing his fur the wrong way. Nelson and I were inconsistent duffers during those early golf outings, shooting in the nineties on many days. "The safest place to be on the course with Willie and Sam is directly in front of them," Larry Trader was fond of saying. "They will drive a golf ball in every direction, but seldom straight down the fairway. Flying buzzards and ground squirrels are in constant danger." In subsequent years, Nelson got much better at the game. I gave it up in disgust when it became obvious that I would never be the next Arnold Palmer.

When I started giving Nelson ink in my *Express-News* column, he seemed grateful. This was long before the world found out about the amazing talent from Abbott, Texas. I recall asking Willie if there were other newspaper writers around the country who recognized his talent and were writing about him. "There are," he said. "They are in pockets around the country. Like you, these guys are willing to go out on a limb for me."

This was a time when Nelson had become disillusioned and disgruntled with the country music recording industry based in Nashville. This was also a time when marijuana possession was still a felony, and Willie was making little attempt to hide his almost open use of the evil weed. "I have decided to record my music in Texas," Willie told me. "I guess people wanting to buy the records will just have to come to Texas to get them."

Those were heady years for us all. Nelson's Saturday-night gigs in Helotes ended at midnight, giving us plenty of time for impromptu visits to San Antonio live-music venues that stayed open until 2:00 a.m. On many of those nights I would pile into Willie's Mercedes with him, Larry Trader, road hand Billy Cooper, and some member of his crew who drove. Two clubs we always hit were the eclectic Bijou and Scotty Young's Scotchman's Club, both on San Pedro Avenue. Sam Noin and Romy Vela owned and operated the Bijou. And after these came the Longneck Club off Blanco Road where Augie Meyers and other top local talent were showcased. Ronnie Branham was the Longneck operator.

The Bijou was one of those rare and ratty little joints that appealed to musicians. It was a musician's bar with a soul of its own. I recall one night with Willie when we entered the Bijou to find Blind George McClain pounding the piano. Blind George was out of Austin. He had only about 10 percent of his eyesight. His aggressive piano style was combined with his loud foot stomping on plywood stage flooring as he rocked the house. When we entered the Bijou that night, Willie quietly slid in next to George at the piano. He whispered something to Blind George and McClain lit up like a brush fire. He instantly knew who was with him on the piano bench. The duet that followed was epic—Blind George and Nelson ripping the house down with Willie's "Bloody Mary Morning."

On another note, I have always wished I had a video clip of Blind George and his equally blind brother-in-law fist-fighting one night out behind the Bijou. They finally punched themselves out, and I don't think either of them landed a single solid blow.

When we visited the Scotchman's Club, Victor Lopez and Los Keys were the house band, a hot group including Jimmy Casas and Bobby Rey. "I look back now and can hardly believe it," Lopez told me shortly before his death in 2017. "When you all came into the club, I would invite Willie up to sing a number. He usually just sang one song or maybe two and got down, always polite and the gentleman. I would thank him and get back to playing. What a dunce I was. Here was one of the greatest songwriters of all time, and I was letting him off my stage with a mere 'thank you.' I should have encouraged him to play all night."

Sam *(far left)* **hanging with Willie Nelson and friends.**

Nelson truly enjoyed club hopping in those earlier times, and so did I. Late one night we stopped at my house to pick up some money and Willie stepped on a dog bone. In those days, we were still feeding the dogs bones and table scraps. The bone went through Willie's tennis shoe. There was blood everywhere. His howl of pain awakened my wife, Vicky, who walked in to find Nelson holding his injured foot and hopping across the living room on the other one. I recall my then wife telling one of her girlfriends: "Yes, I woke up to this horrible noise and could hardly believe my eyes when I walked into my living room to find Willie Nelson hopping on one foot and holding the other one."

Nelson and I were pretty tight in 1973 when I hatched a plan for a world championship menudo cookoff. I had attended the much-ballyhooed first international chili cookoff at the Big Bend ghost town of Terlingua, which featured chili cooks H. Allen Smith and Wick Fowler. By then I was hobnobbing with Luckenbach imagineer Hondo Crouch and future movie star Guich Koock, and I had an idea that we could pump up a pretty good crowd with the right kind of promotion.

Menudo is the Mexican and South Texas soup made from tripe, hominy, chopped onion, serranos, and various spices. Tripe is the rubbery and powerfully pungent lining of a beef stomach. The legends of Mexico have always touted menudo as a hangover cure. I borrowed the name for our cookoff product from a Wheaties cereal box. Our cookoff would feature the true "Breakfast of Champions." It might not be a medically proven hangover cure, I conceded, but a lot of drunks ate menudo and flour tortillas after a hard night on the alcohol sauce. "The Breakfast of Champions" cookoff captured the heart and imagination of San Antonio and South Texas. I started pumping it in my newspaper column, and the results were amazing. Entrants for the cookoff numbered almost a hundred, some of them cooking teams who came from distant towns like Corpus Christi, Brownsville, Harlingen, and Victoria.

On the morning of the big day, it was April and hot. Cars were jamming the access road leading from I-10 to Raymond Russell Park. I will never forget the DPS cop who called me out of Raymond Russell Park and demanded by what authority was I causing a gigantic traffic backup that was endangering human life. I told the cop we were fixing to host the greatest menudo cookoff ever held and that he would need to talk with my co-sponsor for the event for any questions he might want answered.

"Who might your co-sponsor be?" the cop bawled at me.

"Congressman Henry Gonzalez," I answered.

"The United States congressman?" the cop was about to cry.

"One and the same," I told the policeman.

I hadn't bothered to tell Henry that he was co-sponsoring a menudo cookoff, but I felt confident that he would back me up. The poor cop headed back to his cruiser while cars and trucks passed him as they turned into the park.

I recall cringing when I looked up to see a Winnebago full of prostitutes and a big banner proclaiming "Hot Pants Menudo." It was my friend Madam Theresa Brown and some of her working girls, and I recall the little sinking sensation I felt in my belly while trying to figure out what I would do with Theresa. "Damn it, Theresa," I told her. "What the hell are you trying to do to me? I don't need the heat." T-Brown was unfazed, and her smile promised nothing but mischief when she gave me her answer:

Sam in armadillo hat: Samuelito the Armadillo. "My whole life was a bunch of insane shit."

"Fuck you, Sammy. I have forgotten more about cooking menudo than you will ever know." I left her alone and found something else to do.

We would have the Willie Nelson band and others who wanted to join in. Before it was over, we had Johnny Bush and the Bandoleros, plus more than thirty other groups and a midafternoon boxing match that would feature homicide detective Roy Aguilar and criminal attorney Alan Brown.

This captured the fancy of both lawyers and cops, who talked it up for weeks prior to the event in both the courthouse and the police headquarters. Brown was the nephew of bookmaker Jack Hanratty, and Hanratty told me in advance to bet as much money as I could get down on Brown, a former Golden Gloves champion from Edinburg in the Rio Grande Valley.

To the unpracticed eye of most of the spectators, this fistic match between detective and lawyer looked like a mismatch that might result in serious injury to the attorney. Homicide detective Roy Aguilar was a former street fighter and police academy athlete who was built like a steel oil drum with muscled arms and legs. Brown was a couple of shades paler than Aguilar with a shock of hair hanging over one eye and nothing to suggest arm or leg power that could hurt anything much bigger than a long-legged yard toad.

Minutes before the fight was to start, I heard Hanratty holler out: "Two-to-one." Then only seconds before the opening bell I heard him yell "Five-to-one." I was standing next to the old bookie when he upped the odds yet again: "Ten-to-one." I looked at Jack and he said, "You will not lose if you bet on Alan. He has whipped every fighter in the Rio Grande Valley at least once."

It was late spring and blazing hot that day. Jimmy Parks was refereeing the fight.

Aguilar was the aggressor from the opening bell. He charged Brown hard, punching and missing and sweating. "Twenty-to-one," Hanratty yelled. There were no takers. The second round ended with no punch from Brown, just bobbing, weaving, ducking, and dodging.

Roy was dripping sweat when the third and final round started. And then it was over. Alan hit Roy with a crashing right cross that glazed his eyes and turned his legs to spaghetti. And even as Aguilar was plunging to the canvas, Jack Hanratty could be heard in the distance: "Forty-to-one." I recall saying a little prayer at the time—Oh, Lord, don't let Roy be dead.

The great cookoff ended sometime before dawn. Crowd estimates unofficially topped twenty thousand, but we had no official count since no tickets were sold. We did sell rivers of beer with my associates getting away with most of the profits. A few grave stones were upended by vandals in Mission Park Cemetery next door, but nobody got killed that I ever heard about. I did have a deputy sheriff escort a radio station executive off the grounds when he and his wife engaged in a hollering cuss fight that could be heard all over Raymond Russell Park. Hal Davis was general manager of the Doubleday radio stations KITE AM and KEXL FM at the time. I had no information on the Davises, just that they were raising holy hell with each other. Ironically, Davis would play a large part in my future, but I will talk about this when we get there. One of our county commissioners told me later in private that I shouldn't try any more promotions in county parks for a long while.

At this stage, I was hungover, dog tired, and in dire need of rest. But my rest and recovery would be short-lived and fraught with stunning and traumatic upheaval. A few short weeks after my menudo cookoff, I awakened to learn that Australian newspaper billionaire Rupert Murdoch had purchased the *Express-News* from Harte-Hanks for seventeen million dollars. I had an uneasy sensation in my gut upon learning this news. Houston Harte Sr. had hand-raised me in the newspaper business like an orphaned goat, putting up with my kid shenanigans at the *San Angelo Standard-Times* and following my progress in San Antonio when he bought the *San Antonio Express-News*. Don Quixote's Sancho Panza couldn't have had it any better. As I mentioned earlier, the elderly newspaper titan loved to walk into the *Express* city room and plant his rear on a corner of my desk to talk.

Harte Senior installed Conway Craig as the *Express-News* general manager, but Houston Harte Jr. was directly in line to take over when the elderly Craig retired, and I always sensed that my invisible cloak of protection had been passed down from father to son. Houstie liked me as well as his father did, and I knew it.

Charles O. (Charlie) Kilpatrick, our social climber executive editor who was more than half scared of me because of the rapport I had always enjoyed with the Hartes, wasted no time after the newspaper passed into the hands of Rupert Murdoch. Two days after the paper sold, Kilpatrick fired both me and city editor Ken Kennamer, my friend and a strong supporter.

Ken got the axe because he, too, had built an affiliation with the Hartes that probably made Charlie uncomfortable. I had gotten too big for my britches, and I knew what was coming that morning I was summoned to appear in Kilpatrick's office. I was about to be fired from my column writing job. I knew it but had trouble believing it. From hurricanes to uprisings in the onion fields, I had covered it all, putting my heart and soul into the San Antonio newspaper job. I had never made much money, but with childlike faith I had always looked with optimism for some sort of future with the *Express-News.*

When I walked into Kilpatrick's office, I knew. Charlie was looking at the wall somewhere behind me when he spoke. He had wanted to do this for a long time. I could tell. The Hartes were gone and I was standing there like a naked fighting rooster with no spurs. "You are the best writer I have ever been associated with," Kilpatrick said, "but I have to let you go."

I asked for a reason, nothing more. "You associate with criminals and other undesirable people," he said. He named a couple of my San Antonio friends before dropping Willie Nelson's name. "This musician you just had out at Raymond Russell Park is a known dope addict," Kilpatrick said. Then he dropped the name that confirmed what I had suspected. "Paul English," Kilpatrick said. "The Nelson drummer is a pimp. I know for a fact that English is a pimp, and these are the people you have been associating with."

I knew then that Kilpatrick was getting his information from within the Nelson camp. Or very close to the camp. It is true that Paul was a Fort Worth gangster and pimp before he joined the Nelson band, but Charlie Kilpatrick had no way of knowing this. Someone close to Willie fired the torpedo that sank my canoe. I was dumbfounded when it happened. I am pretty sure I know who the Judas was. The sneak is dead now, but my resentment lived for years before I managed to put it behind me.

My hands were shaking when Kilpatrick ended my newspaper career. I recall the surreal feeling I had of being skinned alive and refitted with another person's skin. I looked down at my hands and saw shriveled folds of skin that didn't belong to me as workers from the *Express* press room rolled stacks of boxes filled with copies of my book down the hallway next to Kilpatrick's office. "I have decided to give you your remaining books as severance pay," Kilpatrick said. "The press room workers will help you load them in your vehicle."

The Express Publishing Company had covered some printing costs for the book with a proviso that I would start collecting royalties only after production costs had been met. I don't recall how many books were sold

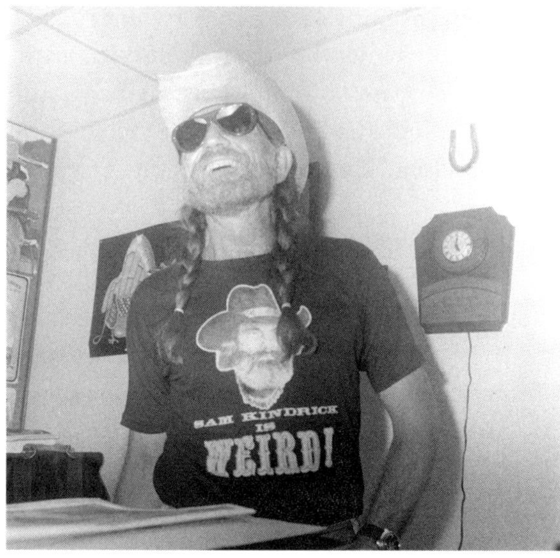

Willie Nelson has always had a penchant for odd-looking T-shirts. Here he wears one that speaks for itself.

by mail. There were many boxes containing unsold books. The newspaper had recouped some printing costs, and I was to get my pay through future book sales. I had no way to market these books. Thousands of them. I had no money. I had school-age kids at home.

I can recall the tangle of emotions that hit me. I felt for a minute like crying; I felt for another minute like going back to Junction and being that carefree little boy running the beautiful South Llano River bottoms of my childhood. Then the anger hit me like a runaway freight. I felt like killing Charlie Kilpatrick. Then I considered offing myself. Then I felt like getting drunk and I did.

Attorney friend Jack Leon offered to sue the *Express-News* in my behalf for wrongful employment termination. "This is illegal," Leon said. "We can get you reinstated."

I remember telling Jack, "If they don't want me, I damn sure don't want to work for them."

I picked up the pieces and went on. I had to quit drinking and I did. I started doing drugs as a substitute, recalling now the words of a musician and songwriting friend who said, "We figured cocaine was the answer to our drinking problem." It wasn't. It was the gateway to another little stretch of hell on earth. I stuck with my mantra: Anything worth doing is worth overdoing. And the insanity got its second wind.

14

THE KEXL RADIO EXPERIENCE

Immediately after my firing at the *Express-News* I was in shock. I knew I couldn't feed myself if I continued the drinking, but what the hell was I to do? Willie Nelson offered to take me in. He said he would find something for me to do on the road, maybe with publicity or something of that nature.

Nelson is like that, generous and kind and well-known for taking in strays. But this was not the time. While I would eventually tour for a short time with Willie and help emcee some of his earlier Fourth of July picnics, I couldn't make myself jump on a Nelson tour bus immediately after my firing from the newspaper. Maybe it was pride, ignorance, or innate stupidity, but I needed to figure some things out on my own.

A couple of years before the newspaper firing I had been offered a job with the *Houston Post*. This opportunity might still have been available, but I didn't want to live in Houston. I accepted a special features job with the onetime rival *San Antonio Light* but quit this short-lived experiment when I was ordered to write color for a Houston Astros playoff game. I still didn't like Houston, and I have never cared for baseball.

Marie Hicks hired me to write a weekly front-page column for the *North Side Recorder,* a San Antonio shopper that was delivered free over most of north San Antonio. The shopper pay was hardly enough to feed my family, but it was helping when my herky-jerky career was to take another hairpin turn.

It was midafternoon and I was shooting nine-ball pool in a beer joint on Oblate at San Pedro when the big voice of Hal Davis interrupted my mindless reverie. "How does it feel to be broke and on your ass?" Davis taunted. He was almost as big as his voice. I recognized him immediately. He was the radio hotshot I had thrown out of the menudo cookoff a couple of weeks before. Davis and his wife were in a hissing cuss fight at the cookoff, and it didn't help matters that I was half drunk at the time. A security cop asked what he should do with the fighting couple, and I told him to pitch them.

When I saw Davis approaching me in that beer joint, I wasn't immediately sure that he wouldn't take a swing at me as he walked up to the pool table. "You don't have to like me, Mister ex-newspaper columnist, but I'm here to offer you a news announcer job on a rock-and-roll hippie radio station if you could lower yourself to such a level."

"I don't believe you," I told Davis. "I have never worked at a radio station."

"Show up at our studios on Data Point Drive at four o'clock in the morning and find out," Davis said. "The starting pay won't be over the rafters, but it will beat hell out of the nothing you are making now."

This couldn't be. It would be impossible. I had never even heard my recorded voice. I was convinced that Hal Davis, general manager of Doubleday Broadcasting's KITE AM and KEXL FM radio stations, would inflict some form of debilitating revenge on me for throwing him and his wife out of the menudo cookoff. Davis might have me arrested for trespassing if I showed up at that radio station at four o'clock in the morning. I told myself this. Or he might have security bulls unceremoniously drag me off the property by the scruff of my neck. It would serve me right. Especially since I had been as drunk as or drunker than Davis at the cookoff and concert. I told Vicky that afternoon. She urged me to try it. Why not? We had no money. Nothing to lose but more face. If there was any face left.

It was pitch dark when I arrived at the building on Data Point. I took the elevator to the second floor. KITE AM and KEXL FM studios were separate, each with control rooms and studio space. Shit, I thought, this can't be happening.

Davis had told me to "ask for Ron." When I entered the KEXL waiting room, I was met by Ron Houston, a controversial disc jockey who possessed the greatest voice San Antonio radio has ever known. Freddy Lee Jones (aka Ron Houston when he worked in his hometown of Karnes City) had been a top jock on AM stations KMAC, KTSA, KFAN, KNUZ in Houston, KMAL in Karnes County, and country FM KBUC. He was now the morning-drive voice on an outlaw free-form rocker the likes of which Texas radio fans had never heard before. It was KEXL FM (104.5), the collective voice of a radio rock music culture in which I was soon to be enmeshed.

Houston and I knew each other from the drinking joints. He was the unrepentant friend of shotgun-packing pimp and three-card monte dealer Bunny Eckert, a fact that didn't exactly endear Houston to polite society and the San Antonio Country Club set, although Houston would later be posthumously named to the Texas Radio Hall of Fame. He called me "Soul" at that first radio station meeting, and he was still calling me "Soul" years later when a massive heart attack took his life.

"What the hell am I supposed to do?" I asked Houston as we sat behind twin microphones looking at each other. I will never forget his answer. "Just start talking, Soul."

That was the improbable beginning. I knew that traditional news was not expected of me. To satisfy federal broadcast requirements, I picked up a few lines from a syndicated service called "News of the Weird," but my main job was to jawbone with Ron Houston about most anything that crossed my mind. "I always wished I had taped our first show together," Houston said many times.

I had a strong voice with an unmistakable Junction, Texas, drawl. Ron and I were to develop a morning-drive show that many believed had no equal. I was the "champion of men and the working girl's friend," and on other mornings, it was simply "the long-haired redneck," an ID I snatched from David Allan Coe. I delighted in sniping on the air at Charlie Kilpatrick, executive editor of the *Express-News* who had fired me.

Hal Davis had been brought in by Doubleday Broadcasting to oversee both KITE AM and KEXL FM stations, and I soon realized that Davis was unimpressed with the aristocracy of San Antonio. While I japed on the air at Charlie Kilpatrick and the social status he longed to capture,

Davis remained conspicuously silent. To denigrate any major radio station executive in the fashion I hassled Kilpatrick would put most any San Antonio media upstart on the chopping block. Yet I was allowed to say stuff on the air like, "I wonder how Charlie Kilpatrick can manage to put on his socks without help from wife Margie this morning. I heard that Margie went out of town for the weekend. Charlie has a lot of trouble with colored socks. And he may not know how to properly use colored toilet paper, either."

Hal Davis allowed me to run wild with caustic drivel such as this. And it didn't take me long to figure out why Davis put me on the air. He had as much pushback renegade in him as I had in me, and I will always believe that Hal Davis pocketed his pride and hired me partly because he believed I was dealt with unjustly and partly because he sensed I might attract listeners.

My growing legions of young listeners were not lost on most of the local radio score keepers. Hal Davis and I became friends. "I just had a hunch," Davis later told me. "I thought those hippie kids would like you and I was right."

I guess Ron Houston knew something too. I just wish he could have been present years later when I was inducted into the San Antonio Radio Hall of Fame. I will always remember those first words out of his mouth. "Start talking, Soul." Talking I did, quickly bonding and blending with the young air staff at KEXL. While Houston was only a few years younger than me, I had a couple of decades on the others. And at this time I was making the big transition from alcohol to the world of the young dopers I found myself surrounded by at KEXL.

I fit right in. I had found my next home. I loved Ron Houston in life and death, and I learned to love the KEXL wild-assed kids who made up the air staff. These young rock music marvels were in a world and time of their own. They included such talents as Barbara (Legs) Marullo, Martha Martinez, Allen (Bubba) Grimm, Sweet Michael Boykin, Nick St. John, Bobby Reyes, Debbie Jecker, Tom Devine, Gordie Ham, and Skip DuCharme. They were light years ahead of the bellowing blowhards who characterized most AM radio and a lot of new FM stations of that era. I made the most noise of any of them, yakking with Ron Houston on the morning drive and shattering the peace and quiet with the commercials I had started to write and record. KEXL jocks were dramatically quiet.

Some of them would enunciate the call letters softly. At other moments, after a segue of tasteful rock album cuts, the jock might reverently whisper them all together into the mike: "Kex-sul, album radio."

Although KEXL FM was outlaw rock in its purest form, there was some method behind the madness. KEXL was officially an AOR station: Album Oriented Rock. Most amazing about KEXL was the formatting. None of it came directly from the front office. Most of it was through staff members like Allen Grimm, who was the longest-tenured KEXL program director, and Martha Martinez. Grimm actually started it all when KEXL was in its infancy at HemisFair Plaza.

Barbara Marullo recalls that KEXL started in the Menger Hotel with the street-level control room looking out onto Alamo Plaza next to the Alamo. "Then we moved to HemisFair Plaza, then Data Point," Marullo recalled. "I will never forget Ron Houston smoking his pipe and peering out that window on Alamo Plaza." Marullo recalls Jerry Pound managing KEXL when it was on Alamo Plaza and at HemisFair Plaza. She said Johnny Solo was program director at HemisFair and Woody Roberts was manager.

Grimm had been dead for a number of years when I prepared this manuscript; Martinez was a lively cancer survivor who helped me fill in some blanks. And Barbara Marullo was the one KEXL sweetheart who could recall most of the music played in those legendary years. Marullo and Martinez were the two foxes I knew and depended on while breaking in at KEXL.

Martha said, "We had a loose format, with certain cuts designated for different day parts; the hardest rocking cuts were saved for late afternoon through about midnight. There were rules about how often cuts were played to keep them from being played too often; we taped paper logs on the albums, where we noted which cut we played at what time."

I recall Bubba Grimm shouting at some errant new jock: "I never want to hear the same album cut more than once over a three-day period!" That might have been a slight exaggeration, but it was close. The program director, or music director, Martha continued, "would listen to each album and note which were the best songs to play for each day part, or, in some cases, which cuts *never* to play. So, while we all had different tastes, the music was really decided by the time you were on."

Sam could be heard regularly on KEXL FM radio. I was an outlaw then.

The KEXL jocks were more than amazing in their uncanny ability to pick hit songs before they became hit songs. Alan Grimm broke Aerosmith before anyone else in Texas had recognized this rock music hit machine, and KEXL's Sweet Michael Boykin broke Jackson Browne in San Antonio.

"I recall Bubba breaking Aerosmith in Texas," Barbara Marullo said. "We were playing groups like Emerson, Lake & Palmer, Rush, Yes, Styx, Montrose, Peter Frampton, the Band and Byrds. . . . See what you have started? And I can recall Martha introducing Bonnie Raitt to South Texas radio listeners for sure. And the Pointer Sisters. Willie had them on his picnic show at Liberty Hill."

Barbara recalled benefits for KEXL that were held at Olmos Park and at Sayers. Despite the huge cult following, and more listeners from the general population than most of the experts could imagine, KEXL was always digging for survival money. These concerts included Shawn Phillips, the Grateful Dead, Augie Meyers, and New Riders of the Purple Sage.

"We played hell out of Bruce Springsteen, starting with his first LP," Marullo said. "That was Bubba and Martha's doing. I recall first seeing him at Armadillo World Headquarters in Austin."

I will never forget my first meeting with new KEXL general manager Rex Tackett, a career radio management type and good guy who was obviously in uncharted waters with management of KEXL FM. Shortly after my air shift with Ron Houston was up and running, Tackett pulled me into his office, where he had two record album jackets sitting on his desk. These big jackets were almost exactly twelve and a half inches square, and the record covers on Tackett's desk looked like they had been run through a shredding machine.

"You are the oldest employee I have on this radio station staff," Tackett said. "I was hoping you could tell me what has been happening to these album jackets. They are torn all to pieces. The lettering is so ripped up I can't even read the names of some songs. It would appear that someone may have cut them with a knife or other sharp instrument."

I lied to Rex Tackett with the straight face of a sixty-year-old San Quentin convict. "I haven't got any idea," I said, hoping Tackett wasn't watching my lying eyes. I knew what had happened to those album covers. Some of the DJs had been using the jackets to chop up and line up cocaine and crystal meth. I was relatively new to the drug culture, but I had been around long enough to recognize razor blade slashes on a cardboard album jacket.

I knew the girls had not been laying out lines of coke and meth. I had no problem figuring out who was doing it. And without a single qualm, I would lie to the boss and protect those young KEXL jocks who were snorting lines of coke and crank off the album jackets. I could not snitch on my fellow radio offenders, and without even realizing it, I had chosen the treacherous path of the "owlhoot." I was one of them. I couldn't bring myself to snitch then, as I could not bring myself to snitch years later when I was facing twenty years in the state penitentiary. Bookmaker Jack Hanratty had called it. I was well on my way to becoming the outlaw journalist.

My intention was never to be a radio personality. I always knew that I would finish my life as a writer. Those two-plus years at KEXL were crazy. It was like something out of a psilocybin mushroom dream. Ron was recording land commercials for G. G. Gale of Timberwood Park fame, while I was writing copy and cutting trailer park spots for S. A. Sam Greene.

I recall some of the lines: "Oaks North Mobile Home Estates, folks, out where the Texas Hills kiss the sky. Big acreage-sized lots and privacy to boot. You don't have to watch your neighbor's old lady hanging out her panty hose at Oaks North. Got room for a hat-stomping and an armadillo race on the same property." Parts of Oaks North can still be seen in the Bulverde area.

Sam Greene was the super San Antonio land huckster who much later established a monastery near Blanco, proclaimed himself to be a monk named Father Benedict, and proceeded to molest every young boy he could get his hands on. Greene's natural flair for the dramatic helped hasten his Waterloo. His monastery's biggest draw was a painting of the Virgin Mary that reportedly wept tears of myrrh. Convicted of sexually molesting novice monks at the monastery, Father Benedict admitted that the weeping icon was bogus and eventually killed himself with a massive overdose of pain meds. While I had suspected that Greene might have been a little strange, I was as surprised as most when salesman Sam was to reinvent himself as Father Benedict with Jesus-style monk sandals and long flowing gray beard.

I know that I had my part in Greene's land scam. I wrote most of the radio copy with little more than a perfunctory description of the property from Greene. One was for Twin Lakes Estates near Lytle. My on-air description of lunker bass thrashing the two lake tops, plus a majestic wild turkey hen soaring over the sparkling water at sunrise, was close to being at least some type of misdemeanor. When I had occasion to view the actual property we had been promoting, I felt like giving someone their money back. The "twin lakes" were greasy little stock tanks with green algae scum on the top and a couple of used Kotex pads lying in plain view. I carried a picture in my head of this sordid scene until Benedict got busted for sodomizing apprentice monks. After that, contrived bass and nonexistent turkeys didn't seem all that bad.

Soon after my arrival at KEXL I learned that all language on the air is regulated by the Federal Communications Commission (FCC). Violators may be fined or jailed or both, and gross offenders may be removed from an air job. I acquired an FCC manual and studied the language requirements. I learned the words that were taboo for radio announcers, but I took it a notch further. To my surprise, I found other words without federal restriction, many of them words that most people would assume to be on the banned list.

When I used the word "horny" in a newscast, my radio associates were shocked to learn that this is not a federal no-no word. Or it wasn't at the time. Neither is the word "wired," no matter in what context it may be used. Or such was the case in the 1970s. To the young drug users of the 1970s, the slang term "wired" meant that one was jacked up, sky high and buzzing on some form of speed, blood pressure elevated and heart thumping like a Harley motor. When I came on the air at five o'clock in the morning and said I was "wired and inspired," vast numbers of young speed freaks connected. A non-doper friend said he almost wrecked his car the first time he heard me make the comment.

When I was on KEXL, the stations were rated by a service called Arbitron. We never hit the top of the rating chart, but we always believed we had as many as or more listeners than any other FM station in the area. Most of the ratings were done by telephone, someone from the ratings service calling residents and asking what radio station they were listening to. The most obvious flaw here was the assumption that all radio listeners had traditional dwellings with telephones.

Many members of the hippie subculture that made up our listener base did not live in traditional houses with traditional telephones. They lived in trailers, Volkswagen buses, apartment pads that belonged to God-only-knows who, and what traditional society refers to as communes. But they had access to radios, and their collective listener muscle would be on display when a hot live rock act was advertised on KEXL.

KEXL was fun for me, a diversion before my inevitable reentry into the writing game. The station promoted a Renaissance fair, and we drew big crowds with the KEXL armadillo races at HemisFair Plaza. Samuelito, my world-champion racing armadillo, successfully defended his crown at the KEXL races, and some of the giddy radio station fans may have actually believed the Samuelito bullshit.

When ZZ Top was breaking into the market, a dozen thirty-second radio ads on KEXL would pack any club in San Antonio. The listeners were always out there, and we always knew it. KEXL jocks enjoyed a special rapport with many of the leading rock musicians of that era. There was always a name act ready to help with a benefit during KEXL's last days.

The sad ending in 1974 was inevitable. Doubleday, the giant book publisher, was closing out its broadcasting arm, and KEXL's last night on the air was noted by our party at Johnny Goode's Village Inn.

The T-shirts I had printed were apropos. They featured a tombstone with the epitaph:

KEXL is Dead
Here Lies the Last Free Radio Station

One armadillo standing by the grave held a Bible. A second armadillo was prone and weeping over the grave.

I think I shed a tear myself that night. I didn't know the how or the why of it all, but I knew I would be going back to the writing business. There was no other place for me in San Antonio radio. I didn't even consider contacting another station.

15

MY FRIEND HONDO CROUCH

Ask me if I knew Hondo Crouch, and you might get a half-straight answer or a half-crooked one. I don't believe there was ever a man, woman, or child who knew Hondo a hundred percent or from gizzard to craw. He was the clown prince of Luckenbach, the inimitable Hill Country Imagineer, and a genuine enigma if there ever was one. Although many never knew it, Hondo Crouch was one of the greatest showmen this world has ever known. Hondo was also an accomplished writer.

I cried the morning Hondo died of a heart attack. That was September 27, 1976. Tex Schofield called with the bad news. Hondo was only fifty-nine. He was my friend and beer-drinking buddy who fired my imagination every time I got around him. There was no such thing as a bad photo of John Russell (Hondo) Crouch. His silvery-white hair and beard did not denote advanced age with Crouch, nor did his other "old man" trappings. Hondo wore jeans stuffed into the high tops of cowboy boots, and sweat-stained moderate-brim western hats that looked like they had been lying out in a sheep pen.

Hondo Crouch was an all-American swimmer at the University of Texas who never wanted to grow up. And he never did. His skin glowed with apparent health, and his blue eyes twinkled with mischief. Hondo was the Hill Country raconteur who whittled and carved on wood, played pranks on friends and strangers alike, and turned a broken-down Central Texas general store and beer joint with separate dance hall into the town of Luckenbach, a magical place that inspired the Willie Nelson/Waylon Jennings hit song "Luckenbach, Texas.

The song will forever remain a part of the Hondo Crouch and Luckenbach legend, right along with Crouch soliloquies like "Luckenbach Moon" and "Luckenbach Daylight." By the light of a campfire and moonlight, Hondo would regale his audience with a goosebump-raising "Luckenbach Moon" dissertation that would stay with them for the rest of their natural lives. I could never forget a "moon that makes haunted houses uglier and ugly girls prettier," nor "a moon that makes little animals see farther and feel closer together."

I met Hondo Crouch in 1967 at the first World Championship Chili Cookoff in the West Texas ghost town of Terlingua. It was a hokey contest between New York author H. Allen Smith and Texas journalist Wick Fowler to see which contestant cooked the best chili. The chili, of course, had nothing to do with this contrived display of insanity and self-grandiosity by some of the world's most shameless narcissists. We were there along with a defrocked Catholic priest; a Hollywood starlet who ran half-naked through the old silver mining town's main drag; two wetback whores (known today as illegal immigrant ladies of ill repute) from the Mexican border town of Ojinaga; a bull rider; chili chefs with handles like Allegani Janie Schoefield and Yeller Dog Marsh; and Luckenbach founder, mayor, and grand pooh-bah Hondo Crouch.

I will never forget that windy, raw morning in Terlingua. A cold norther with plenty of snap was whistling through the Chisos Mountains of the Texas Big Bend when I first laid eyes on Hondo Crouch. People were gathered around fires for warmth, and everyone I saw was wearing coats or jackets. Everyone but Hondo.

Crouch was wearing cowboy boots, his trademark short-brimmed felt with grease creases and goat barn stains, and a set of old-timey long johns with the classic trapdoor seat flap for emergencies. Crouch may have been chewing tobacco that morning. I am sure that he was drinking a Schlitz beer from a can. I'm not sure which of us started the introduction. I do know that we seemed to click. Hondo had some bacon fried, and he was frying an egg when I walked up. He asked me if I would care for an egg or a cold beer. I settled for the beer.

Sam sits on front porch of the Luckenbach Store and Post Office while Hondo sports his buffalo hide coat.

The legend of Hondo Crouch and Luckenbach has been told and retold through the years. John Russell Crouch was "the swimming cowboy" from Hondo, Texas. At the University of Texas, Crouch met his bride-to-be, Helen Ruth (Shatzie) Stieler, daughter of Adolph Stieler, once labeled the goat king of the world by *Life* and *American Sheep and Goat Raiser* magazines.

In 1942, Stieler owned thirty-eight thousand goats, twenty thousand sheep, and one thousand cattle grazing on ninety thousand Texas acres in Kendall, Kimble, Kerr, Gillespie, Blanco, and San Saba Counties. The headquarters has always been Stieler Hill on the Stieler ranch between Comfort and Fredericksburg, where Stieler's daughter and other members of her family live today.

The swimming cowboy adapted to the nickname "Hondo" with little trouble. He never did fit well in the big-money ranching world he married into. For a time, Hondo worked in his father-in-law's Comfort Wool and Mohair Company, but his heart was never in it. While Adolph Stieler made his fortune with hard work and natural skills of a stockman, Hondo never seemed to get serious about anything more than what appeared to be his own brand of tomfoolery. In her book *Hondo My Father*, daughter Becky Crouch Patterson describes her father as "a mystery, a frustrating puzzle."

I recall one lazy summer afternoon when I was hanging out and drinking beer with Hondo at Luckenbach. With no warning, Hondo grabbed my arm and said, "Come on. I want to show you some fun." He invited me into his battered old pickup truck and away we went down Ranch Road 1376. Hondo stepped on the gas, and we were soon hitting forty, fifty, sixty, and then seventy on the rolling ranch-road hills. It was almost scary as the rattletrap pickup topped what must be the highest hill on that stretch of road.

Hondo abruptly killed the engine. We were coasting fast. Down the big hill and up a smaller one before the truck started to lose momentum. As the truck slowed, Hondo put one of his booted feet on the dash. He was totally relaxed and grinning like a possum as the vehicle finally came to a creeping stop. "We just covered a whole mile and several yards running in Mexican overdrive," Hondo said. "It saves gas, and it sure is a lot of fun."

Hondo wrote more than six hundred columns for the *Comfort News* under the heading "Cedar Creek Clippings" and the pseudonym Peter

Cedarstacker. With Hondo's permission, I reproduced a number of the columns in *Action Magazine*. They were parodies or satires of the life and times of country folk from that area, including a family of fictitious cedar choppers and their grubby little boy Jay Elbie. "And when it was cold and nasty," Peter Cedarstacker wrote, "little Jay Elbie's nose kept sticking together." Or when "Uncle Undo died in a red ant nest," it was really bad.

A month before Hondo died, Bob Hope appeared at a benefit at the Nimitz Hotel in Fredericksburg. In the middle of Hope's talk, Hondo walked onto the stage and handed Hope a note that brought tears of mirth to the comedian's eyes. The note read: "Your fly is open." Representing what he facetiously referred to as the Luckenbach Chamber of Commerce, Hondo then presented Hope with an axe handle in lieu of a golf club with this forgettable punchline: "Sorry it doesn't have a head on it. You see, it's hard to get a head in Luckenbach."

Humorist and radio personality John Henry Faulk saw in Hondo what I always saw—a keen mind working behind a facade of country-boy bullshit. "He would act as if he was just an old tobacco-chewing country boy who didn't know nothing," Faulk said, "but he was actually very intelligent and well informed. He took the character he played seriously—too seriously I always felt, because he never stepped out of character. It became real to him."

Always the entertainer, Hondo played guitar and sang Tex-Mex ballads in South Texas Spanish that endeared him to crowds and professional musicians. Hondo was very close to Jerry Jeff Walker, a frequent visitor to Luckenbach who recorded his live *¡Viva Terlingua!* album with the Lost Gonzo Band in the Luckenbach dance hall. And for reasons I never knew, Hondo turned down an invitation to appear with Walker at a Carnegie Hall performance. Hondo was booked to appear on the *Tonight Show* with Johnny Carson when he died.

Jerry Jeff Walker was a familiar figure around Luckenbach. I know that Hondo was a father figure for Jerry Jeff. Walker loved Crouch, and Hondo showed signs that he felt the same. We used to sit at picnic tables behind the Luckenbach store, drinking and listening as Jerry Jeff crafted songs. I was there when Walker wrote his song "Night Rider's Lament." We drank and argued and cussed each other that night about nothing until neither of us could stand on two feet. I think one of us had a bottle of mescal. Walker and I were bowed up at each other and too drunk to

Jerry Jeff Walker (*left*) and Sam. Boy, we were drunk. Jerry Jeff was glassy-eyed and could barely talk. I had to step in to sing for him.

even get up from the picnic table bench when Hondo came walking out of the store. "Well, well," Hondo said. "I can see that this is really going to be a bloody one. Now both of you need to crawl over to your trucks and sleep it off. We will have no fist fights at Luckenbach."

I awakened in my truck the next morning, hungover and dog sick. There was dried vomit in my beard and a pounding in my skull like a blacksmith's hammer meeting cold rebar on an anvil. Dried vomit really stinks. Only a real alcoholic would take another drink of alcohol after a night like that, yet here we were that afternoon. Me and Jerry Jeff. Slugging down one beer after another to calm the shakes and without any memory of what the hell we were arguing about the night before. As Hondo Crouch would put it, probably just a big old nothin'.

Nobody really knew what made Hondo tick, but he had theatrics in his blood. The world was Hondo's stage, but he did make more formal appearances. He appeared on the TV series *To Tell the Truth* as the humorist owner of a Texas town the size of a flyspeck, and he had a film performance in *Pony Express* that was in the can when he died.

Hondo was the leader of a theater troupe known as the Crazy Comfort Bunch. They played in villages such as Comfort, Waring, and Grapetown, and Hondo was the star of a homemade movie that Rex Foster produced, *Blank Dank*. It featured Hondo playing all seven roles. "I never got on a stage," Hondo was fond of saying. "Stages just seemed to get under me."

Luckenbach was always a waiting stage for Hondo, although his self-deprecating manner suggested otherwise. Luckenbach's population was listed as three. The town had one parking meter that didn't work. A mailbox on a pole was designated for "air mail." Every promotion Hondo hatched up was a spoof of somebody or something, although Crouch's motto was "Everybody is somebody in Luckenbach."

The first Great World's Fair at Luckenbach drew a crowd. So did the chili cookoff for women only, a day of celebration to welcome the return of the dirt daubers, and the non-buy centennial that featured a bad-taste award. At the Great World's Fair, Hondo was introduced as mayor. He wore a black wig, a top hat, and a buffalo hide coat for the occasion. Events at the fair included armadillo races, tobacco spitting, chicken flying, and cow-chip throwing. Special invited guests included Elizabeth Taylor and the Prince of Wales. Of their absence, Hondo said, "I guess they decided to stay home."

Hondo attracted people like a magnet picks up horseshoe nails. Hardly ever did I see Hondo when he didn't have a beer in his hand, yet I never saw a drunken Crouch. If a cowboy hobo could look dapper, that was Hondo. He had every situation under total control, and I never saw Hondo upset, rattled, or out of step until that black day at Luckenbach when the British Broadcasting Corporation people rolled into the tiny town. The great Luckenbach catastrophe was about to happen, the one harrowing day that saw Hondo Crouch completely lose his composure and ability to even express himself.

The BBC wanted to film a mini-documentary on Luckenbach. The scenario had already been set with Hondo having a major role in the planning. I don't know how he hooked up with the BBC, but he obviously did, in London with the TV headquarters, we were soon to learn. "We are going on British TV," Hondo said in a telephone call to my office in San Antonio. "I want you here for the filming. We start at first light tomorrow."

Hondo was geared up for this one. The excitement in his voice was electric. He had already selected the players. I must have been about the last one contacted. I had never seen Hondo excited about anything before, but this British television thing had him all but vibrating in his boots. Our British film debut would include Hondo, Jerry Jeff, syndicated cowboy cartoonist Ace Reid of Kerrville, magazine publisher and Hondo crony Sam Kindrick, and Luckenbach fixture and gadfly Rusty Cox, probably the biggest Jerry Jeff Walker groupie who ever lived.

The British film crew arrived in Luckenbach at the crack of dawn. They included a redheaded, freckled, and slightly dumpy female reporter and two male sound camera techies. The techies called the woman reporter "Birdy." It soon became obvious to most of the parties on hand that Birdy was in charge. Most of the parties included everyone but cowboy cartoonist Ace Reid, who was driven from Kerrville to Luckenbach by someone in a really sorry-looking station wagon. The first indication that we were in for a horribly miserable day came when Ace tried to exit the station wagon. He was typically skunk drunk, even at that early hour, and he missed while attempting his first step from the vehicle. Ace had a half-empty pint bottle of whiskey in his hand when he went sprawling headfirst across the Luckenbach store parking lot, a stream of barn yard obscenities pouring from his mouth. I recall some broken whiskey bottle glass, a couple of empty beer bottles, a wad of rusty baling wire, an old copy of the *Goat Gap Gazette*, and other trash spilling out of the wagon with Ace.

This was the BBC's welcome to Luckenbach, Texas. Then came the real fun as Birdy outlined our main screen scene. She had prepared a largely unrehearsed scenario that had Walker picking and singing with the rest of us telling quaint Texas tales as we laughed and joshed with Hondo and one another around the Luckenbach Store bar area.

Birdy wanted a couple of trial runs prior to the actual filming. I sensed trouble as our cast of characters gathered around Walker. At this point, Jerry Jeff started acting like Jerry Jeff. "We can't rehearse this stuff," Walker told Birdy. "We are not actors."

Birdy needed a guitar player who could sing Texas ballads. She beseeched Hondo for help. Her British accent sounded like a foreign tongue in these prickly circumstances. "Come on, Jerry Jeff." Hondo was all but begging. "Let's hear something."

"Come on Jerry Jeff," pleaded Rusty Cox. Rusty could see his one chance for TV stardom evaporating before his eyes. He was clearly distraught.

"To hell with this British TV business," Walker said. "Who wants to be on British TV?"

Everything was going downhill at this point. Nobody knew what to do or say. We had moved out of the store when Birdy chirped bravely in her strange little British accent. "What is this?" She had plucked a strand of Spanish moss from the lower limb of a Luckenbach live oak tree.

Poor little Birdy. She was desperately trying to keep some form of dialogue alive. "That there's Spanish moss, lady," drawled Ace Reid.

"Oh, my," said Birdy. "What is it for?"

"Well, ma'am," Ace said, "the Comanche Indian squaws used to poke it up their pussies when they was menstruating."

Birdy paled and looked like she might faint away. Hondo made a sound like a mortally wounded small animal. Then he said, "Awww Ace, aww no." Hondo was bent over like he might have ingested poison.

Birdy was headed for their rented car. The Brit camera crew was packing their equipment. No British TV for us. Jerry Jeff said little as he left for Austin. Hondo was not the "Clown Prince of Luckenbach" on this black day. He looked to me like he was going to cry, and I wouldn't be surprised if he did. I felt like crying myself just watching him.

THE AMAZING AUGIE MEYERS

I had known Augie Meyers for only a short time back in the 1970s when I was separating from my first wife, Vicky. I had met both Augie and Doug Sahm in casual settings, but little did I suspect that both would reach legendary status during the course of my lifetime or that I would forge a friendship with the iconic Meyers that would endure through the course of our earthly existence.

As I have said many times, Augie Meyers and Johnny Bush became my special soul brothers from the Texas music world. They headlined three of my *Action Magazine* anniversary shows at Tony Talanco's Texas Pride Barbecue near Adkins, and my friendship with Meyers continued after Bush's death from heart failure on October 16, 2020. My last contact with Johnny was Christmas Eve 1919 when my wife Sharon and I attended night services at Trinity Baptist Church with Johnny and his wife Lynda in San Antonio. Sharon and I have also remained close to Meyers and his wife Sara through the years.

It was early in 1976, shortly after I started *Action Magazine*, that I somehow wound up in the farmhouse on the banks of Cibolo Creek in Bulverde that Augie Meyers and his family were leasing. Augie and his first wife, Carol, had returned from California, where they had basked in the sunlight of bigtime success with Doug Sahm and the astonishing Sir

Douglas Quintet, recording such major hits as "Mendocino" and "She's About a Mover." That band had dissolved, and vox organ and accordion master Meyers was getting it going again with his own group, Augie Meyers and the Western Head Band.

I had only a foggy perception of Meyers's connection to the music world when he invited me to visit the farmhouse. I had moved out of our family home in San Antonio, leaving the house to Vicky and my three children. I was looking for a place to live, and Augie Meyers had my answer.

John Avila, who lived across the creek and a short distance from the Meyers house, had a one-bedroom cabin for rent. The price was right. My friend Jake Noll and his wife, Kate, had just purchased the nearby Specht's Store, and things felt right. I moved in the next day, never dreaming whom I would see, hear, and meet over just a few short months through my proximity to the old farmhouse.

Augie Meyers, I soon learned, both knew and commanded the respect of established music greats from various genres, many of whom saw fit to regularly drop by the Bulverde house when their tour vehicles passed through the area. "We had a bunch of musician visitors back there in the 1970s and 1980s," Meyers said. "Kinky Friedman was out there early on, also Jerry Garcia of the Grateful Dead, and Willie before he became Willie Nelson. That was when he was still wearing sport coats and turtleneck sweaters."

Sound slips through the night air of Bulverde with a crisp resonance not found in nightclubs or usual music venues. When I was living near the Meyers house, I heard a lot and I saw a lot. From Dylan and Jerry Garcia to Spanky McFarlane they came, and the spectacle of Leon Russell sitting on a set of rusted-out bedsprings while feeding bread crumbs to a rooster was nothing to get excited about.

Through teardrops and laughter, sickness and hospitals, and personal losses that cut the big victim of childhood polio to the emotional quick, I have been there near Augie. He almost died from kidney failure, diverticulitis, prostate cancer, and God only knows what else, but here we find him—polio-damaged leg swinging in unison with the trademark braided pigtail that reaches to his belt. With Carol on vocals and teenage son Clay on drums, Meyers's Western Head Band included mercurial guitar ace Chris Holzhaus and bassist Harvey Kagan, among others.

The Meyers website sums it up well:

> Augie Meyers's style and his Vox Continental has become one of music's most distinctive keyboard sounds around. Augie can be heard with the Sir Douglas Quintet, Texas Tornados, Meyers' solo efforts as well as on landmark albums by Bob Dylan ("Time Out of Mind" and "Love and Theft") and John Hammond ("Wicked Grin"). Echoes of the Meyers' style and sound can be heard in the music of the Doors, the Kinks, the Animals as well as the Beatles just to name a few.
>
> By fusing Tex-Mex, Cajun, conjunto and soulful rock together along with the power of Meyers' distinctive vox organ, an impact that is still being felt in rock 'n' roll today. While the Sir Douglas Quintet never broke up and never succumbed to the lure of the oldies circuit, when Meyers and his musical cohorts decided they wanted to do something different, they did.

Doug Sahm died from heart failure in 1999. He was lead vocalist and guitarist. I liked Doug, and I believe he liked me, although I never got as close to Sahm as I did to Meyers. A frenetic Scorpio, Doug was genetically wired tighter than a two-dollar watch. He moved fast and talked even faster, leading me to say that interviewing Sahm was a no-brainer. Just turn on the tape recorder, and Doug would interview himself.

The Sir Douglas Quintet left San Antonio in what many considered disgrace following Doug's marijuana arrest. Their destination was California, the land of opportunity where the monster hit "Mendocino" was recorded. When the musicians returned to Texas, Doug anchored in Austin. Augie returned to the San Antonio area and the Bulverde farm his grandparents had owned.

It was just a matter of time until Doug and Augie were to reunite in what many considered to be the Tex-Mex super band of all time. The Texas Tornados also included Flaco Jimenez and Freddy Fender. This group produced a Grammy and continued on with Doug's son Shawn supplying lead vocals after his father's death.

In addition to winning the Grammy, Meyers was feted in 2021 with a lifetime achievement award banquet that was attended by both San Antonio mayor Ron Nirenberg and Bexar County judge Nelson Wolfe. Entertainers for that one included ZZ Top guitarist Billy Gibbons and Asleep at the Wheel leader Ray Benson.

Long before these honors, many could recall Meyers being presented with a special El Corazon de San Antonio Award on the city's Main Plaza. This distinction, which translates as "The Heart of San Antonio," was the city's Main Plaza Conservancy's fourth such presentation, the other three going to Flaco Jimenez, Jesse Borrego Jr., and the late Esteban (Steve) Jordan. The Main Plaza Conservancy press release said Meyers was selected for the award for his big part in establishing a special San Antonio sound, that "unique mix of rock, country, conjunto, blues, and soul, and also for his refusal to lock himself into one style of music."

While Meyers knew that I grew up in the Nashville Hank and Lefty era of country music, he says country has always been a part of his musical soul, but like old pros such as Darrell McCall and Moe Bandy, Augie has trouble identifying with the Nashville sound of the 2020s.

"Doug and I always played some country," Augie says, "but I put out an album of all original country songs that I couldn't even get played on a single San Antonio radio station. The songs on that album, titled *Augie Meyers Country*, don't fit the modern mold of watered-down pop they are calling country. My songs on that album are old-style traditional country, the kind of material that Little Jimmy Dickins would have approved of. My experience with this project really brought something home to me. If Hank Williams himself could rise from the dead and return to the music business, he would have one hell of a hard time getting his music played on what they now call country radio."

Doug Sahm's elder son Shawn was a lead voice with the Texas Tornados, and the admiration and respect Augie Meyers felt for his old running mate's firstborn was all but palpable. "I have known Shawn since the day he was born," Meyers told me. "He never ceases to amaze me. He looks like Doug and he sounds like Doug. Sometimes, when Shawn is singing, I close my eyes and feel the hairs rising on the back of my neck. He is truly a reincarnation of his father. He brings Doug right back to me with the music we love."

Doug Sahm's younger son Shandon became a street musician in the Netherlands, perhaps because of his late father's warm reception in the Netherlands when Sir Douglas Quintet records were number-one sellers in Scandinavia. "We played a lot in Holland and Denmark and other countries in that part of the world," Augie recalls. "I always left early by boat for all of our appearances in the Scandinavian countries. I wouldn't get on an airplane then, and I still won't get on one. I limit my boat rides now to winter cruises I play with my old West Texas buddy T. Gosney Thornton, a great musician I met at the Longneck Club in San Antonio back in the seventies."

While he has dabbled in just about every genre of music, Augie has always called his band's Tex-Mex sound "meskin rock 'n' roll," and his original rendition of "Hey, Baby, Que Paso" has become a South Texas anthem. Augie spelled it "Hey, Baby, Kep Pa So," refusing as always to capitulate with proper linguistic reverence before the racially correct slang police.

Augie's wife is Mexican American, and much to the chagrin of the language puritans, Meyers has never once altered the lyrics of his spirited polka titled "Down in Mexico." The slang term "meskin" has long been considered the Spanish language "N-word," but Augie's Tex-Mex dance hall favorite "Down in Mexico" never fails to get the crowds up and moving. It has a jolly and happy ring to it that promotes goodwill rather than animosity.

> I'm going down, down, down,
> down in the heart of Mexico;
> I'm gonna get me a meskin queen,
> she gonna cook me some refried beans,
> down in the heart of Mexico.

Here is what Bob Dylan had to say about Meyers:

> Augie's my man. He's like an intellectual who goes fishing using bookworms. Seriously though, he's the shining example of a musician, vox player or otherwise, who can break the code. His playing speaks volumes. Speaks in tongue actually. He can bring a song, certainly any one of mine, into the real world. I've loved his playing going all the way back to the Sir Doug days when he was featured and dominant. What makes him so great is that internally speaking, he's the master of syncopation and timing. And this is something that cannot be taught. If you need someone to get you through the shipping lanes and there's no detours, Augie will get you right straight through it. Augie's your man.

After a successful kidney transplant in 2010, Meyers told me as we were having lunch at Garcia's Mexican Restaurant on Fredericksburg Road, "The Lord has been mighty good to me. I have always believed in saints, and now I believe even as strongly in angels, because I have had three of them helping me right here on earth."

My friendship with Augie has endured over the years without a single dustup, and Augie and Sara were among the special few who attended my wedding with Sharon on July 7, 2007, in a little nondenominational Marble Falls church garden overlooking Lake LBJ. Sax great Bobby Rey was at the wedding as was the late Ron Houston, my air shift partner on KEXL. Johnny Bush was invited but unable to attend because of an out-of-state gig. Kate Mangold, owner of Specht's Store at the time, was there with daughter Lisa Noll. Kate baked the wedding cake. Lisa was the kid waitress at Maggie's Restaurant who was there to extinguish the flames and wipe my face when I was nodding off and setting my newspaper afire with lighted cigarettes. It was hard to stay awake when coming down off a three-day speed high. Lisa later became an elementary school vice-principal.

Augie's earth-dwelling angels have been his grandmother, St. Hedwig native Sophie Kosub, who doctored his polio-damaged limbs with mud dauber nest mud when Meyers was scarcely more than a toddler; San Antonio urologist Michael Newell, the physician who removed a cancerous prostate when there was yet time; and Dallas computer programmer Jimmy Lucas, the reborn Christian who donated Meyers a kidney without even knowing that Meyers was a musician, much less a famous one with international recognition.

Augie Meyers received his kidney transplant shortly before his seventy-first birthday. He was taking seventy-seven anti-rejection pills weekly immediately after the procedure. Today at this writing he is eighty-four and still taking most of the medications, still writing songs, and still performing before his adoring Texas fan base. Meyers has never lost his gratitude to the man who saved his life with a donated kidney.

"Jimmy Lucas is a sweetheart," Augie said. "He is a wonderful person, and we have become really close. He made a mighty big sacrifice for nothing in return, a sacrifice that I believe saved my life, and I believe there is a powerful spiritual connection here. Jimmy was out of work when he gave me the kidney, and within two weeks of the transplant operation here in San Antonio, he landed the job in Dallas he had wanted for most of his life."

Lucas made his decision to donate a kidney after hearing Augie's son Clay asking for help on a Dallas radio station. I remember calling Lucas after the operation, and I remember what he told me. He was thirty-nine at the time, and he was incredulous that doctors ordered a psychiatric examination prior to proceeding with the transplant. Such an act of altruism was apparently hard for the doctors to grasp, and they needed to make sure that their patient was in command of his faculties.

Lucas explained: "I had been a Christian for a couple of years. I hadn't led a very good life until I decided to turn my life over to Jesus Christ. Everything had been about me . . . too much me, and I simply wanted to do something good for somebody else. I couldn't have found a better man to help and I have no regrets."

Meyers was near death in July 2009 when he was rushed to the hospital with blood pressure and potassium levels already through the roof, an event that ruined his kidneys. With a portable dialysis machine that Meyers had to stay on eight hours a day, he was still recording music and trying to tour, but many of us could see tombstones in Augie's eyes. He wasn't going to make it much longer, and he knew it. "Without Jimmy Lucas I couldn't have continued much longer," Meyers said. "I now rank him right there in Angel Row with Dr. Newell and my Grandma Sophie. To these people and the grace of God I owe my life."

After removing a cancerous prostate gland that was threatening Augie's life, Dr. Michael Newell became another close friend who still appears at most of Augie's local music events.

The third Augie Meyers angel no longer walks on this earth, but the veteran musician will always love his Grandma Sophie. Farm woman Sophie Kosub knew something the mainstream medical profession was unaware of—the healing properties to be found in the mud nests fashioned by the near-stingerless wasps found in South Texas known as mud daubers.

"I had polio when I was two," Augie said, "the paralysis affecting both an arm and a leg. My grandmother dissolved the nests in water and made poultices from the mud. She rubbed it on my arm and leg on a daily basis for what became months and then years. I didn't walk until I was nine. I might not be alive today had it not been for my Grandma Sophie, and I know I wouldn't be walking and performing today if not for her."

Augie also expresses gratitude for Dr. Francis Wright, the transplant specialist who transferred the kidney from donor Lucas. "I think, on second thought, that Dr. Wright should also be among my earthly angel brigade troopers," Meyers laughs. "He is another God-sent magician." Wright, Meyers noted, is the same specialist who implanted a donor kidney in former Spurs star Sean Elliott, who returned to pro basketball after the operation. Elliott received a kidney from his brother.

Those of us who love and respect Augie Meyers know him to be an upbeat and positive force in this old world, laughing and joking through physical tribulations that would sink a lesser man. The emotional curve balls that have smitten the big musician with the long pigtail have certainly ensured that every day hasn't exactly been Six Flags Over Texas for Augie Meyers. I know because I was there.

I was there when record producer Huey Meaux was sentenced to prison for child sex pornography, a development that threatened to extinguish the light in Augie's soul. Euphemistic would be the word for anything short of true love that Augie felt for Meaux, the "Crazy Cajun" owner of Sugar Hill studios in Houston who helped launch the music careers of so many titans of the industry, from Delbert McClinton and Ronnie Milsap to Clifton Chenier and the Sir Douglas Quintet and many more. Meaux managed the Quintet during their formative years.

In 1996, a police raid of Meaux's office turned up thousands of polaroid shots and videos of girls, mostly underage, in sexual situations. Meaux pleaded guilty to two counts of sexual assault of a child, a drug possession charge, a child pornography charge, and another for jumping bail and briefly fleeing to Mexico. He was sentenced to fifteen years in prison and was released in 2007. Meaux was eighty-two when he died in 2011.

Augie Meyers has never been one to discuss in length the emotional agonies he has been through. On the subject of Huey Meaux, he just turned his head and looked into space. "I will never know why Huey did those things he went to jail for," Meyers said. "I have thought about this many times, and I have never come up with an answer. I don't think Huey knew why he did what he did. Huey helped so many of us musicians. . . . He did so much for so many." Augie wrote Meaux regularly while he was in prison, and he stayed in faithful telephone contact with him until his death.

Of Meyers and Meaux, Margaret Mosher quoted Augie in the *Austin Chronicle*: "Huey managed us: 'Y'all gotta dress, look nice. Don't never go out on stage with holes in your tennis shoes and blue jeans and T-shirts with stains on them. People wanna see nice. They don't wanna see what they look like.' So we dressed all the time. At first, Huey said wear white gloves, so when we went on stage we would take our gloves off and throw them to the audience. After two months, Huey said, 'We've been through 500 pairs of gloves, and they cost $2 apiece. No more glove throwing. We didn't throw no more gloves." Augie said, "I loved Huey Meaux." And that ended that.

The breakup of Meyers's first marriage to Carol stunned the local music community. It seemed to friends and close acquaintances like the idyllic musician family, Carol on tambourine and singing harmonies, while son Clay was proving to be a drummer who could hold his own with many of the older and more experienced musicians in that field. For reasons known only to her, Carol went to New York and joined a contingent of female vocalists who performed briefly around the Big Apple. It was during this time that the marriage began to fall apart. Augie never wanted to talk about it, and I never pushed him for details. It was none of my business then, and it is none of my business now. But I saw and felt Augie's hurt, and I know today that the divorce was one of the lowest points in his life.

Time passed, and the family members reached a form of cordiality in later years. Happier times were in the mix when Augie married Sara Ramirez. Augie had known her father, and he bonded naturally with Sara. She accompanies her husband on many of his gigs, handles record sales, and provides merchandise designs.

Carol never remarried. At this writing she occupied a trailer on Bulverde property owned by son Clay. She always speaks highly of Augie, and Clay stays close to both of his parents.

While the divorce and death of Huey Meaux were traumatic events for Augie Meyers, the loss of Doug Sahm was stunning and probably the most unexpected. Doug died at age fifty-eight in Taos, New Mexico, following a massive heart attack. "I heard it and I couldn't believe it," Augie said. "Doug was like my brother . . . more than my brother. We were part of each other, joined in spirit and the love we shared. We traveled some high roads and some low roads, but we were always there for each other." Life without Doug has been like learning how to walk all over again for Augie. Meyers says he still feels the presence, the Doug ghost who stays close and watchful.

Augie Meyers first broke out on the San Antonio music scene in the late 1960s with some fuzzy-cheeked compadres who called themselves

Augie Meyers is a huge part of the Sam Kindrick story. He has seen me at my worst and my best, and a better friend no man could have.

Lord August and the Visions of Lite. These young music makers included Harvey Kagan, Pineapple Marconi, Publio Casias, and Augie Meyers. They starred at such venues as the Pusi-Kat Club and Sam Kinsey's Teen Canteen.

In 2022, the Augie Meyers Band included son Clay on drums, Al Gomez on trumpet, and a scattering of musical pros who have been with Augie on varying projects and tours, including original Sir Douglas Quintet bass guitarist Jack Barber. The later years have seen Meyers's limp becoming more pronounced as he battles what is known as post-polio syndrome, a condition that often attacks polio survivors as late as fifty years or longer after their initial bout with the crippling disease. "It's a weakening of the muscles," Meyers said. "There is some pain, and I know I may have to soon return to walking with a cane, but my gratitude to God and all of the people who have helped me outweighs it all."

Meyers still peppers his friends with a never-ending stream of cornball jokes. It's just what he does. But he gets serious on matters that mean the most to his many friends. Over my entire life, I can honestly say that I have had two musician friends who called on a consistent basis to check on my well-being. They are Southside San Antonio guitar slinger Jimmy Spacek and Augie Meyers.

17

THE DRUG BUST HORRORS

While growing up in Junction, I had no awareness of street drugs. We didn't have them. My cousin Gordon (Stick) Bishop brought two sickly-looking little marijuana cigarettes home when he finished his army tour in Korea. They had been hand-rolled and twisted up on both ends. We went down under the South Llano River bridge and tried to smoke the weed with no success. Stick's weed did nothing for us. I think he had carried it around until it lost the THC power needed to produce even a tiny high. "We would get more jump rolling Bull Durham," Stick proclaimed, and that was that for the evil weed.

The prospect of anyone around Junction doing heroin or cocaine in 1955 was laughable. The closest any of us ever got to hard drugs was watching *The Man with the Golden Arm* at Irma Ragsdale's Texan Theater on Junction's Main Street. This was the controversial 1955 film about a drug addict who gets clean while in prison but struggles to stay that way when released. The highly acclaimed movie starred Frank Sinatra, Kim Novak, Darren McGavin, and Eleanor Parker. Sinatra played the part of Frankie Machine, a Chicago drummer who was hooked on a drug that was never named in the film. It was always presumed to be heroin as the movie's leading man injected it with a hypodermic needle: the "golden arm."

So, to us Junctionites, the dirty hard drugs were little more than shadowy fiction reserved for incomprehensible metropolises like Chicago and

New York City. Nobody around Junction would ever dream of shooting up drugs with a needle or snorting crystal fire up both nostrils and into the brain through a soda straw or tightly rolled dollar bill. We all had better sense, or so I had wrongly assumed.

After my arrival in San Antonio, and through the bars and nightclubs I was to frequent, I met the first two dope addicts I had ever laid eyes on—Leroy Badarocco, a heroin junkie, and Robin Johnson, a pool hustler who shot up all of the Demerol he could lay hands on, even when it meant breaking into drugstores to get his fixes. Leroy came from a nice family who owned a little restaurant on McCullough Avenue. I do know he was hooked on heroin and that he tried multiple times to kick the habit. Robin became addicted to the pain medication Demerol through legitimate physician prescriptions for migraine headaches.

With the exception of Rudolph Wonderone Jr. (aka Minnesota Fats) and a former road hustler and pool hall owner known as Bananas Rodriguez, my friend Robin Johnson was the smoothest nine-ball pool player I had ever met or written articles about. Robin would never dream of shooting heroin. To him, heroin was a dirty street drug used by his abject inferiors. Demerol was a legitimate medicine prescribed by legitimate professionals, but there were too many legitimate professionals willing to write Robin the scripts that eventually took his freedom and then his life.

The last time he was arrested for breaking into a pharmacy to steal Demerol, police found him passed out in a drug-induced stupor and with a needle rig hanging out of his arm. He tried many times to kick the habit but finally threw in the towel. Robin was to die from a deliberate overdose of Demerol.

My first book was copyrighted in 1973 by the *Express-News* and printed that same year by Davis Brothers Publishing of Waco. In this book was to appear the tragic story of a young married couple identified as Freddie and Vikki. They were parents of a two-year-old boy, and both were heroin addicts. Freddie was a burglar; Vikki, a prostitute.

Freddie's description of intravenous drug beginnings and withdrawals was the most believable and equally terrifying that I ever heard. He said, "When you first start, it's a luxury. It's the greatest, a panacea. If you've got athlete's foot, it doesn't itch anymore. If you've got sinus troubles, your head clears. Your mind is clear. You have everything in perspective.

Time, everything. You feel like a Dudley Do-Right. But when you get hooked hard like me, you need the fix just to feel half normal. When you don't get it, everything is wrong with you. Your bowels run, your nose runs, your eyes run, and you feel like you are coming to pieces. You feel like you are in hell."

As I neared the end of my drinking hell, symptoms much like these began to appear.

When I finally started pulling away from alcohol and sampling a few speed pills we called black mollies, along with powerful downers known as quaaludes, my tortured mind-set had shifted to the wrong side of the legal railroad tracks. With all of the drug misery I had witnessed first-hand, who would believe that I would make such a choice? But self-knowledge availed me nothing.

The pills at first seemed to help, energizing my alcohol-soaked body and dormant brain cells. I sensed that I was making a grave error when I started popping mostly speed pills. I have a vivid mental picture of this happening, from law-abiding citizen to drug criminal procuring illegal dope from a combination drug lab and chop shop near my home in Bulverde. The drug lab was producing high-grade methamphetamine. In the chop shop, skilled welders and body men were dismantling stolen cars and trucks for parts that would be sold. Anchored in my memory is a scene from those days that makes no more sense than the insanity I was exhibiting.

I was sitting on a cedar stump outside the lab/chop shop, drinking straight I. W. Harper Bourbon from a bottle, snorting uncut meth from a pocket mirror, and fervently asking God to make me a better person. I was in the transition period from drugs and alcohol to straight drugs, ranging from pills to powdered poison such as cocaine and then methamphetamine. While my denial process kept me from ever joining those despicable knights of the hollow sword, I had no moral boundaries when it came to breaking ounces of meth down to eighths and grams for sale to friends and close associates.

The term "drug dealer" has a disgusting connotation because it is a disgusting practice, and I had no excuse even though my sole intent was to cover the cost of my own insatiable needs. Poor boys with two-hundred-dollar daily drug habits have few choices. It was an accepted truism in the drug world I was entering: It was either deal or steal, and I knew I could never cut it as a cat burglar.

The morning after my firing at the *Express-News*, I knew that I had to quit drinking alcohol or die. I was soon to quit drinking. My musician friend said it for the both of us. We thought coke would be the answer to our drinking problem. It was not, of course, and the irony of it was that I would eventually find salvation in a God-based recovery program known worldwide. But not before I was near death and on the doorstep of the state penitentiary.

My years in full-blown drug addiction were the blackest, most-humiliating, and soul-smashing times of my life. I was destroying my career; my marriage to Vicky, who never did anything to deserve the humiliation and neglect she got from me; my children's right to a father they might be proud of; and what fell just short of my freedom to walk on Texas soil without chain shackles on my ankles and steel cuffs on my wrists.

My first and last arrests on felony drug charges made headlines in both San Antonio newspapers. The *San Antonio Express*, the newspaper for which I once wrote a daily column and garnered a Pulitzer nomination for excellence in breaking news coverage, ran my drug busts on the metro section front page. The rival *San Antonio Light* delivered a page-one gut punch after one of the drug busts that I felt certain was designed to deprive me of little reason to keep on living in the San Antonio area.

Accompanying that article was a photograph of me in a circuit-riding preacher attire that I had worn in the filming of a failed comedy titled *The Adventures of Jody Shannon*. My role in the movie, which never made it past the cutting-room floor, was that of Preacher Sam, a hypocritical whiskey-drinking, dice-shooting, whore-chasing minister who rode a jughead mule. The old movie promo shot featured me in flat-brim hat, arms raised in facetious supplication to a deity that didn't exist in a heaven of acrimonious scorn for Junction hicks who dared, and failed, to hack it on the big-city stage.

When that unholy scene assaulted my senses from the front page of the *San Antonio Light*, my reaction was short and unforgettable: a sense of indescribable pain and the emptiness of total loss. I have never found words to adequately recreate this awful portrait of self-doom. And I have never understood what kept this godawful image from striking me dead in my tracks. I remember saying the first real prayer that ever escaped my lips: "God help me. Lord, please help me."

Preacher Sam praying to the heavens. The son of a deeply religious mother knew the part inside out.

Before I discovered cocaine and the meth trade, I purchased my dope from two renegade ex-physicians, Steven Pollock and Ted Norris. Pollock grew psilocybin mushrooms and sold them from his north San Antonio home. He died late one night when burglars ransacked his home and shot him between the eyes. There were two strong suspects, but no one was ever convicted of the crime.

Ted Norris would write prescriptions for any drug his customers ordered. When I told him I wanted one hundred Preludin pills, he wrote the prescription, then asked me how well the super speed worked. "I've never tried those," he told me. "Save me a pill from your prescription. I might get a script of my own."

I graduated from pills to powdered cocaine and methamphetamine with someone offering me a line of coke that had been chopped with a razor blade and arranged on a pocket mirror. As was customary in the drug world I was entering, I snorted the line of cocaine with a tightly rolled dollar bill, eschewing any thought of shooting cocaine and later methamphetamine with a hypodermic needle, a practice known as "running the dope," and a drug culture habit that brought with it the filthy, debilitating term that all proper society has come to loathe: "junkie."

I was no damn junkie, I told myself. I was a snorter and not a shooter, a user and not an abuser, even though I was inhaling near the end of my drug addiction career (snorting) in powdered form enough high-grade methamphetamine to kill a moose. The high cost of cocaine soon drove me to the less-expensive but equally damaging man-made killer known on the streets as "meth." And snorting large quantities of cocaine had resulted in geyser-like nose bleeds that progressed to my filling a handkerchief with pieces of nasal tissue I called "coke meat." Strangely enough, the meth that threatened to wreck my brain had little noticeable effect on my sinus passages. It just burned like hell. By this time, I was escalating my withdrawal from the human race.

There are 3.5 grams in an eighth of an ounce of powdered drug, known on the streets as an eight-ball, and I was consuming almost an eighth of an ounce of meth every two days and sometimes daily when my drug world ended in handcuffs and total demoralization. Harlon Copeland was the Bexar County sheriff when I was first arrested and jailed on aggravated possession of methamphetamine charges. A conviction on this charge could result in a prison sentence of from ten to ninety-nine years. My office was in a strip center on San Antonio's Wurzbach Road. Just across the street was a topless club known as Baby Dolls.

Sheriff Copeland and his troops hit my office late one morning. The memory of that drug bust is still a surreal media circus that included reporters from what seemed like every TV and radio station in San Antonio. To spice up the morning show was a gaggle of titty-bar dancers who drifted over from Baby Dolls.

After deputies came crashing through my office door, Sheriff Copeland appeared in person to oversee all details of what he obviously viewed as a prestigious feather in the cap of Bexar County law enforcement. Copeland kept me handcuffed for almost two hours as two of his deputies called what seemed like every TV and radio station in Texas, plus both the *San Antonio Express-News* and the *San Antonio Light*.

"You have written some really bad things about the sheriff's department for a number of years," Copeland reminded me. "But we have got you now." As his deputies wound up their telephone calls to local media, Copeland stood in front of a large wall mirror I had in my office. When he had his hair combed to satisfaction, the sheriff turned to me and said, "Well, Sam, it's time for us to go meet the press."

The parking lot was filled with reporters and camera crews, many of whom I knew personally. My mood was worse than foul. A WOAI TV cameraman shoved a microphone in my face and really let me have it. "You are live on Channel 4," he said. "What do you have to say?"

It came out before my brain really registered. "Fuck Harlon Copeland," I said. The cameraman recoiled as if from some horrible odor. I don't know what he said to his live audience. I felt as though I was being regarded with less appeal than a turd roller beetle.

"Enough of that," Copeland said. "Now you are going to jail." The sheriff escorted me to his personal car. One of his deputies drove while Copeland and I occupied the back seat. I was handcuffed. "How do you feel now?" the sheriff asked.

I recall my answer as if it were yesterday. "I feel like jumping into a big dark hole and dragging you right in behind me." This evoked a short laugh.

After that, and as we completed the ride to jail and a booking procedure, Copeland was almost jovial. He told me that he felt sure I would have a good lawyer. He did everything but wish me well. The circus was over. Copeland got what he wanted. As I was unloaded at the jail, I will swear that Harlon Copeland gave my shoulder a reassuring squeeze. I never knew what he was thinking.

It is hard to believe, but I escaped from this arrest with a ten-year probated sentence, thanks to high-powered attorney friends like Alan Brown and A. L. Hernden. Less than a year went by before I was busted again on felony drug charges, this time in *Action Magazine* offices I occupied on the main street of Castle Hills. There was no fanfare or media hoopla with this bust. It came at night by members of the Alamo Area Narcotics Task Force, headed by New Braunfels Sheriff Department officer Sumner Bowen.

This arrest, I was convinced, would be the end of my life in the free world. My ten-year probated sentence from the Copeland arrest would be revoked, I was almost positive. Sumner Bowen also knew the stakes I was facing when he offered me the chance to turn informant. I will never forget the soul torture generated by the option Bowen offered.

The narcotics cop was folksy and congenial when he laid out his pitch. The other officers had left the room. I sat handcuffed with Bowen on another chair directly in front of me. I will never forget what transpired next. Bowen's words were seared into my consciousness like the Ten Commandments Moses received from God. "I have been reading you for years," Bowen said. "And I have been a fan of yours for years. I don't know how you got tangled up with people in the dope world, but I do know one thing. None of those people would do anything to help you. They would never get down for you when it counted. I think it's about time you got down for yourself. And that is exactly what I am prepared to offer, a chance for you to do something for yourself."

I knew what was coming next. It was like my mind and body were encased in a steel coffin that I couldn't open. I had been around the criminal element long enough to know what happens to the informants known as "snitches." Some die violent deaths; some don't. Nothing is lower than a scumbag who will send another man to prison just to save his own ass.

"You have a choice here tonight," Sumner Bowen said. "You can go to jail and then on to prison with your record, which you will never be able to escape, or we can go down to Maggie's for breakfast and coffee, and then you will be free to go on about your life." Bowen paused long and hard before he said it: "Just give me the name of the person with the lab."

He wanted me to give up the individual who manufactured the drugs found in my office. The so-called lab was a small mom-and-pop operation when compared with most meth mills, but it was big enough to warrant the trade-out Bowen was offering. Strange as it may seem, the image and words of Willie Nelson drummer Paul English were flashing before my eyes and playing through my mind. Paul was a Fort Worth gangster before he straightened out and joined the Nelson band. He was what they called a "police character" in that day and time. "The cops didn't name us police characters," Paul told me. "We named ourselves characters because we had character. We never ratted on our fellow man."

I wondered about my own sanity when I rejected Bowen's offer. "I can't do it," I said. "You can take me on to jail." I was loaded into an unmarked police car when Sumner Bowen leaned in an open window to say: "I think you are nuts, but I respect your position."

I have thought long and hard about my decision that night. What would have happened had I given up the couple who manufactured the meth in their country chop shop? Would it have been as Bowen promised? Would I have been free to go after a cup of coffee?

I think I turned down the snitch offer more out of raw fear than any sense of nobility. I had a sick feeling in my gut when I entered the unmarked sheriff car for the ride to jail. I had been around the criminal element long enough to know the fate of many informants. I didn't want to spend the rest of my life looking over my shoulder and listening for footsteps, either real or imagined. And for whatever reason, I am glad today that I didn't snitch.

18

THE MIRACLE OF 144TH DISTRICT COURT

The sun was shining and the birds were singing as I rode my bicycle on that bright spring morning near my Bulverde home. A year had passed since my last drug bust at the hands of Sumner Bowen and the Alamo Area Drug Task Force, and I had been sober and drug-free for an entire year after joining a popular God-based recovery program. I had violated a ten-year probated sentence for drug possession with that final arrest, and a probation revocation and sentencing hearing would be the inevitable end to my freedom. I had posted bond, and there was nothing more to do but wait.

Days turned into weeks and weeks turned into months as I waited to hear from the court system. Nothing happened as I attended daily meetings in the recovery program. I had heard nothing from my lawyer, and I told myself that I might be off the hook. Maybe my case just slipped through a crack in the legal apparatus. Apprehension turned into relief, and I had all but forgotten about the case when an unmarked sheriff's car pulled my bicycle over in front of the Honey Creek Grocery Store at the intersection of Texas Highway 46 and Blanco Road.

I was arrested by deputies from the drug task force. My probation had been revoked, and I was headed for jail to await a sentencing hearing before 144th District Court judge Susan D. Reed, the toughest and most uncompromising jurist in the system when it came to drug cases. I was going before the "Hanging Judge," as Reed was known to the criminal element. For some still unexplainable reason, my paperwork had been mislaid until it landed on Reed's court docket.

The Honey Creek Grocery no longer exists. It was a one-woman enterprise, owned and operated at the time of the arrest by my friend Mary Lou (Kelly) Gibson. Kelly and her friend Marcie Snyder were on the grocery front porch as I was being handcuffed. I recall Kelly wringing her hands in consternation. Kelly and Marcie agreed to take charge of my bicycle since I was headed for jail with no bond in the offing. I gave them a phone number for my son Grady. I also asked them to notify my Bulverde friend Sam Lowrey.

When we reached the Bexar County Jail, my incarceration education was to begin. I was first placed in a holding cell to await fingerprinting and other processing procedures. There was one other prisoner in the little cell, a middle-aged Hispanic inmate who must have weighed three hundred pounds. Restroom facilities consisted of a sink and one barren commode sitting in the middle of the room. I have never forgotten my horrendous introduction to captivity. The big boy was on the thunder mug, emptying his bowels with grunts and groans befitting a dying hippopotamus, and the gaseous stench from that monster shit filled that little holding cell like a Nazi gas chamber.

The prayer I uttered was simple and heartfelt: "Oh Lord, get me out of here and I swear I will never do another drug or take another drink of alcohol for the rest of my life."

Everything seemed surreal as I was to spend the better part of a month behind bars. I was being hand-searched every time I turned around. Damn it to hell. I was wearing an orange monkey suit, and nobody gave a damn about my college degree and Pulitzer nomination. My smart mouth was no asset, and I soon learned the hard way to keep it shut.

The guard searching my person ran his hand too near my privates for my liking. "I reckon you might be having fun doing that," I smarted off. The guard brought his fist into my crotch with sufficient force to take away my breath and any notion I might have had for further wise-ass comment. It was an old-fashioned nut cracking worth remembering.

Welcome to the Bexar County Jail, Mr. newspaper columnist. Social stratification has always been alive and well in the jail. It is a sort of caste system determined by the inmates. When I was jailed in the 1970s, the Texas prisons were overcrowded and many inmates were allowed to serve their prison sentences in county lockups. Hispanics were in the majority, followed by blacks, and then the whites like me who were the third largest in number.

I was one of the oldest of jail inmates at the time, and good fortune or maybe providence from the get-go provided me with a jailhouse angel known by one and all as the "Wizard." He was a career Hispanic burglar whose Christian designation was Danny, but everyone in the jail referred to him simply as Wizard. And he looked like a wizard with sharply chiseled features and pointed goatee. Since I was one of the oldest inmates on the cell block, Wizard christened me "Pops" and the appellation stuck. In jail jargon, Wizard was known as a "house man." He had been in and out of jails and prisons for most of his adult life of thirty-five-plus years, and he could get just about any substance delivered to his cell.

Discrimination was rampant in the Bexar County Jail in the 1970s. *Mayate* is the "N-word" in Spanish, and Wizard was the first person I ever heard use it. My jailhouse indoctrination came from a concerned Wizard who took it upon himself to give me all the protection at his command.

Nodding toward a group of black inmates (they usually stayed grouped together when possible), Wizard said, "Pops, you need to know a few things if you are going to survive in here. Shit happens sometimes, and you need to be on the right side. It happens between the Chicanos and the *mayates*. You are a gringo and you white boys are the minority in jail. When the bad shit goes down, you need to be with us Mexicans. Not with the *mayates*. We always win because there are more of us."

Conversely to the Wizard's warning, my other good jail friend was a big black guy named Frank. Before the Wizard helped me get commissary money in my jail account, Frank generously shared his much-coveted Bugler tobacco and rolling papers with me. A murder-one parolee, Frank's parole had been compromised simply because Frank had failed to report in person to his parole officer.

"Damn it, Frank," I said. "How in hell could you fail to report when it meant you would go back to prison?"

Frank's answer was almost typical of the jailbird whose apathy probably stems from a life with little hope or meaning. "Hell, I didn't go and report because I just didn't feel like it," Frank said. "I was out on the East Side frying me some bacon and eggs that morning I was supposed to report, and I just didn't go in."

Early on in my incarceration, Frank and I shared a cell, me on the top bunk and Frank on the bottom. I had heard scary tales of sodomy and gang rapes in the Texas prison system. I was nervous and on edge my first night in jail. All prisoners had been racked up in their bunks when I called down to Frank in a loud whisper. I was jittery at this point. I was trying to keep things light and in what I hoped would sound like a joking vein when I said, "Hey Frank, you awake?"

"Yeah, what do you want?" Frank sounded like he was half asleep when I voiced my concerns of the night.

"I'm old and tough, and I would really be an awful piece of ass for anybody who might want to try," I said.

Frank's voice was loud enough to be heard all over the cell block. "Goddamn it, Pops, will you shut the fuck up and go to sleep. There's some of us in here trying to get some rest."

The jail had pay phones when I was locked up, and when Wizard's wife, Rose, called, he would put me on the line for one of Rose's encouraging pep talks. I can all but hear her today. "Everything is gonna be fine, Pops. You and Wizard will be out before you know it. I'm here keeping the home fire going. We will have us a big party at our house. Don't you fret about it. TDC [Texas Department of Corrections] will be smoother than county, so keep your chin up."

The sobriety program that basically saved my life puts belief in a higher power before self-reliance, and I was intrigued when I saw the Wizard on his knees by his bunk making the sign of the cross.

"What are you doing?" I asked him.

"Praying," he said.

"Praying for what?"

"I'm praying to God for help doing my time."

The Wizard explained that prayer and a positive attitude were all I needed. "Look, Pops," he said. "You are looking at a ten-year sentence. With good behavior, you might do eighteen months, maybe three years at the most. You can stand on your head and spear grapes with your tongue for eighteen months. Time is just time. God will help you do it."

The thought popped into my head and I verbalized it to the Wizard. I asked him if he had ever considered asking God to remove the compulsion to burglarize houses.

"Shit no," he said. "That's what I do for a living."

That's when the realization hit me. I didn't want to do prison time, with or without God's help. And there I was, all but standing in the shadow of the state penitentiary. I felt like the late Billy Joe Shaver's "Georgia on a Fast Train" lyrics: "I got a good Christian raisin' and an eighth-grade education, ain't no need in y'all treatin' me this way."

It seemed like an eternity before the day arrived for my sentencing hearing in Judge Reed's court. I was in leg irons and my orange inmate jumpsuit when a county van transported me from the jail to the courthouse for the 9:00 a.m. hearing. The only visitor I had during my incarceration had been my oldest son, Grady, who had picked up where the Wizard left off in supplying me with commissary money for tobacco and soap. Regular jail-issue bath soap was like the cheap, scentless little slivers prevalent in flop-house motels of that day. With commissary money supplied by my son, I was able to purchase real and wonderfully strong-scented Irish Spring bath soap. I have Irish Spring in my bathroom today, an everlasting reminder of where I came from.

When the court bailiff called my case, reality sounded in my brain like a death knell. I knew this was it. I was going to state prison for ten years. My little *Action Magazine* would be no more. Could I survive in the prison population? I didn't snitch when Sumner Bowen made his offer. If I got shanked to death, then I would get shanked to death. By God, I would not bend over and grab my ankles. My head was processing horror scenario after horror scenario, when the judge asked if the defense had any witnesses to present.

This hit me like a hidden land mine. I didn't even know that favorable testimony from character witnesses might be possible, that such testimony could even mitigate the severity of a court sentence. My lawyer friend Alan Brown was with me that morning, working pro bono and as surprised as everyone else when the first wave of volunteer witnesses started coming through the courtroom door. I later asked Brown why he hadn't mentioned character witnesses to me, and his answer was, "I was positive it would do no good. Susan Reed had never ruled for a multiple bond violator on drug charges. It just didn't happen with her."

My volunteer surprise character witnesses were entering the courtroom when Susan Reed issued her call for witnesses we might want to present. My first witness was writer friend Joseph Harmes, another member of the recovery group I was in. I was to later learn that Harmes had mounted a telephone campaign through most of the night, rallying other potential witnesses from our substance-abuse group who, as it turned out, were willing and even eager to help. They were all ready to testify that I had been sober for a year and that I was ready to turn my life around.

I never knew the name of the diminutive prosecutor the district attorney's office assigned to my case. He was short, balding, and snotty as hell, a bantam rooster with a sarcastic leer that looked like it had been stitched onto his mouth with fishing line. The hateful gash all but dripped with vitriol.

I recognized most of my witnesses as they entered the courtroom. My lawyer knew none of them. The courtroom was filling fast as other lawyers and a couple of curious judges joined the audience. The Sam Kindrick Circus was free of charge.

"Who should I call?" Brown asked me.

"Joseph Harmes," I whispered.

When Harmes settled into the witness chair, it was plain that the bantam rooster was in attack mode and ready to denigrate any witness we might call. "What might I ask do you do for a living, Mr. Harmes?"

"I am a writer," Joseph answered.

This evoked a veritable cackle from the prosecutor. It was almost a hoot of joy. "A writer, eh. And would you tell this court, Mr. Harmes, exactly who you write for and where this so-called writing appears."

Joseph has always had a poker face. And he didn't move a facial muscle when he answered the prosecutor. "Yes, sir, *People Magazine*."

The rooster was incredulous. He was sneering openly. "Are you telling this court, Mr. Harmes, that you write for the national publication *People Magazine*?"

"I do write for *People*," Joseph answered. You can verify that by checking the magazine masthead. My name is in it."

There was a collective gasp from the gallery, and then the courtroom fell silent as an Egyptian tomb.

"Next witness."

Next came my friend Peter, another recovered alcoholic who, even at that time, was an accomplished upper-echelon corporate attorney in the San Antonio and Bexar County legal system. Reed's jaw seemed to drop when she recognized Peter. "Don't you practice law, and haven't you worked in this court?" Reed asked the witness. "And are you telling the court that you are another of these alcoholics?"

"I am a recovering alcoholic," Peter said, "and I am here to offer testimony which I hope can help this defendant."

"Next witness."

Then came Steve, a broker with the Dean Witter stock brokerage. Following Steve was Roger, owner of two high-end Mexican restaurants. The witness after Roger was owner of San Antonio's largest ambulance and medical supply company.

If we had been given a month to assemble character witnesses, we could never have gathered a group of people with the honest and obvious quality to match this bunch of recovering drunks and dopers. More potential witnesses were filing through the courtroom door when Judge Reed called a stop to the proceedings. With both hands extended toward the audience, witnesses, and lawyers, Reed said, "We will stop all proceedings here. I have heard enough."

The judge then shocked everyone concerned when she said, "I will take this case under advisement and make a final ruling one week from today." She then recessed the court, and the rest is history. She put me back on another ten years of probation, and I was free to go. There was no community service that I knew anything about, but Reed did have me report monthly to the adult probation department for urine samples over what turned out to be seven years.

There were some who believed a benevolent spirit of unknown origin entered Susan Reed's body that morning, prompting her to cut me loose. My friend Madonna, who worked in the court system and knew Judge Reed personally, said, "I don't know who that judge was who set you free after three probation violations, but I do know it wasn't Susan Reed." Others attributed my third probated sentence to a stroke of raw luck. I have always been prone to agree with those who called my stunning release the "Miracle of 144th District Court." It was an act of God, and I have always known it. I have since marveled that the Spirit of the Universe would favor me in such dramatic fashion.

I think it must have been in about 1970 when my friend Mike Sfair barred me from the Commander's Room. Fast-forward this narrative to April 1998. It was late one foggy and misty night. I had been alcohol- and drug-free for nine years, and I was out delivering copies of *Action Maga-*

zine to nightclubs when I approached the club on San Antonio's West Avenue that I had always avoided. The little neon sign read Sfair's Cocktails.

Brothers Mike and George Sfair were long divorced from their big, booming Commander's Room in San Antonio's downtown. They were eking out a modest living in this little bar. Visibility was poor that night, but I had no trouble identifying the man out front. It was Mike, leaning against a street lamp pole and smoking a cigarette. I hadn't seen him in over thirty years, but here he was, looking older and gaunt but unmistakable.

I drove slowly by Sfair's that night, my head seized by both disbelief and fear. Two days before Mike barred me from the Commander's so many years ago, I had borrowed two hundred dollars to pay off a football gambling debt. Hurt, angry, and ashamed, I made no attempt to pay back the money. The months turned into years, and I reasoned that Mike would probably have me arrested or thrown out of his club if I ever approached him.

Yet I never forgot the debt I owed. I drove slowly by Mike on that eventful night. The truck crept on for another couple of blocks before it started turning around, seemingly by its own volition. I drove back and dug two hundred dollars out of my wallet, more money than I usually carried, but I had it on me that night for whatever reason.

"Remember me?" I asked Mike.

"I would never forget," he said.

I handed him two one-hundred dollar bills. He held the money for a few seconds, then reached out and jammed them into my shirt pocket. I tried to push the money into his hand. He would not take it. "Money is not important," he said. "What is important is that you came back." We both cried that night. We hugged in the mist with a street lamp being the only witness to our reunion.

It was only a couple of weeks before I spotted Mike's obituary in the morning paper. He died of natural causes. I know in my heart that God kept him around just long enough for me to make my amends and for us to rekindle our friendship. Mike Sfair is buried at Fort Sam Houston National Cemetery, San Antonio, Bexar County, Texas USA, Plot Section CE Site 48.

19

MADAM THERESA BROWN

She was foxy, plucky, irreverent, and dressed to the nines, a working girl who would become both famous and infamous in the city of San Antonio. Some even called her beautiful. This was my friend Madam Theresa Brown. On the day we met, I was a cub reporter for the *San Antonio Express-News*, and she was getting her brothel business recognized and well-known. It was in the early 1960s.

We were in Phil Sfair's Navy Club on Pecan Street, one of the most popular of San Antonio's after-hours emporiums. It was frequented then by judges, lawyers, media people, and sports figures. I had asked the bartender about the looker chick on the barstool a few stools down from me.

"Theresa Brown," the bartender said.

I knew the name and the reputation. When I walked over to introduce myself, T-Brown (by her own eye-twinkling admission "the biggest whore in town"), turned to me with a knowing and mocking smile. "The newspaperman," she said. "I know who you are."

Maybe she thought I was hitting on her. And maybe I was, depending on the level of Jack Black I had in my system. It's hard to remember now. But I never forgot her words. "You can't afford me, newspaper boy. So don't even try. But I'm gonna buy you a drink. Maybe more than one. And you better not go back to that newspaper and write something about me."

T-Brown, as I always called her, and I sat right there and got shit-faced drunk together. I think she picked up the tab. She probably did for I had little spending money in those days. I can't recall all we discussed that evening and night. I do know we didn't leave there and jump into the sack, and I know that our Navy Club meeting was the beginning of a friendship that would endure for more than fifty years.

Theresa was right. I couldn't afford her. Little did we guess at the time that Theresa would help get me and golf great Lee Trevino kicked out of a popular San Antonio restaurant; or that T-Brown would someday run against a man she called one of her former whorehouse clients for a seat on the San Antonio City Council; or that Brown would terrorize the Bexar County Courthouse and political environs with a three-thousand-name trick list that she threatened to make public.

T-Brown was a rebel with a cause. A divorcée with two little boys to feed, she put her back to the snapping dogs of derision and faced the world of shame and disclaim like the tigress she was. She was tough as old gator leather in many ways. She called the manager of the Old San Francisco Steakhouse a motherfucker in a screaming imbroglio for the ages, but deep down inside was a sad little girl with a sweet and caring spirit that few got to witness. When my son Grady died, T-Brown was one of the first to offer love and comfort. And I was able to reciprocate when her son Cecil died in a one-car rollover. We both meant it from the bottom of our hearts when we expressed our mutual sorrow.

But her unique sense of humor was always there, an omnipotent threat to the sensibilities of the sanctimonious and the phony. Especially those good ol' politico boys who had trouble keeping their peckers in their britches.

As mentioned earlier, my World Championship Menudo Cookoff was about to kick off in Raymond Russell Park when Theresa was to make her grand entrance, arriving in a Winnebago with untrammeled fanfare and a huge sign that proclaimed "Hot Pants Menudo." Theresa didn't do this to cause me grief. I am convinced of that. It was just another part of the T-Brown justification crusade that was a loss she never fully accepted. She didn't want things to be the way they were; she wanted people to react to her in a positive way that could never be.

As the years rolled by, Theresa's notoriety increased exponentially. She was living in Kyle between San Marcos and Austin when she died in a San Antonio hospital of natural causes. We had maintained an email connection until shortly before her death on September 18, 2012. When the standard funeral home death notice reached the *Express-News* city desk, the editors didn't realize whose passing they were publicizing. Theresa merited only a short obit with her name listed as Theresa Brown Burquette and nothing about her sensational background. A young and beautiful photo of Theresa accompanied the printed copy. No cause of death was given, and the notice asked that all donations go to the San Antonio Battered Women's Shelter. The official obit did note that Theresa "will always be remembered for her adventurous nature and love of travel."

Once again, the *Express-News* city desk had blown it, opening the door for my full-blown Theresa Brown column in *Action Magazine*, identifying her as the notorious San Antonio madam who terrorized politicians and hobnobbed with sports stars and members of "the fourth estate." An *Express-News* staffer called me in a panic after the Brown column in *Action Magazine*.

Yes, I told the newspaper person. This was indeed the famed Theresa Brown, and, yes, I had been her longtime friend. The *San Antonio Express* then quoted me in a comprehensive obituary that covered the sensational and troubled life of San Antonio's Madam Theresa Brown. Here is part of that newspaper story:

> Theresa Brown, who has died at age 78, was a brothel madam from San Antonio, Texas, who caused palpitations in many American households after it was revealed that she had carefully maintained a catalogue of more than 3,000 men—politicians, sports stars, religious "pillars of the community," and at least one district judge—who had visited her establishment.
>
> The so-called "Trick List," whose existence was revealed after the FBI raided her bordello in 1980, was made even more combustible by the fact that, alongside the names, Theresa Brown had noted each man's sexual preferences and peccadillos. America's Establishment breathed a sigh of relief when the lawmen who had confiscated the list burned it, but agonies were later renewed when it transpired that Theresa Brown had kept a back-up.
>
> At some point after her arrest she was said to have given the list to a journalist working for a leftist local newspaper, but she later regretted doing so and won a temporary restraining order preventing the paper from publishing it. The paper, meanwhile, found itself

deluged with threats from husbands and phone calls from wives anxious to know if their husbands' names were on the list.

In February 1981 the chief district judge William Sessions [later director of the FBI] decided not to renew the order and the paper subsequently published the names of 19 of Theresa Brown's alleged "high and mighty" clients, whose sexual preferences, the paper claimed, were "too indecent to print."

Theresa Brown was subsequently sentenced to five years of probation, and in 1982 the remnants of her brothel, including a selection of clients' underwear and a circular bed bearing the legend "please remove your clothes" were sold off.

Theresa Brown never divulged the identities of other clients, though for years local and national newspapers continued to speculate about its contents. For many men, the possibility that the list might someday be published in full remained a Sword of Damocles hanging over their lives.

Theresa Brown was born in San Antonio in 1934. According to a later interview she had two children and worked as a bookkeeper and clerk before opening her brothel in the 1960s. "I was getting $50 a month for both kids, and we lived in a [housing estate] project," she explained. "I decided to better myself in the grand tradition of free enterprise."

In the ranks of such establishments, Theresa Brown's brothel operated to the highest standards—and prices were set accordingly. House rules banned her girls from wearing religious symbols or wedding rings during working hours and instructed them never to use drugs, to bathe daily, to keep the house clean and to wear shoes when clients were arriving or leaving. After her establishment was closed down, she ran a bric-a-brac store for a short time and also ran, unsuccessfully, for San Antonio City Council—against an alleged former client, Gene Canavan.

Canavan, of course, denied the allegation, but Theresa said Canavan was one of her tricks and I believed her. She also told me that District Judge Ted Butler was on the list, no big secret since the entire courthouse crowd knew of Judge Ted's affinity for Theresa's damsels of ill repute. But Theresa never publicly identified any of her johns. By court order in 1985, San Antonio police had torched the original list confiscated when they raided the bordello at 315 Northtrail Drive in San Antonio. The publication Theresa gave the backup trick list was a left-leaning west side tab called *El Pueblo.* The reporter who received the index card file of client names was one Amanda Saldivar, and it was Saldivar who passed the list on to *El Pueblo*'s editorial board.

I know Theresa never wanted the list published. When *El Pueblo* named nineteen of Brown's clients, Theresa flew into a rage. She didn't want the wives and the children hurt.

The tabloid called those clients "the high and mighty of San Antonio, who in the past have constantly accused the Blacks, the Mexicans, the poor and working people of being immoral, corrupt, and law breakers."

Represented by ace San Antonio attorney Pat Maloney, Theresa sought and was granted a temporary restraining order against the paper. Maloney told the Associated Press: "She is terribly, terribly worried about the families of these poor men. Theresa Brown is not a kiss-and-tell person. This is viciously and tragically unfair."

The backup list was eventually returned to Theresa. She promised to torch it, too, but nobody knows what happened to the list. In later years, I asked Brown why she didn't turn her list over to me. She fairly cackled: "I never thought of it at the time, but that's what I should have done. Wow. You wouldn't print the list, but you just having it would have been enough to scare the shit out of the entire world. Why didn't we think of it?"

That October 1980 was a wild and rollicking time in San Antonio history. Jack Hanratty was running his Castle Hills sports book, much to the chagrin of several DAs. And shotgun-toting Arthur Harry (Bunny) Eckert was blasting fellow pimps into eternity with his trusted sawed-off 12-gauge. What seemed like the eyes of the world were on Theresa Brown when vice cops came swooping down on her stylish whorehouse.

Theresa had a hand in getting me and golfing great Lee Trevino kicked out of the Old San Francisco Steakhouse. But the true villain in that little caper was notorious sports bookmaker Jack Hanratty, who took a perverse delight in walking bar and restaurant tabs, the bigger the bills the better. Golfing great Trevino was here for the Texas Open. Larry Trader, who had caddied for Lee the Flea, was there at the restaurant with me, bookie Hanratty, Theresa Brown, and a few others from the club scene. Trevino was an unrepentant Brown friend who visited Theresa on every San Antonio visit.

Famed San Antonio madam Theresa Brown was a celebrity entry in the World Championship Menudo Cookoff which featured Willie and many other musicians.

With an expansive wave of his hand, Hanratty ordered porterhouse steaks for our party, then excused himself for a break in the men's room. In predictable Hanratty fashion, Jack never returned, and when the maître d' tried to present Trevino the bill, Theresa blew a fuse, chastising the waitperson for bringing embarrassment to the "world's greatest golfer."

I didn't have any money, and "the world's greatest golfer" had left his in his hotel room. Jack Hanratty had disappeared, along with Larry Trader, and when security kicked us out of the restaurant, Theresa Brown left in a cab, probably with more money in her purse than the rest of us had combined. Trevino was on foot. I don't even know how he got to the restaurant. But I gave him a ride to his hotel, where he fished a roll of hundred-dollar bills from under a mattress. We returned to the restaurant, where Lee paid the bill.

I never learned exactly what caused Theresa's death. She told me by phone a year or so before her death that her health was failing. Quietly and without publicity or the usual fanfare, Theresa went quietly about her charitable avocation of helping disabled and underprivileged women.

Theresa and I exchanged Christmas cards until shortly before her passing. She had embraced Christianity several years after selling her bordello property and dropping off the local radar.

"I have Jesus Christ in my life," she said. And that was it. No more rhetoric on the subject. T-Brown was the real product. And I believe the same could have been said about Mary Magdalen. I will always harbor a corner of love and respect in my heart for Madam Theresa Brown.

20

BUNNY AND KID DEATH

I have known and written about all manner of characters over the years. One of the most notorious was Arthur Harry (Bunny) Eckert, the local pimp and pill head known for killing numerous other denizens of San Antonio's darker side of society. Bunny disappeared March 2, 1986, from the Eckert home on Overhill Drive in San Antonio. On that same night, someone killed Bunny's mother, Lela Mae Eckert. Bunny's body has never been located. His mother was found in the home with her throat cut. I think I know who killed Bunny and his mother, but no proof of either killing has ever been uncovered. I have heard the two killings were done by two men. The motive was bragging rights for Eckert's death.

Bunny is an underground legend now, reportedly sleeping with concrete boots in the darkest and deepest part of Canyon Lake in Comal County. Another story has Eckert's killers disposing of his body with acid.

I was writing for the *Express-News* when Eckert killed George Gabitch and Champ Carter, both gamblers well-known to San Antonio police. I also covered a court hearing for Eckert after he shotgunned to death two black soldiers in an East San Antonio nightclub called the Sat-El-Lite. They were PFC Steven Parker, twenty-five, and PFC Alonzo Williams, twenty-eight. Eckert was ostensibly defending the honor of a redheaded bartender named Judy Jones when he blasted the two hapless Sat-El-Lite Club victims.

I was in the courtroom for that hearing, and I distinctly recall the exchange between Judy Jones and the prosecuting attorney.

"You saw Bunny Eckert kill the two men," the prosecutor said to Judy Jones.

"Yes I did," replied Miss Jones.

"And then what did you say, Miss Jones? What did you say to Bunny Eckert?"

I never forgot her answer: "Wow, Bunny, you really got 'em!"

Renowned criminal lawyer Fred Semaan represented Bunny in these and numerous other killings, gaining acquittals or dismissals through a variety of nebulous legal defense ploys.

I heard that Eckert killed fourteen men, but I never got reliable statistics. The San Antonio Police Department Historical Society records have him down for more than fifty arrests and little jail time. In my first book, I have Bunny on record for seven arrests for unlawfully carrying a weapon, twenty-five for crap shooting, three for making threats, two assault to murder charges, six for possession of drugs, and a murder charge in the killing of gambler George Gabitch.

Testimony showed that Gabitch had been chasing Eckert around a house with a pistol when Bunny gained enough lead to grab his trusty shotgun from his parked car. The blunderbuss roared and George fell dead. I'm not sure, but I believe Eckert killed Champ Carter in a card game dispute. A district judge told me once that Eckert escaped murder convictions simply because most of the people he killed were so low on the social pole that nobody really cared.

Bunny left San Antonio to spend a couple of years in New Orleans, working gaming tables for mafia boss Carlos Marcello. He returned to San Antonio, where he got into the methamphetamine business, an occupation that netted him at least two prison sentences.

Eckert was born on February 14, 1933, Valentine's Day. When I noted in my daily newspaper column that Eckert was born on the anniversary of the St. Valentine's Day massacre in Chicago, Bunny called me at the *Express-News* city room to lodge his reasonable complaint. "Hey, man, what the hell is going on? My mother reads your column religiously, and neither of us can be blamed for me being born on the anniversary of the St. Valentine's Day massacre. Give me a break."

Eckert raced quarter horses, and his friends would attest to his loyalty and generosity. After being sentenced to federal prison a second time on drug charges, Eckert was allowed to check himself into La Tuna Federal Bureau of Prisons near El Paso after completing a series of medical procedures to remove his acne scars. He told the feds he would be prompt to start serving his sentence, and they granted him the extra time.

I wrote about it at the time, noting that Eckert said what he meant and meant what he said. I know he liked me. Knowing my penchant at the time for turquoise and silver jewelry, Bunny sent me a silver and turquoise belt buckle with a bear claw inlaid between the stones. I still have it. He had one of his working girls deliver the buckle.

Ron Houston was a top DJ on KTSA radio during most of Bunny Eckert's run as San Antonio's most notorious bad boy. Houston was an unapologetic friend of Eckert, and he remained Bunny's friend until Eckert's presumed murder. When Houston and I were working a morning-drive show on KEXL FM, Houston always dedicated a Willie Nelson or Charlie Daniels song to Bunny Eckert on Valentine's Day. Houston told me that Eckert had cleaned up his act and was devoting most of his time to the racehorses when he was killed.

The lineup of friends and less-than-ordinary characters who have crossed my journalistic radar seems endless upon reflection. They range from gamblers to preachers, from madams to lawyers, from outlaws to musicians, and they include other strange, frightening, and beautiful people.

I was fairly new to San Antonio when I met Al Juergens, a rugged boxer and self-taught acrobat who waged and won more fights in saloons than he did in the ring. My first encounter with Juergens was at San Antonio's old Five Points Cafe, a late-night and early-morning hangout for sports figures, newspaper people, and late-night drinkers. I was introduced to Juergens by Dan Cook, sports editor of the *San Antonio Evening News* at that time, and the three of us were sitting at a table when two cops entered the restaurant and ordered Juergens to stand up.

"It wasn't me," Al protested. "I have been right here sitting with these newspaper reporters, minding my own business and waiting for breakfast." I noticed that Juergens had skinned knuckles on his left hand, but none of us said anything to the cops. We learned later that someone had knocked a truck driver cold during an altercation in the parking lot. The police were all too familiar with Juergens.

The ring wars between Al Juergens and a double-tough Mexican fighter by the name of Santiago Gutierrez distinguished the colorful Juergens among other fighters. His major weapon was an explosive left hook that left most of his opponents down and senseless on the ring canvas. Juergens had curly black hair, thick eyebrows crisscrossed by scar tissue, and a nose that had been rearranged multiple times. Juergens had ropy arm and leg muscles and a rub board belly. The fighter displayed no discernible fear. He was a classic brawler who would take two punches to land one of his own, and I don't think Juergens was ever knocked out in the ring.

No matter how the fight ended, whether a knockout or referee decision, Al Juergens performed his signature back flip in the center of the ring, followed by a simulated "bird" for his many detractors. Juergens couldn't flip the finger with boxing gloves on both hands, but he got the message across by jamming one fist high into the air with vigorous pumping motions that were painfully unmistakable. Fuck you, and you, and you, and you . . . while the boos were all but deafening.

In San Antonio, most of the fighters were Mexican Americans, and the vast majority of fight fans who attended the boxing matches in San Antonio's old Municipal Auditorium were Hispanics. They didn't like Al Juergens, and the acrimony was mutual. Al didn't like his brown-skinned opponents.

A natural welterweight, Al was fighting out of his weight class in his battles with the larger Gutierrez, a true middleweight. There were no more Texas welterweight-class fighters left that Juergens hadn't already whipped. Juergens and the larger Gutierrez had several fights, the number I cannot recall. Juergens may have won one of them. I know they fought to a draw at least once. But Gutierrez won more of the battles on points. Neither Al Juergens nor Santiago Gutierrez ever scored a knockout over the other. They literally fought to a bloody standstill every time.

Just days before the first time I ever saw Juergens in the ring, I can distinctly remember the newspaper headline: "Fighter Jailed for Theft of Vitamin Pills." Al had dropped a bottle of vitamin pills into his coat pocket while visiting the Walgreens on Houston Street. A store clerk summoned a beat policeman, who promptly arrested the fighter. Juergens posted bond after a petty theft charge that was eventually dismissed when Al successfully argued that he had innocently dropped the pill bottle into his pocket. Al said he had other merchandise in his arms at the time and simply forgot the pills in his pocket when he was checking out. The judge believed him, and the theft charges were dropped, but not before the newspaper headlines broke the day before Juergens was to fight at the auditorium.

This was the first time I ever saw Al fight. I don't recall the name of his Mexican American opponent, but I remember Juergens winning by a knockout. I attended the fight with sports editor Dan Cook, and what I remember with clarity was the crowd chanting something in unison I couldn't understand.

"What are they saying?" I yelled at Cook.

The chant was a roar. "They are saying vitamin, vitamin, vitamin," Cook said.

Those San Antonio fight crowds loved to hate Al Juergens, and he wasn't about to disappoint them. After what I always referred to as the vitamin fight, Juergens performed his customary back flip in the center of the ring and then shot his boxing glove "bird" to the derisive crowd. I was both amazed and impressed, and I watched every San Antonio fight Al Juergens had from that day forward. That nobody ever killed him remains a mystery to this day.

For reasons known only to him, Al Juergens moved from San Antonio to Belleville, Illinois, and it was years later before I was to hear from him again. I was working an air shift on KEXL FM radio when—out of the blue—Juergens called from Illinois on the telephone. He was excited.

"Man, am I glad that I found you," he said. "I am coming back to San Antonio with my new invention that is going to make us both million-aires. I will have it with me the next time I see you. Believe it or not, but I have invented a device that will enable a gasoline engine car to run on water. I know it sounds crazy but it works. I thought of you when I came up with the invention. You can help me promote it. A water-powered car. We are going to get rich."

That was the last time I heard a word from Juergens. And I never saw him again.

I always wondered if perhaps Santiago Gutierrez might have hit Al in the head one time too many. I have hoped not. Those back flips and boxing glove "birds" are among my most cherished memories. Vitamin, vitamin, vitamin . . . There was only one Al Juergens.

Unlike Al Juergens, Bobby (Kid Death) Thomas was no skilled ring warrior, but he was a seemingly indestructible character whose relatively brief and spotty boxing ring career followed survival episodes that included second- and third-degree burns over 65 percent of his body in a drag racing fuel explosion; broken neck, and both arms, and one leg in a fall from a second-story roof that bordered a sixty-foot canyon; and a point-blank .357 Magnum gunshot to the gut that resulted in surgeons removing part of his pancreas, spleen, and all of one lung.

I was there for most of it. Bobby was my friend. He always called me "Sambo." Bobby was a drag car builder and racer in his younger days, but he can best be defined as an unrepentant scam artist with a vivid imagination. When I first encountered Bobby Thomas, he was selling what he purported to be baby polar bear skins. The juvenile "polar bear" hides, priced at two hundred dollars apiece, were the size of sheepskins because that is exactly what they were. Bobby was hawking them in San Antonio nightclub parking lots. I don't know where he got the sheepskins.

Thomas discovered that he could run an ordinary sheepskin through the neighborhood laundromat's deep-cleansing and high-temperature drying processes with amazing results. The lanolin-free sheep hides came out as snow-white and fluffy as any baby bear that ever came frolicking out of the land of the midnight sun. I don't know how many of the bogus bear hides Bobby managed to sell. He wouldn't say when I asked him about it.

The patchwork of burn scars visible on Thomas's arms and neck did little to detract from his movie star looks. He looked good even when he lay half dead on a hospital gurney. Bobby's older brother Roy recalled the nitromethane explosion that left the younger Thomas minus one ear and with burns over 65 percent of his body. Roy and Bobby were operating a drag race shop at the time—Thomas Brothers Perfection Enterprises on San Antonio's Basse Road—but the racing fuel mishap happened in their mother's front yard. The can with highly sensitive nitromethane got bumped and up it blew.

"Bobby saw it coming," Roy told me. "He stepped in to shield two of our little nieces at the time. They were four and five years old. The kids were unhurt, but Bobby was engulfed in flames. One of his ears was burned completely off."

The fire was before I met Bobby Thomas, but I knew him well when he fell from a huge two-story roof and to the bottom of a sixty-foot canyon in the Bulverde area where we both lived at the time. I was never sure whether Bobby was leasing the house or using it with permission of the owner. I do know that he was repairing wind damage on the roof when it started raining, causing him to slip on the wet aluminum roof and plunge from the house top to the canyon floor far below. After a relatively short hospital stay, Thomas was released with a metal hoop contraption bolted to his vertebrae and completely encircling his head. He looked like a *Star Wars* nightmare. I saw the doctor's official report. Bobby suffered a fractured neck, fractured right wrist, fractured left elbow, fractured right knee, and two broken ribs.Bobby's entrance into the world of professional boxing came through trainer and boxing manager Tony Ayala. The father of an entire stable of fighters that included world featherweight contender Mike Ayala, Sammy Ayala, and Tony Ayala (Little Tony) Jr., Big Tony, as he was known, took a fancy to Bobby Thomas. The elder Ayala took Thomas into his stable of fighters, carefully selecting opponents he knew Bobby could beat.

"It wasn't that Bobby had great potential as a fighter," Tony Jr. told me. "The old man liked him because he was tough, more than a little bit crazy, and an Anglo who could expand on the Ayala Mexican family fan base."

Big Tony could pick the undercard opponents for an Ayala fight until Mike Ayala landed a world title fight with featherweight world champion Danny (Little Red) Lopez, one of the greatest boxers to hold the world title in that weight division. Bobby wanted to fight on the undercard against Dennis Haggerty, a fighter from the Lopez camp. Big Tony was against it. He knew nothing about Haggerty but suspected he might be formidable as he was part of the Danny Lopez package. Bobby all but begged Ayala to put him on the card, a decision Big Tony finally made with much trepidation.

I was there for the title fight. It was April 10, 1979, and the old Hemis-Fair Arena was packed to the scuppers for what *Ring Magazine* later dubbed one of the greatest fights of all time. Mike Ayala put up a fight for the ages, falling in the fifteenth round to a thunderous Lopez knockout right. When Mike finally hit the canvas, most of the undercard had been forgotten, including Dennis Haggerty's defeat of Bobby Thomas, a knockout after forty-five seconds of the first round that left Bobby with a broken jaw. I asked Bobby about the ignominious knockout, and his answer was vintage Thomas: "It was no knockout, Sambo. I have never been knocked out. Knocked stupid but never out."

The younger Ayala, Tony Jr., had world title attributes, but it was not to be. He served prison time in New Jersey for raping a schoolteacher and later died in San Antonio from an overdose of heroin.

Bobby Thomas was to appear on a few more Ayala fight undercards, but the fistic fiasco that was to garner the most attention unfolded in a circus tent, where actor Guich Koock hosted what he called the Luckenbach World's Fair at Fredericksburg on the fairgrounds. This was a follow-up to the original Luckenbach World's Fair hatched by Koock and Hondo Crouch, who were originally co-owners of Luckenbach.

Entertainment for the Fredericksburg outing included a motorcycle daredevil who called himself Even Steven and what was to become known as the "Great World's Fight," a dubious appellation I hung on a contest of brainless brawn between Bobby Thomas and martial arts participant and instructor Johnny Hernandez. There was bad blood between Thomas and Hernandez from the outset, probably the result of some long-forgotten barroom imbroglio. It was during the buildup for the Great World's Fight that Bobby crowned himself "Kid Death," a misnomer if there ever was one. "Sambo," Thomas told me before the opening bell, "you are getting ready to see Kid Death kill a big Mexican."

Nobody killed anybody, and the nearest we got to the great beyond under that circus tent was from spectators who all but laughed themselves to death before the Great World's Fight came to a merciful end. It was billed as a battle to the end, when one of the fighters was unable to continue. The referee was Jimmy Parks, an attorney and onetime amateur boxer whose sole duty was declaring a winner.

Hernandez, who outweighed Thomas by a good fifty pounds, showed up with his fists heavily taped and with objects of unknown identity under the tape. Thomas was wearing weird-looking work gloves that bulged with what we were to later learn was a form of powdered lead. Thomas and Hernandez flailed away, neither landing a decent punch. Bobby couldn't keep up his guard, probably because his lead-weighted gloves were too heavy for him to hold up. The heavier Hernandez finally prevailed when the self-anointed Kid Death could no longer muster enough wind to stand upright on his feet. Referee Parks called it for Hernandez.

Bobby's response to this one was predictable. "Sambo, this one will be finally decided when I catch him on the street."

The caper that almost cost Bobby Thomas his life came outside a San Antonio discotheque known as Sugar Daddy's. Trouble had been brewing for some time between Thomas and Ernie Hoessley, owner of Sugar Daddy's and other nightclub establishments. I don't recall Bobby's take on the beef, but my friend Joe Cardenas said Thomas had threatened Hoessley in some sort of protection racket attempt.

Bobby took a .357 Magnum slug to his gut while approaching the front door of the nightclub on a late morning. The word quickly spread that Ernie Hoessley had shot Bobby Thomas, but that is not what happened. Bobby was shot by a Hoessley lieutenant and Sugar Daddy's door man we all knew only as Little Rudy. The last name slipped my mind, but I recall Little Rudy as a congenial sort whom most of the disco customers liked.

I was in my office on Broadway the morning Thomas was shot. It was only about a half mile to the Baptist Hospital emergency room where he was rushed. I don't recall who called me, but I distinctly remember what transpired that morning. When I walked into the emergency room, nobody tried to stop me. Bobby was on a gurney, bathed in his own blood, and as white as one of his bleached "polar bear" skins.

Somehow, he recognized me. "Sambo, come closer." His lips were blue. His eyes were sunken. His voice was a raspy whisper, but I will never forget the exact words that escaped his mouth. "Sambo, they drygulched me."

Those were his exact words. I have never forgotten those words or the last ones he uttered before I left that emergency room. "Sambo, tell Ernie that vengeance is mine."

Thankfully for all concerned, Thomas never followed up on the threat. The years slipped by, and the next time I saw Bobby was many years later outside the Cove nightclub and restaurant on Cypress Street. "Sambo," Bobby said. "My kidneys are playing out, and I know I won't be around much longer. I was always glad to have you for a friend." Bobby's kidneys quit on March 28, 2015. He died in his mother's apartment at the age of sixty-eight.

21

THE COSMIC SWEETHEART

I will never forget the Cosmic Sweetheart and her cadre of foxy followers. They took the San Antonio nightclub scene by storm in the rowdy and rip-snorting 1970s and 1980s. The first time I laid eyes on Carol Cannon, she was tending bar at Al Hoxey's Horse Feathers Saloon on Wurzbach Road. The power of first impressions can never be underestimated. Big Carol was a visual extravaganza who gave new meaning to an epic of cosmic dimensions.

Standing six foot two inches in her bare feet, San Antonio's Cosmic Sweetheart sported the blond beauty of a screen actress and showmanship befitting a carnival queen. She moved with fluid bare-midriff grace, jingling and jangling and rattling in a cacophony of ankle bells and hoop earrings big enough for a trained seal to jump through. In high school, she said, she was five foot eleven inches tall and very curvy. "The other kids called me Boom Boom Cannon," Carol laughed. She has a big, boisterous laugh to go with it all. There was always something mysteriously exotic about Carol Cannon, an intelligence that spoke of far more than a tall bar girl.

Inspired by Rolling Stones front man Mick Jagger, the Cosmic Sweetheart had a twinkling half-karat diamond that belonged to her grandmother inlaid in one of her front teeth, and she was truly built like the proverbial brick shithouse. All of this and her college teaching degree and her time as a high school teacher, plus early work as a musician with the Fort Worth Symphony, produced a combination that would help land Carol Cannon speaking parts in two major movies and position her to become a major nightclub owner and operator on the San Antonio scene. She also helped form a small Fort Worth production company that discovered legendary Texas rock band ZZ Top. The fact that Carol went on to become a bank vice president and stockbroker in later life was no coincidence. She also married high school sweetheart Larry Carpenter in 2002, officially making her Carol Cannon Carpenter, but for identification clarity she will be referred to as Carol Cannon for the remainder of this account.

The "Cosmic Sweetheart" is a nickname Carol carried from college. And that's what she named what might have been the only third-world discotheque in the country. Like most of San Antonio's major discotheques of the time, the Cosmic Sweetheart Discotheque was owned and operated by Ronnie Branham under the auspices of Alex Habeeb and El Dorado Vending.

Although she worked in numerous San Antonio nightclubs, "Big Carol," as she was known to many, is best remembered for her tenure as owner/ operator of the Foxy Lady Saloon on Perrin Beitel Road. This came about when Alex Habeeb said, "Carol, we need to put you in your own club. I have been watching you, and I know you can handle it. I believe we can make a lot of money." The Foxy Lady Saloon was born.

Carol's Foxy Lady bartenders and waitstaff were all female stunners who worked under such titillating titles as "Miss Joyful," "Patty Perfect," "Annie Oakley," "Teen Angel," and the "Diamond Princess." All were fitting nicknames for a Cosmic Sweetheart's earthly domain that was to attract country music stars like Willie Nelson and casting directors for major films such as *Race with the Devil* and *Logan's Run*.

I recall the night that we crowded into Willie Nelson's Mercedes out behind the Foxy Lady Saloon to hear the completed tape of *Redheaded Stranger*, the album that would go platinum and catapult Nelson into almost instant national stardom. Carol, Willie, Larry Trader, Billy Cooper, and I were jammed into the Mercedes. The marijuana smoke was so dense we could barely see. Willie was as excited as I had ever seen him. Trader and Cooper were working for Nelson at the time. Of the new album, he said, "This one is the real motherfucker." And those were his exact words.

Willie Nelson (*left*) and Sam. We were stoned. But I never did like marijuana. I liked speed.

Carol recalls Willie's penchant for tequila sunrises and Joy Gandy, the dimpled waitress with long, flowing raven tresses who answered to the nickname "Miss Joyful." Joy was a stone fox, an eyeful befitting her stage name. "Willie was married to his second wife, Connie, at the time, and the crush he had on Joy was just a big crush," Carol recalls. "But everyone had a crush on Joy. Willie and Joy never dated. She was beautiful with the huge dimples and long black hair. Willie was the biggest name visiting the Foxy Lady at the time, although we did get a call from the Eagles. They were playing San Antonio when someone from their group called and asked for directions, but the Eagles never showed up."

Carol said, "I have always had a Plan B. When I left a school teaching job in Fort Worth for San Antonio in the early 1970s, I never dreamed that San Antonio would be my forever home. I was in a marriage that wasn't working, and my best friend, Joy Gandy, was waiting tables and tending bar in a jumping San Antonio discotheque called Tiffany Palace.

Joy recommended me to the club owners and I was hired. My life was never the same again."

In those days, the major San Antonio disco nightclubs were built and largely controlled by shrewd and astute business individuals and amalgamations of the same. When Carol Cannon was hired at Tiffany Palace, the club was being bankrolled by El Dorado Vending, a company comprising Alex Habeeb, Joe Friesenhahn, and John Fitzpatrick. Ronnie Branham was the club operator/owner, and he hired Carol at the suggestion of Habeeb.

"They were buying and developing these properties all over the city," Carol said. "They were fixing them up and installing renters (titular "owners") to operate them. They got their rent from the club operator, plus proceeds from all vending machines their company supplied, including juke boxes, pool tables, and game machines. The money was literally flowing."

El Dorado Vending was made up of an unlikely combo as Carol recalls them.

"One was Lebanese, one was a Jew, and the third was an Irish Catholic. They couldn't have been better or more efficient at what they did. Habeeb was in for the bucks and the lifestyle. Fitzpatrick and Friesenhahn were in it for the money. John was married, and Friesenhahn couldn't have been any lower profile than he was. Alex Habeeb liked the lifestyle, but his main focus was always the money, and he was a financial genius who knew how to deal with people."

Malcolm Gildart, owner of Allcoin Equipment Co., was also partnered with Habeeb and Freisenhahn in bankrolling many of the Ronnie Branham clubs. Gildart put Jack Mikulenka in business with the numerous Jack clubs. They all worked together. Branham also operated the country music Longneck Club. The manager and trouble shooter/bouncer for the Branham clubs was Cotton Stout, a tough cookie from Oklahoma who owned the Austin Highway Squirrel Cage club in his own right.

When he was dying of cancer, Cotton asked that I conduct his funeral at Porter Loring Funeral Home. "He doesn't want a preacher," Ronnie Branham told me. "He wants you to do the funeral."

Carol Cannon recalls those crazy times, although she didn't attend Stout's funeral. I had just undergone an emergency appendectomy, and I was bleeding through my suit coat when I officiated at Cotton's last rites. Funeral home owner Porter Loring was on hand for that one, and

I could tell he was nervous. "What are you going to say?" Porter Loring asked me.

I told him I had no idea as I had never preached a funeral. I remembered the Ten Commandments from my Sunday School class at the Junction First Baptist Church. I stated that Cotton hadn't broken any of them that I knew about, and the service went without a hitch.

During her earlier years in Fort Worth, Carol Cannon was raised in a family of musicians. "My mother once worked the road with Glen Campbell. And I was playing with the Fort Worth Symphony when I was very young. I played violin, viola, and cello. My mom was a violinist."

Carol had an affinity for all things music, and the importance of secondary education was part of her upbringing. Carol's natural flair for the dramatic was always near the surface, though, and while she worked her way through three universities and into a junior high teaching job, Big Carol was busily helping form a production company that was largely responsible for discovering the Texas rock phenomenon ZZ Top.

> I graduated from Texas Wesleyan in Fort Worth. I also attended TCU and the University of the Americas in Mexico City. I was teaching Spanish at the junior high level when I left Fort Worth for San Antonio. I think one of my biggest accomplishments while in Fort Worth was teaming up with my friend Jack Ford and a few other little hippie types to sign ZZ Top for a Texas outlaw tour. Each of us put in a few thousand dollars. It's like I said, I have always had a Plan B. We called our group Brotherhood Productions. The band was unknown when we started this tour through twenty-two Texas towns and a few cities. We had an old van with ZZ Top painted on both sides in gigantic letters. It was an attention getter, and ZZ was really starting to click with the public. We were making some good money when our tour wound up in Dallas. By then we could afford a good hotel, and I recall Billy Gibbons looking out one of the hotel windows at a line of people forming for the show at a nearby venue. He was realizing that his life was never going to be the same again.

Asked what happened with ZZ Top after the tour, Carol replied with a sharp edge in her voice: "Stone City Productions of San Antonio stole them right out from under us. Just like that, here today and gone tomorrow."

Carol grew up in Fort Worth, and she did what a number of young women of that day were expected to do. She graduated from college, got married, and started teaching school. The marriage was Carol's first of four, and there were major problems from the outset. "The poor guy had served in Vietnam," Carol said. "He was suffering from PTSD in a big way. I didn't know what it was at the time. He was about to drive me crazy when I came to San Antonio to visit my friend Joy Gandy. Her husband was military and stationed in San Antonio. I had no intention of staying for any real length of time, but Joy was tending bar and doing well at the Tiffany Palace, one of the city's largest discos, and I jumped at a waitress position that came after Joy recommended me."

This new nightclub gig was a turning point for Big Carol, and one that took no lengthy contemplation on her part: "Teaching junior high I had been making $392 a month after takeouts for taxes and United Way. I was twenty-five years old at the time, and when I made $94 in tips my first night at Tiffany Palace, it was like wow and yes, I was in the wrong business. I could make more in one week at the discotheque than I was making in a month teaching in the Fort Worth school system. Alex Habeeb of Eldorado Vending told Ronnie Branham to hire me."

It was the beginning of a long and fruitful relationship. Branham was to operate other large and successful discos such as Deja Vu, Hallelujah Hollywood, Last National Bank, Sugar Daddy's, and the live country music Longneck Club. Carol and Ronnie had much in common, the most obvious trait they shared being a propensity for show. Branham tooled around the city in Bentleys, Auburn Boat Tail Speedsters, and other expensive and exotic automobiles, while Carol made a fashion statement that few young women would have the nerve to emulate. She paid San Antonio dentist Jerry Beckel to drill a hole in a perfectly healthy front tooth for the diamond implant Carol was still flashing at age seventy-one when this writing took place. And Beckel was still practicing dentistry. Said Carol: "He was a little hesitant about drilling into my perfectly good tooth, but I kept after him until he agreed to do it. The diamond idea came from Mick Jagger. I have always been a Jagger freak, and I was intrigued when I saw a diamond implanted in one of Jagger's side teeth."

Carol said she met the Rolling Stones lead singer in the old Marriott Hotel Bar on San Antonio's Austin Highway when Jagger was dating the Texas girl he eventually married. She has seen eleven Rolling Stones shows, the most memorable and thrilling of them all being the San Antonio Municipal Auditorium performance when the glint of her diamond-studded incisor caught Jagger's eye. "He saw the diamond, and when he saw it, he moved out to the edge of the stage in front of me and poured champagne on my head," Carol said. "It was his way of acknowledgment and his approval of my diamond smile."

Attention with a flair for drama was always Big Carol's forte. At a convention center Taste of the Town event that featured displays by restaurants and pricey bistros from all over the city, Carol Cannon was the focal point for the Branham discotheques. She showed up in a silver lamé spacesuit topped by a blinking lighted turban powered by a battery pack. With platform shoes, Carol said she stood six foot seven while heat from the turban all but fried her brain. "It was a statement," she said. "The Branham clubs were there and represented with the best eateries in the city."

If there is a touch of narcissism in Big Carol's makeup, nobody ever objected, let alone the spectators and film techies who watched her bare-assed naked interviews with two major film casting directors. "A bunch of us were in the Foxy Lady when this guy walked through the door. He handed me a card and said he was a casting director. He said, 'Well, you must be the Cosmic Sweetheart.' He told me a number of people had recommended me for a part in the movie. If I wanted to try for a part, I was to meet him the next day at one of the bigger hotels downtown."

Carol eventually wound up with speaking parts in *Race with the Devil* with Peter Fonda, Warren Oates, and Loretta Swit, and in *Logan's Run* with Farah Fawcett and Peter Ustinov. *Logan's Run* was Fawcett's first movie. The casting director for both films was the same, and the Cosmic Sweetheart was required to appear naked for both casting sessions.

She vividly recalled that first casting session for *Race with the Devil*: "I took Teen Angel with me. She was eighteen and gorgeous. The hotel lobby sign said '20th Century Fox Casting.' I'm all dressed up for the occasion, mingling and jingling, wearing a yellow dress that was barely tied in the front. There were about thirty people sitting around this big room. They watched me walk and listened to my voice. Then the casting director told me he wanted me to take off all my clothes. I thought, Whoa, what is this? But I went into the dressing room and came out wearing nothing but high heels."

Boom Boom Cannon had scored a direct hit. "They called the next day and told me I had a part. I think more than two hundred girls had been considered." Carol got parts for Joy Gandy in both films. Carol was called in to audition for *Logan's Run*, where, once again, she was required to completely disrobe. Carol said, "I played the head witch in *Race with the Devil*, an American action horror film. My part was in a human sacrifice scene." *Logan's Run*, Carol said, was a futuristic film in which nobody lived to be older than thirty. She played a dancer in the Love Shop.

In the San Antonio nightclub industry of the 1970s and 1980s, every club owner with a brain knew the value of a charismatic and physically attractive "day girl" bartender. The nights took care of themselves, but daytime business often depended on the looks and steady line of bullshit produced by the great "day girls" of the time. Although horny male customers who sat for hours in rapt anticipation were seldom afforded even a sniff of the tantalizing day bartender goodies, they stuck around nevertheless until the shift ended. No matter how remote and unlikely it might be, there was always the hope a bright and loquacious day bar girl could stoke and nurture until the inevitable end: No pussy, boys, just a lot of happy hot air.

To the club owner, female day bartenders with these attributes were worth their weight in ten-dollar bills. It ain't easy to tell six different off-color jokes to six different bar patrons at the same time without losing a name or a punchline while mixing and shaking margaritas and daiquiris and washing dirty glasses without missing a beat. These girls were deceptive mistresses of illusion, and the suckers never tired of them.

Lana Seekatz of Squirrel Cage and Sugar Shack fame was one of San Antonio's best day girl bartenders. Lana also sold ads for *Action Magazine*. And there were a limited number of others who fit this special bar category. But none of them ever eclipsed the Cosmic Sweetheart when it came to keeping a day bar full of restless roosters entertained.

Such was the case when Big Carol took Patty Wall (aka Patty Perfect) to work a celebrated day gig on the Boerne, Texas, main drag. Carol couldn't recall the exact name of the saloon, but she won't ever forget the opening day. Enter Janet Quist, the Cosmic Sweetheart's friend who just happened to be Hugh Hefner's December 1978 *Playboy* centerfold model. Big Carol had invited her up to sign some *Playboy* magazines for the Boerne cowboys. The Boerne saloon was jammed to the scuppers. Carol said the testosterone was all but dripping from the rafters. "I think every cowboy in Kendall County might have been in the joint," Carol said. "They were pushing and shoving, all eager for Janet to sign their copies of *Playboy*. I never smelled so much Old Spice in one place at one time in my life."

The Cosmic Sweetheart Discotheque operation will forever be seared into Carol Cannon's memory. It was truly a third-world disco, staffed by large waitresses of varied nationalities and patronized by an odd mixture of Middle Eastern men (Saudis and Iranians) who were in pilot training at Lackland Air Force Base on San Antonio's southwest side. Those were the days before the Islamic revolution when the US-friendly shah of Iran was in power. The military exchange situation we had with that country is now part of our contentious history with the Iranians.

"The Arabs loved large women, and a lot of the waitresses I hired were big ones," Carol said. "We had waitresses of Chinese, Hispanic, and Vietnamese descent, and our clientele consisted almost exclusively of Arabs, both Saudis and Iranians, plus the big mamas who followed them. This arrangement proved to be tricky at times because the Iranians and Saudis hated each other."

Branham and his associates picked the right girl for this job, for few others could have maintained order and some semblance of sanity and still realized a profit in a club like the Cosmic Sweetheart. Carol was the DJ who spun the records and the manager who served as sergeant of arms.

"We catered to the Arabs," Carol said. "No one else in town wanted them. They all drank Johnny Walker Red scotch with orange juice, and every single one of them smoked Marlboro cigarettes. And we had a rule that kept the Iranians and Saudis from declaring all-out war on one another. Anyone who got out of line had his picture taken by our house photographer. That photo was put on the wall, and the offender was barred for life." Carol said the Middle Eastern pilot trainees were constantly on edge. "The Saudis were okay with the Arab designation," Carol said. "But don't call an Iranian an Arab, although that's what they are. They insist upon being referred to as Iranians."

The club regulars called Big Carol "the Sword" in Arabic. They had it right. One of Carol's biggest thrills was a trip to the Apollo Theater in New York's Harlem, courtesy of the politically connected Sutton family of San Antonio. G. J. Sutton was a powerhouse on San Antonio's East Side for years, while his brother Percy owned the New York theater. Included in the San Antonio entourage were Carol, friend Karen (Red on the Head)

Dittman and her boyfriend, and longtime friend Michael Teas and his partner.

"We took the A-train to Harlem in 1985," Carol said. "It was billed as 'Motown Returns to the Apollo.' It was an incredible show and gathering with the greatest names in show business there. Bill Cosby emceed, and the performances were unbelievable. We saw and heard Little Richard, Patty Labelle, Sammy Davis Jr., the Four Tops, Etta James, and Diana Ross. It was televised. Boy George was there along with Rod Stewart. Jesse Jackson and Coretta King. Just too many names for me to remember them all."

As disco was born with John Travolta and *Saturday Night Fever*, disco was to die with the advent of Travolta and *Urban Cowboy*. "The disco dancers all went to the two-step," Carol said. "That was when I moved on to work for John McCormick at the Dallas Nightclub. John owned several clubs, including the Midnight Rodeo. I worked for more than ten years as John's inspector general. This included doing payrolls and even carrying a tool belt to work on club air conditioners and other equipment."

Finally weary of the nightclub scene, Big Carol applied for a job at Citibank, was accepted, and eventually retired as a vice president in the bank's brokerage department. She always had a Plan B.

Boom Boom Cannon was retired at this writing. She is now Boom Boom Cannon Carpenter, living happily in San Antonio with her husband, Larry Carpenter, and their two dogs. Carol is now an ordained minister of the Universal Life Church, and she has performed her first wedding ceremony. She says the church is about everything spiritual. She says that's where she is today.

While Larry stays home with the dogs, Carol travels abroad about three times a year. She recently returned from the Holy Land. She laughs a lot, and when she smiles, one may see a diamond's twinkle. And think, perhaps, of Jagger and the Stones. Maybe about longevity. Or maybe about large females with cosmic insight and X-ray eyes that can see your soul.

"I think we die the first time when we quit breathing," Carol said. "The second time we die is when people stop talking about us. You and I may live for eons."

PETEY THE WONDER DOG

When Sharon and I first started dating, a little Jack Russell Terrier named Petey helped us realize that we truly wanted to be a family. He became an integral part of everything we did, and Sharon insisted that this final *Action Magazine* column I wrote on Petey be a part of this book. Here is the column.

This will be the final report on Petey the Wonder Dog, my tough little Jack Russell Terrier who guarded our truck and slept under my covers for the better part of sixteen years.

Petey is gone now. I had to put the ornery little booger down on May 9, 2008. It was the hardest decision I have ever made, and my roiled emotions and shattered heart have delayed this column until the present. I learned the true meaning of tough from Petey.

When he was about nine months of age, a Honda Civic backed squarely over his back with both front and back wheels, mashing him down into deep caliche mud that somehow spared his life and enabled him to crawl out unscathed.

Then, when he was barely two years of age, Petey espied some sort of varmint, bird, or offending shadow as I drove east on I-35 somewhere near the Weidner Road exit. It was early afternoon. I was hitting sixty-five or seventy, and eighteen-wheelers were rumbling behind me and on the left flank.

That's when the Jack Russell "Terror" chose to leap head-on out of the passenger side window, which was rolled down during those times of little money and no air conditioning.

In my rearview mirror, I saw my beloved little bundle of solid muscle and high-wired energy hit the pavement and bounce like a ping-pong ball directly between two eastbound Mack diesels. My heart fell to the pit of my stomach as I somehow managed to pull my truck over next to the concrete side wall, which offered little shoulder for the hot and screaming traffic lane.

When I got my truck stopped, I looked back to locate the dead and flattened mass of white and black fur that would surely mark the death site for Petey. Instead, I saw a very lively little Jack Russell Terrier, somewhat bloody but unbent, dodging eighteen-wheelers and running like a little white ground missile after my truck. When I managed to get the passenger side door open, Petey exploded into the truck cab, his elbows and feet skinned and raw, and an expression on his wishbone-like face that seemed to implore: "Come on, Pops, let's get the hell out of here."

At the Acorn Hill Animal Hospital on Perrin Beitel Road, vet Don Johnson was checking Petey's limbs, neck, back, and skull as I related what had happened, and I could hardly believe my ears when the doc started laughing.

"What's funny?" I asked.

"This dog," said Dr. Johnson. "There is nothing broken. Absolutely nothing. If most any other breed of dog had jumped out of that truck, you would have had to scrape him up with a shovel. I find Petey here to be rather amazing."

And that's what Petey the Wonder Dog was. Amazing. He was also my friend and running mate who never had the misfortune of seeing me drunk or wired on speed. I met Petey shortly after quitting drugs and alcohol. I consider our meeting to be spiritual fate. I have had dogs since I was a kid—mutts, Catahoula Leopard Dogs, Treeing Walker Coonhounds, and a little female Fox Terrier I called Echo. She was the last dog I owned before meeting Petey, and the loss of Echo was a morale-busting tragedy that was threatening to unwind my emotional mainspring for good when my friend Collin Aldrich stepped into the picture.

Those were hard days. I was flat broke and on the second ten-year probation for drug possession when someone stole the junker of a truck I had bought for seven hundred dollars shortly after leaving jail for the final time. Losing the wheels was a blow, but the real dagger in my gut came when the truck thieves took Echo with the stolen vehicle. The old truck was later found stripped and worthless, but I never recovered my little dog, although I had offered all the reward money I could afford.

Collin Aldrich offered me friendship, help, and the greatest gift I could ever have received, although I couldn't see it at the time.

Aldrich offered me a year-old Jack Russell Terrier named Petey, free of charge, and with no strings attached. Petey and his father, Collin's other Jack Russell named Hollywood, were as intent as only Jack Russells can be on the proposition of killing each other, and Aldrich had learned what most Jack Russell breeders and owners already knew—two male "Jacks" in proximity are a likely combination for mayhem and possibly even death.

"I would come home from work and find them locked onto each other's throats, blood all over the place," Collin said. "I knew that one of them would eventually die, and I figured it would be Hollywood. Petey was obviously the stronger of the two."

Aldrich said, "Take him if you want him," and that's what I did. But not without some serious misgivings and doubt that any sort of bond could ever exist between myself and this barrel-chested little rebel who planted his feet and growled his defiance the first time I ordered him to drop a huge green beetle he held wiggling between his teeth.

"Drop the bug, Petey! Now!"

I'll never forget that first clash of wills. He took two steps back, growled again deep in his throat, and swallowed the big nasty bug in one mighty gulp.

As he gagged and dry-heaved, trying mightily to get the offensive obstruction out of his innards, I sat down and laughed at him until tears of joy flowed from my eyes. And there began the Petey dog years, a deep love affair between me and the Jack Russell Terrier who taught me a lot about grit, gumption, raw courage, survival, and the mortality of both man and beast.

Since I didn't raise Petey from eight-week-old puppyhood, I wondered for some time if a true bond between me and this strong-willed little bruiser would ever take shape. And Petey was certainly no easy sell.

He was never a lick-the-master's hand sycophant who would jump through hoops and cower for crumbs of affection. Not this little Jack. Petey was a fierce competitor who bloodied me on numerous occasions as we roughhoused in tough love play. He was twenty-three pounds of twisted steel and panther piss, as they would say up on the South Llano River near Junction, and he would fight a circular saw and tell you which tooth of the blade hit him in the butt as he sailed through the door.

Petey would sink his fangs into a tennis ball and hold on with the tenacity of a vise as I swung him in circles above my head. Dobermans and Rottweilers failed to impress this little Jack Russell, and I do believe Petey would have bowed up and attacked a grizzly bear had one of the big bruins crossed his trail. He hated thunder and Harley Davidson motorcycles with equal intensity, and his prowess as a hunter was without equal.

Petey caught and killed cottontail rabbits before they could get out of our rural yard near Bulverde. He chased raccoons, possums, lizards, low-flying birds, butterflies, and "boogers" that appeared in the night. Petey located and bayed every single scorpion that ever invaded our Bulverde cabin. He would grab the stinger-ready scorpion between his teeth, pitch it into the air, and repeat the process until I arrived to stomp on the dangerous insect. And he would kill wasps that ventured close enough for him to grab them.

The city home I also occupy with wife-to-be Sharon was also Petey's domain, and there were some hairy fang-to-fang encounters between the Jack and Sharon's cocker-mix pound refugee Princess, whose unlikely name belied her street dog nature and vicious survival instincts. Male dogs don't usually attack females, but Petey made exceptions to this dubious rule of general dog society anytime Princess even thought about getting near his food. In retaliation, Princess almost chewed off Petey's hind foot on one occasion, but the worst encounter of all came when the female ventured too near the burial site of a squirrel that Petey had killed and stashed for future use. He damn near snuffed her on that occasion.

The closeness between Petey and me was first made manifest by his territorial dedication to guarding the truck in which he rode with me almost everywhere. I noticed that he was following me to the bathroom and sitting patiently by the door until I emerged. Petey had the uncanny ability to sense when I was sick or upset, nosing closer and closer to me during such times of pain or stress, and only Petey and I really knew that he could understand the English language when he wanted to listen. There was a spiritual connection I cannot explain.

Denial, they say, ain't a river in Egypt, but I refused to toss in the towel as Petey began to decline. Two years ago his liver failed, but we got a reprieve through numerous medications and a lot of sheer determination on his part. His hearing went, his joints ached, and his hindquarters began to sag as the onetime jumping bean and lightning-quick varmint killer struggled to get over even the shortest door stoop.

With the failing liver came a cardiac cough that only steroids could control, and when I wasn't poking liver pills and steroids down my little old fella, I was dosing him with baby Tylenol and Robitussin to help with the cough. I had to lift Petey into the truck, and up onto the couch, and into my bed. And as he began to lose control of his kidneys, I covered the bed with an old rain slicker to deflect the dog pee as we continued to sleep together as always.

Someone asked me if I wanted my dog to live forever. "That," I said, "is exactly what I want." The person who asked the stupid question turned and walked away.

Sharon and I never knew Princess's exact age, since she was a refugee from the city pound. But we had her almost as long as I had Petey, and her death from cancer in March both shocked and saddened us. Then, just two months later, Petey's time came.

I knew the days were numbered, and I prayed that I would get some sign when the last day arrived. And I did, but just five days before his death, the mighty little Jack Russell hobbled out of the back door and came back into the house with a baby possum scrunched between his gray jaws.

"Hot, damn, Petey," I cheered. "You still have it." He couldn't handle an adult possum, but he did manage to crunch a miserable infant marsupial that I had to mercifully finish off with a stick.

Then my prayer was answered. Petey walked out the back door and sank to the ground. He couldn't rise, and the sad, almost apologetic look in his eyes seemed to say it all—I'm sorry, Pops, but I believe I have hoed out my row . . . caught my last rabbit . . . cornered my last scorpion. I guess I'm ready to go.

I held Petey and tears flooded my face as Dr. Johnson administered my dog his last shot. Petey stretched, seemed to sigh, and then he was gone.

It took some praying, bawling, and deep reflection and self-searching before I was fit to write this piece.

Petey and Princess were both cremated at the Paws in Heaven pet crematory in Sattler, and their remains now sit side by side in two little white jugs on our den bookcase.

Life goes on, too, as sure as death will catch up to us all, and the new lights in our lives are two wild-assed Jack Russell rocket puppies named Henry and Annie.

No dog could ever replace Petey in my heart. But there are spiritual things I could never hope to understand. The new male pup bites blood out of my arms, holds on to a tennis ball as I hoist him almost belt high, and he sits by the bathroom door every time I visit the donnicker. I'm waiting now for him to corner his first scorpion.

And then there was my recent discovery in the weeds out by the Bulverde cabin. I poked at one of Petey's last dried-out old calling cards with a stick as a tear rolled down my cheek.

Many people could never understand, but there are a few animal nuts out there who know how a grown man could cry over a crumbly old dog turd.

23

MY KEY TO SURVIVAL

I have survived both bladder and thyroid cancer. A ruptured appendix many years ago almost did me in, and I received third-degree leg burns in a senseless gasoline fire that could have killed me. Such minor inconveniences are hardly worth mentioning.

The physical pain from the surgeon's scalpel and mishaps inflicted by the machinery of man are nothing when compared with the emotional pain of irretrievable loss. I experienced that loss on the night of February 15, 1993. My firstborn child, son Grady Michael Kindrick, killed himself with a .38-caliber pistol in the backyard of his mother's home on Harriett Street in San Antonio. He had just broken up with his longtime girlfriend. It was the day after Valentine's Day. He was thirty-six.

I was working late in my small *Action Magazine* office on Broadway when I got the call. I was recently divorced at the time. The call was from my youngest son, Steven, who with his older brother, Grady, had been staying with his mother in what had been our family home. Our daughter, Gena, my youngest, was living with her mother, Vicky. Grady was living in the home on Harriett Street after separating from the girlfriend, and Steve had recently moved back from Florida where he had been working in the nursing home industry.

I picked up the phone.

"Daddy . . ."

Steven was hyperventilating. I knew something was wrong.

"Daddy, you have to get over here. Grady shot himself. He's dead." This could not be. I could not make myself believe this. Some kind of crazy hallucination on Steve's part. Someone must have given him a laced joint.

I went numb as I drove to my ex-wife's house. It was close to midnight. I saw flashing lights. Police cars. An ambulance. Two cops were waiting for me when I arrived. One escorted me through the house and into the backyard. I saw Grady on the ground. He had shot himself in the head. His body was covered by a sheet.

I think they were waiting for a coroner. At the time of Grady's suicide, I hadn't had a drink of alcohol or any drug for three years. Some predicted that I would drink over Grady's death. I didn't want to drink. I wanted to die. The night of Grady's death I drove back to the tarpaper shack in Bulverde where I lived alone with my dog. I recall dropping to my knees and trying to look skyward through a flood of tears.

Dear Jesus in Heaven, I prayed. Please bring my boy back and take me instead. I was raised by a Christian mother, attending services and Sunday school in the Junction First Baptist Church. But I didn't make a real contact with God until I sobered up in a recovery program that stressed belief in a power greater than myself.

I sobbed and hated the uncontrollable tears. It was years later that I was to take comfort in the words on tears by nineteenth-century writer Washington Irving: "There is a sacredness in tears. They are not a sign of weakness, but of power. They speak more eloquently than ten thousand tongues. They are the messengers of overwhelming grief, of deep contrition, and of unspeakable love."

Grady's sister, Gena, found his body. She had been to a concert with a friend when she stopped at the White Room, a nightclub she frequented with her older brother. Gena recalled, "Me and a friend stopped at the White Room and a guy we knew said Grady asked him for bullets. I have no idea if he got any from him. The bartender gave me a cocktail napkin that Grady had written on, listing all the jewelry he was wearing. I had a bad feeling, so I went home to look for him and found him in the backyard already dead."

One of the policemen at the scene of Grady's death put his arm around my shoulders and said, "I know who you are, and I know you might not care for policemen. But I truly feel for you, and I want you to know that this is the hardest part of police work for me. I will say a prayer for you tonight."

I didn't get the cop's name. I never forgot him. My hard shell of resentment for authority was showing its first crack.

While driving away from my former home and the scene of my son's death, I can recall mental flashbacks that have faded but never disappeared from my soul and my human psyche. I held Grady in the palm of my hand after his premature birth in a Bay City hospital. My first job after college was editorship of a tiny weekly called the *Bay City News*. Grady weighed 3.5 pounds at birth. Vicky and I were overwhelmed with both joy and apprehension. Would he even make it? By the time he was a year old, he was the size of a normal yearling.

The scenes rocketing through my brain on that fateful night were vivid and raw. Grady on the little stool. He was about three then, and his hair was curly and golden-blond. Short pants and little white shoes. The cutest little kid God ever made. Grady in the visitor's booth at Bexar County Jail. He brought me soap and tobacco. He was my only visitor when I was locked up. Grady trying to find me a lawyer. He had no money, but he tried. I learned from friends that he worried about me. Grady the night before Willie's first picnic when Nelson introduced him to his idol—Leon Russell.

The memories, the guilt. The physical fight I had with my son. Why didn't I do better? Why didn't we go fishing more? Why didn't I do more? I know now that I was never really unselfish and mature enough to be a real father to my son. I was a friend, a running mate, and a confidant. We loved each other until it literally hurt, but I didn't know what to do with it at the time.

Grady dropped out of Robert E. Lee High School, later passing a General Educational Development (GED) test. He wrote a couple of record reviews for *Action Magazine*. I could see the talent and the potential, but the kid didn't get the direction and help that he needed. When I started *Action Magazine* in 1975, Grady wanted to work for me. I wore turquoise jewelry. Grady wore turquoise jewelry. I wore cowboy boots. Grady wore cowboy boots.

Grady helped me with photography and some photo lab work, but the little magazine just didn't bring in enough revenue for the two of us. He

Grady, my oldest son, was a rock-and-roller and every bit the outlaw I was. Leon Russell turned the kid on to Willie Nelson. Grady's death haunts me.

bounced from one odd job to the next, telling me once shortly before his death: "I have never done one damn thing for myself. I have wasted so much."

A red flag. Perhaps. But I didn't see it. Who in the hell in my world had ever heard of something called clinical depression?

The bewilderment and sense of disbelief when one loses a child like I lost Grady must certainly have some spiritual connection to God's animal kingdom. I saw it when my Jack Russell Terrier Henry caught and killed a baby redbird that had left its nest in a hanging plant on our front porch. Three other fledglings had apparently left the nest successfully, leaving this last one. It was the baby's first and last attempt at flight.

I knew the fledgling cardinals were feathered out and ready for flight. I should have locked the dog in the backyard. It was my fault, not Henry's. Jack Russell Terriers are hunters, born and bred to attack and kill. They are lightning quick. When the baby redbird fluttered down on the yard grass, the dog ended its life.

It was a poignant lesson for Sharon and me. The hardest part was watching the adult redbirds after their baby's death. Cardinals mate for life, both mother and father feeding the young. With nothing but scattered feathers left of their baby, the parents were obviously in a high state of stress, squawking piteously as they flew to their now-empty nest, then to the ground, then back to the nest. They had lost their baby. They were frantic. They could not understand. In their own fashion, I am sure they were crying. I knew the near panic of inscrutable emptiness and the need to cry out. To scream for help.

Since Grady's death, my faith has strengthened. Although I have not been a regular church man, my Higher Power is the God of my childhood. My God walked on water and raised a man from the dead some two thousand years ago, and, yes, his name is Jesus Christ. His spirit still saves and heals, springing drunks and dope addicts I have known and worked with from their own furnace of man-made fire. I will never get over Grady's death; but with God's help, I have been able to get through it.

I know I will see Grady and other loved ones again. For me, heaven will surely include the beautiful, burbling clear waters of the South Llano River where I grew up. My wife, Sharon, and all of my loved ones, including my former wife, Vicky, will be there, and every dog and cat I ever owned will be on hand to greet me. And I won't be surprised if a certain

Sharon Kindrick, my wife and steady partner in sober living and faith.

My late son Steven and daughter Gena. Steven died of small cell lung cancer. Gena is my only surviving child.

little redbird is there, sitting safely on a high branch and keeping a sharp eye on Henry the Jack Russell Terrier.

As this autobiography winds down, some might wonder why I withheld my son's suicide until the last of this project. It was not part of a script. It was part of my personal pain that I put off as long as my mind would allow.

My younger son, Steven Howard Kindrick, died January 3, 2019, from small-cell lung cancer. He was born August 23, 1958, in Shannon Memorial Hospital in San Angelo while I worked for the *San Angelo Standard-Times*. Vicky Kindrick, my former wife and mother of my three children, died of natural causes on January 22, 2021, in San Antonio. She was born June 30, 1937. My daughter, Gena, is my lone surviving child at this writing. Born October 20, 1963, in San Antonio's downtown Baptist Hospital, Gena graduated from Robert E. Lee High School before attending San Antonio College for a couple of years. She is now retired from restaurant management. Gena was a starter on the Lee girls' basketball team, and I couldn't have been prouder. I attended every game possible. Both of my sons attended Lee, and both later received GEDs. Patti Boerner, Gena's partner for over twenty-five years, is loved and considered to be another daughter by both me and Sharon.

There were bright spots in the latter days of *Action Magazine*, three anniversary shows at Texas Pride Barbecue that showcased musicians who ranged from Kinky Friedman, Augie Meyers, and Johnny Bush to Alex Harvey and Johnny Rodriguez. Others included Dub Robinson of the Drugstore Cowboys and Randy and Russ Toman of the Toman Brothers, Hector and David Saldaña, and Sylvia Kirk, Darrell McCall, and many more artists who graced the pages of *Action* for forty-four years.

The big surprise for me was my inclusion into the Wittliff Collections at Texas State University, a huge honor that sees my work included with such Texas writer giants as Larry McMurtry and Cormac McCarthy, as well as musicians the likes of Willie Nelson, Ray Benson, and Jerry Jeff Walker. I graduated from the San Marcos university in 1957 when it was Southwest Texas State Teachers College. Sadly, Bill Wittliff, who started the museum on Texas talent, died before I had a chance to meet him. He was the Texas screenwriter who coproduced *The Redheaded Stranger* movie with Willie Nelson and crafted the screen version of *Lonesome Dove*.

My entrance into the Wittliff can be attributed to former *San Antonio Express-News* music columnist Hector Saldaña, now music curator at the Wittliff and the talented leader of San Antonio's Tex-Mex rock band the Krayolas. I wrote the first story ever printed on the Krayolas when Hector and his brother David were teenagers. Now Hector's boys are in the band.

The Wittliff Collections represent a giant museum of works by Texas writers, photographers, musicians, and screenwriters. This vast body of works encompasses the entire seventh floor of the Texas State Alkek Library, and it continues to grow.

My Wittliff exhibit ties in with the outlaw country music outbreak of the 1970s when Willie Nelson, Commander Cody, Waylon Jennings, Rusty Wier, Willis Allen Ramsey, B. W. Stevenson, Ray Benson, Ray Wylie Hubbard, Jerry Jeff Walker, David Allan Coe, and a few others led a limited exodus of artists from the constraints of Nashville. These were the so-called outlaws of country music who traded their traditional sequined coats and ostrich boots for head rags and tennis shoes, who broke from the giant record label sounds and sheen of Nashville, choosing instead to sign with smaller independent labels while hiring their own record producers, engineers, and side men for the recording sessions.

If these were the "outlaws" of country music, then I became the outlaw journalist who hung out with them and wrote about them. I never considered *Action Magazine* to be a music magazine, and I did not place myself in a position to judge or evaluate the music or the musicians who made it. *Action* was an entertainment magazine. I did not publish personal record reviews in *Action Magazine*. I always said that *Action* covered the real action, whether an armadillo race, a cow pasture boxing match, or a picking party under the stars. Texas musicians never needed a tweedy, ponderous, self-anointed pundit to analyze their work or their worth. Texas musicians have always delivered far more than any audience had any right to expect.

I sat in the cab of a pickup truck in a saloon parking lot and got whiskey-sloshed with the great Townes Van Zandt. I recall asking Townes what or who might have inspired him to write his great hit song "Pancho and Lefty." Was the story line about a drug deal gone bad as many believed? Or was it following a plot even more mysterious and obscure? Townes looked me straight in the eye and said, "I don't know for sure what the song is all about. The meaning kept changing on me while I was writing it."

I never doubted that Van Zandt was telling it exactly as it was. The same went with my friend Billy Joe Shaver. This was the great mystery surrounding those great poets of song who took their secrets to the grave. Billy Joe Shaver told me he climbed to the high cliffs overlooking the Narrows of Tennessee's Harpeth River for the explicit purpose of deliberately plunging to his death. "I was ready to jump," Shaver told me, "when the song lyrics started forming in my mind. I wasn't much, but I could see possibilities. I was just an old chunk of coal, but I was going to be a diamond in my dreams."

When Shaver climbed down from the Harpeth River Narrows, he had written "Old Chunk of Coal," the song that John Anderson turned into a country music hit. "I'm just an Old Chunk of Coal, but I'm going to be a diamond someday."

My exhibit at the Wittliff Collections at Texas State features me in a Mexican sombrero with a very suspicious-looking cigarette smoking

Sam in sombrero, with joint, at the zenith of his gonzo journalist persona and defiant as hell.

between two of my fingers. *Action Magazine* copies covering forty-four years are stored and on display in my Wittliff exhibit, as well as old columns that go back to my 1960s and early 1970s years as a reporter and columnist for the *San Antonio Express-News*.

So here we are, maybe at the ending for me and maybe not. Bill Shakespeare would say I seem to have survived the slings and arrows of outrageous fortune. Bill Wilson would say that God has transformed me from a churlish foul-mouthed Mr. Hyde into a much happier and much more pleasant Dr. Jekyll.

Some refer to this transformation as a spiritual awakening or a psychic change. Sobriety for me means far more than abstinence from alcohol and drugs. Sobriety means sanity, gratitude, and a spiritual way of life that defies adequate description. While my Higher Power is a Jewish carpenter, my state of spirituality goes beyond the structure of organized religion.

I love my wife, Sharon, and I will tell anyone who will listen that I have a five-foot wife and a kick-ass fairy-tale life, all the result of sobriety and my faith in God. I was a deer hunter who now feeds the animals at my kitchen gate. I was a white wing dove hunter who now grieves the death of a baby redbird. Does this make me less the mucho, macho stud-duck image I had painted for myself? I can't explain it but God can. An old spiritual adviser I had many years ago passed me the key. His name was Jack Forrest.

"Get down on your knees beside your bed every night," Jack said. "Thank God for keeping you sober one more day. Then put your boots under the bed. When you crawl down the next morning to get the boots, ask God for another day of sobriety while you are still on your knees."

It works. And I still pray on my knees.

My faith tells me that we are all heading for another show, a garden of love with old bronc breakers, sparkling spring water, our loved ones and friends, hounds and terriers and country music by Hank and Lefty and Willie, and the one component of the human psyche that every man, woman, and child has longed for since the beginning of time—just one single soul who gives a shit. I'm holding on for the very best possible spiritual scenario, and I will brook no argument for a second-place finish. I know the next life for me will be a good one.

Index